Charles Simic

UNDER DISCUSSION

Annie Finch and Marilyn Hacker, General Editors
Donald Hall, Founding Editor

Volumes in the Under Discussion series collect reviews and essays about individual poets. The series is concerned with contemporary American and English poets about whom the consensus has not yet been formed and the final vote has not been taken. Titles in the series include:

On Frank Bidart: Fastening the Voice to the Page
edited by Liam Rector and Tree Swenson
On Louise Glück: Change What You See
edited by Joanne Feit Diehl
On James Tate
edited by Brian Henry
Robert Hayden
edited by Laurence Goldstein and Robert Chrisman
Charles Simic
edited by Bruce Weigl
On Gwendolyn Brooks
edited by Stephen Caldwell Wright
On William Stafford
edited by Tom Andrews
Denise Levertov
edited with an introduction by Albert Gelpi
The Poetry of W. D. Snodgrass
edited by Stephen Haven
On the Poetry of Philip Levine
edited by Christopher Buckley
James Wright
edited by Peter Stitt and Frank Graziano
Anne Sexton
edited by Steven E. Colburn
On the Poetry of Galway Kinnell
edited by Howard Nelson
Robert Creeley's Life and Work
edited by John Wilson
On the Poetry of Allen Ginsberg
edited by Lewis Hyde
Reading Adrienne Rich
edited by Jane Roberta Cooper
Elizabeth Bishop and Her Art
edited by Lloyd Schwartz and Sybil P. Estess

Charles Simic

Essays on the Poetry

Edited by Bruce Weigl

Ann Arbor

THE UNIVERSITY OF MICHIGAN PRESS

To all our friends . . .

First paperback edition 2008

Published in the United States of America by
The University of Michigan Press
Manufactured in the United States of America
⊗Printed on acid-free paper
2011 2010 2009 2008 5 4 3 2

A CIP catalog record for this book is available from the British Library

Charles Simic : essays on the poetry / edited by Bruce Weigl.
p. cm.
Includes bibliographical references (p.).
ISBN 0-472-10713-5 (alk. paper)
1. Simic, Charles, 1938—Criticism and interpretation.
I. Weigl, Bruce, 1949– .
PS3569.I4725Z58 1996
811'.54—dc20
96-25334
CIP

ISBN 978-0-472-10713-1 (cloth : alk. paper)
ISBN-13: 978-0-472-03290-7 (pbk : alk. paper)
ISBN-10: 0-472-03290-9 (pbk : alk. paper)

Acknowledgments

Special acknowledgment and appreciation should go to Brian Avery. He contributed an important study of Charles Simic's poetry to this collection and compiled an inclusive bibliography; he also made valuable contributions at every level of the editing and preparation of this manuscript. Without his writing, research, and editorial skills and assistance, this book could not have been created.

I am also appreciative of the support, editorial work, and guidance of David Lehman and of LeAnn Fields.

Thanks also to CS and JKW for their support.

Contents

Introduction

> In the beginning, always, a myth of origins of the poetic act . . . to recreate what is unspoken and enduring in words, and thus live twice as it were.

Charles Simic remains an enigma, even within the eclectic tradition of postmodern American poetry. He is a poet difficult to categorize, difficult to generalize about, set apart from his contemporaries by a particularly inclusive and worldly vision and by a Cartesian duality of speech and being. "Simic's isolation," Brad Crenshaw has written, "within the labyrinth of discourse corresponds with an estrangement from his own body, where the island of consciousness is sequestered."[1] It is precisely because of this isolation, I believe, that very few extended studies of his work, very few longer essays or articles, have been published, though the critical reception of Simic's work has been largely favorable since his first collection appeared over twenty-five years ago. Simic is one of our most popular American poets, whose growing body of work continues to attract new readers, yet critics have shied away from his poetry. The reasons for this reluctance are not so mysterious. Those who try to teach or write about Simic's poetry quickly realize that they must first deal with a language that has been pared to a primal minimum. This book attempts, by coming at the poetry from several different perspectives, to get at the primacy of language and thought that is the hearthstone of Simic's poetry.

The design of this book is straightforward. Part I comprises critical responses to individual works by Simic. It begins with the earliest short reviews, notable in spite of their brevity for their fundamental insights into a poetry few critics were willing to take on, and for their struggle to find a diction suitable to describe it. Gathered in part I with these early responses are a variety of later reviews and essays, organized (with a few exceptions for thematic purposes) chronologically, so that the reader may discover an unfolding of the critical reception of Simic's work during the past twenty-five years. The reader will observe a metamorphosizing relationship between the poet and critic as if, in an ideal critical context, they have learned from each other.

Part 2 includes essays that focus, from sometimes radically different points of view, on the whole of Simic's poetic vision—not only the poetry, but the aesthetic from which it emerges. Part 3 is made up of a selection of Simic's own critical and autobiographical writing and an interview, conducted through the mails during a two-year period, that includes an extended discussion of Simic's expansive and wise notions of form in poetry.

As Crenshaw has written, the differences for Simic "in language, cultural forms, political institutions and especially civil freedoms have heightened [his] sensitivity to the inevitable oppressions practiced upon the individual by the state."[2] In response to that oppression, Simic's poetry often centers on seemingly oblique images of political violence, abandonment, loss, hunger, and exile experienced, in their most basic and corrupt ways, as a child living through World War II in Yugoslavia and during his immigrant's journey. Simic's poetry, therefore, seems at times irreducible to even the highest critical consideration. An urgent linguistic primacy struggles on the page and in the heart and mind to remain always apart from mere statement or fact; a darkly universal discourse dominated by an imaginatively epistemological sensibility; a sorcerer doing alchemy behind the scenes. Simic has managed to strip down to a few notes, or images, or brushstrokes things as they are. Remarkably, an entire universe is projected, as in Klee and Matisse, a mental and concrete landscape of ideas and the technological implements of our own undoing that take shape in real people's lives dramatized in Simic's haunting minimalist vignettes. Particular to a great deal of Simic's poetry is his habit of setting the spectacular alongside the mundane, the comic in bed with the tragic, and a powerful sense of the brute forces of history and nature intruding on the reality of the poems. There is also the overwhelming presence of myth or mythic consciousness in the poetry from the beginning, personalized so that Simic forces myth to make sense in our time and in our lives, an elemental aspect of his work that many of his critics have explored. Many of the poems echo the history of our humanness: from an ancient and nearly silent time when the details of our tribal memory were assembled, right up to the present moment, when words often seem like hot coals on our tongues, so that we are unable to speak clearly in the face of the bureaucrats and dictators who want to control our discourse and therefore our lives. The voice that speaks these poems seems to have seen and spoken all of our cultural memory, an Ishmael to history's Ahabs.

An eclectic critical response to Simic's poetry is therefore essential. One must be willing to enter a wildly imaginative world, willing to jump into the fray surrounded by strangely human and magnificently cosmic forces that radiate within the expansive vistas of his imagination. In the poems one can find jazz and blues—not simply the expansive forms of jazz but the atmosphere too, the sensibility that the jazz age brought to us—and one can find history and its dark secrets, politics, opera, drama, romance, love in the various forms of its many "offices," the pathology of domesticity, the great philosophical ideas laid alongside knives, forks, and spoons that take on a rich new life animated by Simic's energy and imagination.

Simic's journey as a poet, from the early somewhat abstract, somewhat surreal, so-called object poems, to the most recent work, which shows clear manifestations of autobiographical experience, has been a journey of discovery, an archaeological dig of sorts, a diving into an historical past that seems, under his inscrutable eye, to be inextricably part of a personal past. He begins in *What the Grass Says* and *Somewhere Among Us a Stone Is Taking Notes* (1967 and 1969, respectively) with a kind of Cartesian nothingness in which he seeks to reexamine our world and its objective reality so as to resurrect the magic that he knows is inherently there. Simic wants to decreate "the world in an effort to forestall its nonexistence,"[3] and through this metaphysical reexamination, he begins to recreate a landscape of oddly juxtaposed objects he then peoples with the menagerie of characters necessary to tell his expanding historical experience. But however odd this landscape and its characters and props may seem, however otherworldly, we should not be too quick to go symbol hunting. Rather than describe what Simic accomplishes as simply metaphor, it might be more advantageous to think of his method as a layering of consciousness juxtaposed against different levels of the literal. "If I say 'rats in diapers,' " Simic has averred, "I mean 'rats in diapers.' " There is a logic to Simic's mythology, as to Blake's, a palpable shape to his cosmos.

Many of the poems in Simic's considerable body of work are difficult to enter initially, not unlike the *Parables and Paradoxes* of Kafka, for how they assert themselves obliquely. Other poems are pure illuminations one can pick right off the page, captured moments of a life the poet describes as "a beautiful mystery on the verge of understanding, always on the verge." Stephen Hawking has said that all galaxies visible to us, and probably all galaxies in the universe, are moving away from ours, a lonely thought, even for the scientist. In fact, he says that if one could stand anywhere in the universe, the rest of cosmic existence would appear to be moving away, expanding in some profoundly inexplicable way. One senses, reading Hawking, that there exists an illusive equation that could solve the problem of this constantly expanding universe, and one senses this same emotion reading the poetry of Charles Simic: a deeply emotional conviction that you are on the verge of some great revelation, some great understanding. And Simic's poems are like Hawking's galaxies: spinning away from us, visible, but impossible to fully embrace, impossible to prevent from escaping our attempts to hold them down and make them fully a part of us.

My hope is that the essays and the interview gathered here are varied and inclusive enough so that they will invite the readers' own participation in the vision of the poems. That should be the aim of all criticism: to inspire the reader to turn back to the poems. Once in their presence, there is little doubt that you'll come away wiser, amused at the irony of your own existence and revitalized by a poetic voice singular in our time for its quality of empathy, for its cosmic logic enriched by imagination, and for its deep and abiding clarity.

Charles Simic has published sixteen books of poetry, including *Charon's Cosmology,* nominated for a National Book Award in 1977, *Classic Ballroom Dances,* which won the 1980 di Castagnola Award and the Harriet Monroe Poetry Award, and *The World Doesn't End,* which was awarded the Pulitzer Prize for poetry in 1990. In addition, Simic has been honored with a Guggenheim Fellowship, a MacArthur Foundation Fellowship, grants from the National Endowment for the Arts, the Edgar Allan Poe Award, and awards from the National Institute of Arts and Letters and the American Academy of Arts and Letters. Simic is also an important translator of Yugoslavian, South American, and French poetry, winning two PEN International Translation Awards. He has coedited two anthologies of poetry and has published two collections of essays. At the University of New Hampshire, where he has taught for over twenty years, Simic attracts a large following of students, many of whom have gone on to their own writing and publishing careers. Among his fellow poets and other members of the audience for contemporary poetry, Simic is read widely in this country, in France (where his work is translated by Madeline Follain, writer and widow of Jean Follain), and in his native Yugoslavia. He has read at over one hundred universities, libraries, and poetry centers internationally.

Those are the vital statistics of a distinguished career in American poetry. But what matters most of course is the poetry itself: how it holds up to time; how it continues to mean in new and expanding ways; how it lasts. What better measure of a poetry than its longevity? Already we have been reading Charles Simic for twenty-five years, and there is good reason to believe that we'll be reading him for another twenty-five as well. This collection is a celebration of that poetry, and an inquiry into the nature of its origins and the development of its style.

NOTES

1. Brad Crenshaw, "Charles Simic," *Critical Survey of Poetry, English Language Series,* ed. Frank N. Magill, Vol. 6 (Inglewood Cliffs, N.J.: Salem Press, 1982), 2590–98.
2. Ibid.
3. Ibid.

PART ONE *Out of Poverty*

Out of poverty
To begin again . . .

WILLIAM MATTHEWS

Charles Simic's *What the Grass Says*

In these poems by Charles Simic an impulse towards speech wars against an impulse towards silence. Continually we find images of silence:

> Further ahead, someone
> Even more silent
> Passes over the grass
> Without bending it

and

> In the midst of that silence
> It seems possible
> To live simply
> On the earth

all are from the first poem, "Summer Morning."

Another predominant motif is smallness. In the first poem there is "the little school of the corn field" and "the tiny soul of the caterpillar." In another poem:

> This is the hour in which I want to
> Travel through bodies of sleeping children
> Extracting something infinitely small
> Like that singular grain of sand
> The sea has lost to the land.

Often this miniaturization is a move towards silence, away from the huge buzzing world. It is an expression of sympathy for the still, small, and vulnerable in nature. There is a risky and, ultimately, bad sentimental poem, "Sparrow," about holding a sparrow cupped in the hands "The way God holds mine / In the

---

From a review of *What the Grass Says* by William Matthews, *Lillabulero* 2, no. 1 (winter 1968).

grip of the earth." The tenderness is genuine, but the poem cheats by carefully enlisting our emotions to the situation, so that when those two lines about the grip of the earth arrive, we accept them only because we are already leaning that way, as if we had been drawn offside.

In the book's better poems a similar tenderness is directed toward humankind. In these poems people are restored to a real role in the natural world. In the poems emphasizing stillness and smallness man seems a grotesque, clumsy giant, a blatant bull in Mother Nature's china shop. It is not really a natural world we know about from living in, but one Simic invents to oppose man's rapacious use of nature and other men. Because Simic's invention is so rich and his hatred of rapine so well directed, we nearly come to believe in this invented nature. But poems like "Fear," "Five Naked Men Lined Up for Army Physicals," "The Boss Hires," "To All Hog-Raisers, My Ancestors," "Working on the Pennsylvania Railroad in Winter," and "Marching" remind us that it is otherwise. "Marching" goes like this:

> After I forgot about the horses
> And when the fire turned into cool water flowing,
> And the old woman took off her mourning to enter a coffin
> At the end of a long life
>
> A horse stood like an apparition,
> A dream of a drowned girl cast out by the sea,
> Suddenly he turned his head, bugler turning his bugle
> To face the moon shining like a new laid egg.
>
> Then I rose in my house among my sons,
> I put on my old clothes and my muddy boots,
> My clothes smelling of wolves and deep snow,
> My boots that have trodden men's faces.
>
> I remembered the swamps, grass taller than horses,
> Fast rivers softer than chicken flesh,
> Where I'll stumble into deep hollows, dark eyelids,
> Until I am buried under human droppings.
>
> Blood rose into my head shaking its little bells.
> In the valley the glow died in the udder of the cow.
> The trees ceased playing with their apples
> And the wind brought the sound of men marching.

A dog went along the road in front of marching soldiers,
A man who was to be hanged went along the road,
His head was bent, his face was dark and twisted
As if death meant straining to empty one's bowels.

So close the doors and windows and do not look,
The stars will come into the autumn sky
Like boats looking for survivors at sea
But no son of yours will rise from the deep.

Though none mar the poems, it has problems. These days the appearance of a horse in a poem is like the death of a small child in a Victorian novel, designed to produce a sure-fire effect. More important, the poem is too long, too diffuse.

It is still, though crippled, a true and courageous poem. Simic takes great risks—imagine even thinking of writing a poem about cupping an injured sparrow in one's hand—and when they work, the effect is wonderful. The man's dark and twisted face could have ruined the entire poem, nearly does, but is somehow just right. More important than these touches, though, is the true view of man in nature. In some of his poems we get the impression that nature is too good for man: here we know that man lives in it and participates in its strange processes ("My clothing smelling of wolves and deep snow, / My boots that have trodden men's faces"). Even more than wolves and deep snow, the sense of man's involvement in a natural world as vicious as it is tender reminds me of John Haines' *Winter News*.

There is another reason why this group of poems stands out from the others in the book, and it has to do with the war between silence and speech. I think of the lines near the end of "Working on the Pennsylvania Railroad in Winter."

I am the one eternally stinking of poverty.
The nigger, the convict, the dirty foreigner.
I am the one they've built the prisons for.
The one who cannot keep his mouth shut.

Despite all the poems about silence, about the deep and the dark, we know Simic is the one who cannot keep his mouth shut.

I think Simic's poems about the stillness and smallness of nature are intended to be about the possibility of leading a spiritual life ("It seems possible / To live simply / On the earth"). Earlier this century, writers like Knut Hamsun and D. H. Lawrence were interested in Pan while others mourned the death of God (every funeral has its late-comers). Part of each writer's intention was to explore the possibilities of living in and through the energies symbolized by Pan. Recently, American poets like Roethke, Bly, Haines, Snyder, and now Simic (each in quite different ways) have made this one of their themes.

But while Simic's attitude toward nature is religious, his theology is Jansenist. We find too little of the demonic or vicious, too little of the grandiose. Nature in his poems often resembles a perfectly landscaped English estate; standing among sculpted hedges, we cannot imagine earthquakes, the grinding of glaciers, or even that there are bodies of water as huge as oceans. This is because he converts nature to religious purposes, rather than writing about in and out of it. Too often in his poems nature represents his longing for peace, for the cessation of spiritual struggle. In one poem he writes, "Make me inert." The man who knows he is "the one who cannot keep his mouth shut" cannot really mean such a wish. It is ultimately a dangerous wish, rising out of the frustration that a spiritual life seems impossible. It sounds like a fantasy of a child who wishes he were dead so his parents would realize how badly they treated him.

Not being able to keep your mouth shut means you are the nigger, the foreigner, the convict, because you take on their pain and talk (write) about it. You are the gabby one, the busybody, the common scold, but never the silent saint.

Simic's poems about human suffering are better. They are both tender and tough-minded enough to sneak past our hatred and suspicion of the sentimental liberal ethic.

The best poem in the book is "Bones." It surpasses the good poems about suffering because it attacks directly the real question Simic is worrying about in all the poems, which is the relationship between the suffering of others and his own need to lead a spiritual life.

> My roof is covered with pigeon bones.
> I do not disturb them. I leave them
> Where they are, warm
> In their bed of feathers.
>
> At night I think I hear the bones,
> The little skulls cracking against the tin,
> For the wind is blowing softly, so softly,
> As if a cricket were singing inside a tulip. . . .

What is joy to me is grief to others.
I feel grief all around my house
Like a ring of beasts circling a campfire
Before dawn.

Here we find the uneasy presence of both the spiritual life Simic needs and wants, and the lives of other humans, with the strange and perhaps dangerous demands those lives make on us. I think the crucial line in the poem is "What is joy to me is grief to others." He doesn't write "What is grief to others is joy to . . . ," as the jubilant advocates of mystical secession would have said, but states simply and powerfully the deep dilemma his poems raise.

I found *What the Grass Says* exciting, even though most of the poems struck me as false. Some will complain that the style is false, but if that is true it is because, in my judgment, most of the poems are working with false content. They are exploratory poems, whose ultimate value is to find Simic's true content by following false trails to dead ends. In "Bones" the style has the shocking inevitability of having grown out of the content. What I like in Simic's poems—even though I like few of them as objects—is his seriousness. There are no slight or occasional poems here, no chocolate-covered marshmallows. I am impatient to read more of his poems, and I hope he will give over the dreams of inert silence for poems which rise from the knowledge in that superb line in "Bones."

DIANE WAKOSKI

Charles Simic's *Somewhere Among Us a Stone Is Taking Notes*

I have not yet decided whether Charles Simic is America's greatest living surrealist poet, a children's writer, a religious writer, or simple-minded. My decision in this matter is irrelevant actually because, whatever he is, his poetry is cryptic and fascinating. He has published two books with Kayak Press, one of the most beautiful and interesting of the little-magazine presses. One of my favorite poems in this book is called "Poem" and it contains all the elements which I admire in Simic's work. He begins the poem with his father writing and when he says he "writes in his coffin" the poem has been transferred into a metaphor perhaps for the poet himself.

> I look at times over his shoulders
> At all that whiteness. The snow is falling.
> As you'd expect. A drop of ink
> Gets buried easily, like a footprint,

he says in the second stanza, and you have a metaphor for man in the natural world. Then Simic adds, "I, too, would get lost but there's his shadow / On the wall," and I start thinking the poet is writing about God, perhaps death. And he ends the poem:

> When the bottle empties
> His great dark hand
> Bigger than the earth
> Feels for the moon's spigot.

This kind of poem you can turn inside out, make symbolic, make metaphoric, make religious, make aesthetic, and still have a beautiful cryptic little piece, written as if it were a folk poem or

---

From "Songs and Notes" by Diane Wakoski, *Poetry* 118 (September 1971).

perhaps a child's verse that wasn't intended to be complex at all. I like those qualities in poetry. They always restore my faith in the poem; make me feel that we should all stop talking about poetry and sit down and memorize some of the poems we love.

VICTOR CONTOSKI

At the Stone's Heart: Charles Simic's *Dismantling the Silence*

Charles Simic has previously published two books of poetry with George Hitchcock's Kayak Press, *What the Grass Says* and *Somewhere Among Us a Stone Is Taking Notes*. The first is in its second printing and is still available from Kayak, while the second is out of print. *Dismantling the Silence* features a selection of poetry from these two books (the poet has omitted seventeen poems from his first book and nine from his second) plus eight new poems. It is an impressive collection.

Simplicity has become one of the trademarks of Simic's poetry—not a simplicity of treatment but a simplicity of subject. His work concerns everyday things: forks, knives, spoons, tables, fingers, bones, spiders, and stones. In "Summer Morning," one of the first poems in this collection, the poet assumes a Whitmanesque character. He stretches out on his bed and imagines the ordinary, public business of a summer morning. He sees a man washing his face with a hose, a butterfly stirring. He is able to enter into the secrets of things: a stone turning over in its sleep, a tree talking. He concludes, "—And all of a sudden / In the midst of that silence / It seems possible / To live simply / On the earth."

This poem, like so many of his, happens in silence. (The tree hushes as he approaches.) Silence, in fact, is one of Simic's standard poetic devices. He is a listener rather than a speaker, and a listener to the tiny voices of things. People, it seems, have nothing really to say to him. In the title poem, the first thing one does in dismantling silence is to take down its ears. When one gets to the bones, he slips them under his skin, so silence becomes part of reader and poet. And not just silence but *the* silence. The concluding stanza is remarkable.

From "At the Stone's Heart" by Victor Contoski, *Modern Poetry Studies* 2 (1971).

It is now completely dark.
Slowly and with patience
Feel its heart. You will need to haul
A heavy chest of drawers
Into its emptiness
To make it creak
On its wheel.

The reader, having dismantled the silence, gets to the heart of the mystery—but he or she finds emptiness, almost. He is left with the problem of mortal man trying to understand immortal things. One can do so only by resorting to something artificial—like poetry. One brings a chest of drawers (a typical, everyday Simic symbol) into the dismantled silence "to make it creak / On its wheel." At first the wheel seems rather anticlimactic, but the word is beautifully chosen. There is a sense of direction in the silence after all, though puny man may not be able to discern it. But he can hear the wheel creaking so he knows it exists. And the wheel, the soul of man, continues to exist when the body of silence is dismantled. In the final sentence one is transported from his bedroom to a universe wheeling in space.

Coupled with Simic's simplicity is, paradoxically, a kind of aristocratic attitude towards his art, a combination that makes his work unique indeed. If at times Simic's persona seems like Walt Whitman hovering over the fields on a summer morning, usually it is less involved in life. The speaker of the poems seems to stand far off from them, as if he were not only not of this world but not of this universe. Can such a speaker really see the same things we do when he looks at our lives? Moreover, this person, looking at life through such a distance (of time as well as space), ignores many of the usual requirements of poetry. There are virtually no transitions, as if the speaker cannot or does not wish to make them. The result is a concentration of words that are concerned with the poem, not with helping the reader understand it. It is a poetry of bricks, not putty. "Eating Out the Angel of Death" begins:

Now my body is the evening sky
And I'm the smoke rising towards it,

Slowly since I watch for the wind,
Carefully, since I'm blind
And my dog and cane have been taken away.

The situation at this point is a rather familiar one, the separation of the body and spirit, though the usual places are reversed—the body seems to be in the heavens and the "I," the soul, is on earth ascending to meet it. The second stanza describes the delicacy with which the soul tries to reunite with its body; yet at this point—just when the reader thinks he or she is about to understand the poem—the poet breaks off.

> I hear gnashing: those bones are afraid.
> They imagine a raven: a lethal speck of summer.
>
> I'm like a cold glass of milk
> The stars will drink before going to bed.

What has the gnashing to do with the poem? And what or whose bones are referred to? Are they the poet's? Could his body be in the sky and his bones be left behind? Or are his bones in the sky as part of his body? My reading posits the "I" as having both body and soul, yet going to meet his "body" in a larger sense when he dies and becomes part of the universe. The third and fourth stanzas form a nice contrast. The bones, with their human fears, symbolize the life the poet is leaving, and the cool, refreshing glass of milk shows the life of peace to which he aspires. Both bones and milk are being consumed, changed to another substance; but their different attitudes towards metamorphosis set the basic conflict of the poem, a conflict that reaches its climax in the startling imagery of the final stanza.

> O there's nothing more beautiful than this climb
> With its bearded, haggard and open fist
> Like the last barbarian
> On the border of an invisible empire.

An open fist? A bearded fist? The poem depends almost entirely on personification and oxymoron; yet the final stanza with its equations of climb = fist = barbarian is still shocking and puzzling. One does get, however, a sense of a new and better life, a life where fists are open, a life that puzzles barbarians. Simic's poetry, like that of T. S. Eliot, can make its meaning felt first. The rational explanations come afterwards. And like Eliot's best poetry, it remains untranslatable into prose, for all of my attempts in the paragraph above.

Thus behind a mask of simplicity there remains a core of mystery in all of his poems, even the most simple. Take "Wind" for example, a poem of two lines.

> Touching me, you touch
> The country that has exiled you.

Who exactly is touching what or whom? Is the you of the poem the wind, the reader, or the poet? (The poet has just assumed the character of a forest in the previous poem.) If the reader touches the wind, it becomes a symbol of nature which has exiled humankind. But if the poem is addressed to the wind, then the man is the active agent; he has shut nature out of his life. And there is also the possibility that the poem may be addressed to the reader or to a lover, whose touch is like a wind on the skin of the poet.

Such poetry depends a great deal on the imagination of the reader who, when he or she reads Simic, can turn to no convenient myths or prose explications but is forced back upon his own experiences. Which explanation, then, does one take? For me, at least, it makes no difference. Why not all? The important things in the poem remain the same regardless of details—the sense of touch, the alienation of the two who were once close.

The music of Simic's poetry is a dull, thumping rhythm. The speaker talks simply in direct, declarative sentences, the way one talks to a foreigner who understands little English. What few rhymes he uses have a deliberate thud.

> There is a wooden slab where bones are broken,
> Scraped clean:—a river dried to its bed
> Where I am fed,
> Where deep in the night I hear a voice.
>
> (From "Butcher Shop")

> Nobody answers.
> Lead. Bullet. With names
> Such as these
> The sleep is deep and long.
>
> (From "Poem without a Title")

Yet when the context calls for poetic rhapsodies, his technique is fully equal to the task.

You must understand that I write this at night
Their sleep surrounds me like an ocean.
Her name is Mary, the most mysterious of all.
She's a forest, standing at the beginning of time.
I'm someone lying within it. This light is our sperm.
The forest is old, older than sleep,
Older than this psalm I'm singing right to the end.

(From "Psalm")

I find few faults in the work, but at times the poetic persona calls too much attention to himself and his manipulations rather than to what he is saying.

I'm Joseph of the Joseph of the Joseph who rode on a donkey,
A wind-mill on the tongue humming with stars,
Columbus himself chained to a chair,
I'm anyone looking for a broom-closet.

(From "Psalm")

And when the speaker intrudes at the end of a poem, he seems to be pushing the meaning, ending with a self-satisfied exclamation point. Look at the last two lines of "Hunger": "She's a bee, you are her flower. / That's all the explanation I find necessary." And at times he is given to melodramatic overstatement, as in the beginning of "Fork": "This strange thing must have crept / Right out of hell."

Yet, all in all, Charles Simic writes fascinating, exciting poetry. It invests mundane objects with universal significance. One rubs them in his work and they take him above or below the earth to secret places from which he gains a new perspective. Only one or two living American poets can evoke a sense of wonder so consistently.

PETER SCHMIDT

White: Charles Simic's Thumbnail Epic

> We search everywhere for the unconditional absolute, but all we find are the conditions.
>
> Novalis

The number of Charles Simic's readers has been increasing steadily during the last two decades, for those who come across his work tend to seek out more and show what they've found to others. His early volumes of poems from George Braziller, *Dismantling the Silence* (1971), *Return to a Place Lit by a Glass of Milk* (1974), *Charon's Cosmology* (1977), and *Classic Ballroom Dances* (1980), have steadfastly stayed in print, an unusual fate for poetry these days, and he has recently published the kinds of works that suggest a poet in the full powers of mid-career: a *Selected Poems,* also from Braziller; a collection of interviews and essays, *The Uncertain Certainty;* and a new volume of poems from a new publisher *(Unending Blues,* 1986). Furthermore, in 1984 Simic became one of the few American poets to be honored with a MacArthur Foundation Grant, providing full support for five years of travel, study, and writing. Such an award indicates both the esteem that Simic's readers have for him and, because of its timing, their sense that Simic's career is perhaps about to enter a new phase—one that may be as marked by this five-year period of study as the first half of his career was shaped by the intense period in the early 1960s he undertook at the New York City Public Library, when he browsed voraciously through the stacks reading poetry, folklore, mythology, anthropology, early eighteenth-century textbooks of science, the journals of explorers, and the literature of various utopian sects.[1]

Simic's long poem *White* occupies a crucial place in the first half of Simic's career. Not only is it the only extended poetic sequence he has so far written, but it was worked on for an entire decade and published twice: Simic now dates it 1970–1980, and has called it

---

From "*White:* Charles Simic's Thumbnail Epic" by Peter Schmidt, *Contemporary Literature* 23 (fall 1982). Reprinted with the permission of University of Wisconsin Press.

his "favorite poem" *(Uncertain Certainty,* 29). Yet the poem is also somewhat of an anomaly in Simic's publishing history, for while most of his other books have had wide publicity and distribution, *White* has been published by small presses only, and has unfortunately never remained in print for long. It is even rarely read at Simic's readings, for he generally refuses to read just parts of it, stressing that the poem is a set of lyrics which must be appreciated as part of a sequence, not in isolation.[2]

Since *White* explores the absence, uncertainty, and erasure that is at the heart of all language, there is something rather ironic in the book's fate. It has become a kind of hidden orphan shadowing the family of Simic's other works, unveiling their secret history, questioning whatever claims they may make to be finished wholes. The lyrics in *White* provide a behind-the-scenes glimpse of many of Simic's most recognizable characters and settings as they might first emerge in his notebooks, before they are fully portrayed in the lyrics which make up the Braziller collections. It is Simic's private collection of beginnings, of summonings—the daily record of the battles he had confronting the white page.

White is also a distinguished attempt to solve a problem which many other poets of Simic's generation are now facing—the creation of a long poem out of a sequence of shorter ones. The last two decades in America have seen renewed interest in the genuinely epic-length poem: work by James Merrill, for example, or Evan Connell, Daniel Hoffman, Marilyn Hacker, Ed Dorn, Robert Duncan, A. R. Ammons. Equally interesting, however, has been the publication of medium-length lyrics or lyric sequences that suggest the ambition of the long poem in scope if not in length: besides *White,* other examples include work by John Ashbery, Mark Strand, David Young, Ruth Whitman, Rachel Blau DuPlessis, Michael S. Harper, Douglas Crase, David Antin. Such writing has been accompanied by increased attention to long poems or lyric sequences by Rilke, Tolson, H.D., Char, Celan, Neruda, Vallejo, Césaire, Tranströmer, and Popa, among others, that have not traditionally been read and compared with those of such canonical Modernist writers as Eliot and Pound and Yeats.

For American poets, particularly those like Simic working in unrhymed forms, one other presence looms large when they contemplate writing a long poem: Walt Whitman. Simic has mentioned how he began his career reading Eliot, Whitman, Sandburg, and Lindsay, but that the poems written under their inspiration were destroyed in the late 1950s when he was in the Army. He then turned to Roethke's *The Lost Son* and *Praise to the End,* the surrealist poets, and his discoveries in the New York Public Library to make a new start for himself. But just as Simic's public career began to be very successful in the early 1970s, Simic deliberately changed direction with *White,* swerving away from the accomplishments of the first book, particularly the short surrealist "object poems" for which he had became quite famous, and returning to a powerful earlier influence, Walt Whitman, so that influence could be rediscovered and rethought (*Uncertain Certainty,* 27–32).

Simic is widely known for the supposedly "foreign" material that he has brought to enrich American poetry—his accent; his experience growing up in Yugoslavia during World War II before his family emigrated to Chicago; his wide reading in European folklore, the French surrealists, modern German and French philosophy, and other topics; his translation of the Yugoslavian mythographer-poet Vasko Popa; and the anthology of translations of writers from Middle and Eastern Europe and Latin America, *Another Republic,* that he edited with Mark Strand. But Simic has also said that he thinks of himself as an *American* poet above all, and his most recent interviews and collections have stressed his umbilical ties to American culture, mentioning in particular both jazz (especially blues lyrics from the 1920s and 1930s) and Walt Whitman and Emily Dickinson. *White* thus gains additional interest because, of all the poems Simic has written, it is the one in which he most determinedly considers his American poetic origins.

I.

> In a philosophical text all the propositions ought to be equally close to the center.
>
> —Theodor Adorno, *Negative Dialectics* (71)

White is composed of three parts. The first two are spoken by the poet and consist of ten ten-line lyrics each, totalling twenty poems. The concluding section, two twenty-line poems, contains the reply of "White" to the poet and is entitled "What the White Had to Say." The "White" of the poem's title is a particular state of mind that the poet seeks to reach during the writing of each short poem, with the first two ten-part sections of *White* being the sum of these incantations. White is *a tabula rasa et alba,* a realm of pure possibility, new selves, new words, and new names, and may be said to be a modern version of the absolute expectancy of divine grace which was the desired climax of the meditative procedures employed by Catholic and Protestant poets in the Renaissance. "All that is near, / I no longer give it a name," the poet says in the second poem of *White,* and later adds, "There are words I need. / They are not near men" (4, 8). Each poem is thus a summoning of the muse of strangeness and new selfhood; White is the only power that can help him shed his past selves and begin again. Instead of using a Willowware cup and a Ouija board, as has James Merrill, another contemporary poet of meditation, Simic places the "five ears" of his fingertips "Against the white page" (12), listening for signs of the descent of his daemon-muse, the White who speaks at the poem's conclusion. During each ten-poem sequence, Simic uses all the strategies he possesses, from prayer and propitiation to temptation and trickery, to summon her. He puts on many masks, including those of an orphan child, a bridegroom and a hermit scholar, and envisions White appearing in many forms, from bestial to celestial. *White*'s persistent quest for a center, a source, plus its infinite evasions and decenterings, make it a deeply philosophical poem in Adorno's sense, a reflection on the mysteries of inspiration and writing.

In the first poem, the poet prays that White will descend and teach him how to divest himself of his old identity and its possessions. He also prays that White will give him a new self, a spiritual marriage. He desires to "touch what I can / Of the quick" and be carried across the threshold dividing one life from another:

> Out of poverty
> To begin again:
>
> With the color of the bride
> And that of blindness,
>
> Touch what I can
> Of the quick,
>
> Speak and then wait,
> As if this light

Will continue to linger
On the threshold.

(3)

His voice is humble and hushed, and he speaks in infinitives ("to begin") and hypotheses ("as if") as though what he desires and describes has not yet been created. He seems both an aspiring young groom and a hermit scholar determined to marry into spiritual wealth by taking a vow of poverty.

With the second poem, we see the poet beginning in earnest his task of shedding his old self. Habit has become a hardening of the senses, a learned deafness, as the objects of this world, represented by a stone and a knife, are appropriated and turned into tools. The poet's response is to impoverish himself, to make the familiar strange:

All that is near,
I no longer give it a name.

Once a stone hard of hearing,
Once sharpened into a knife . . .

Now only a chill
Slipping through.

Enough glow to kneel by and ask
To be tied to its tail

When it goes marrying
Its cousins, the stars.

(4)

This poem has the same mix of humility and resoluteness that the first did. But now there is also an edge of fear: the proposed wedding between the poet and his muse may turn violent. At first, the violence in the lines may be hard to see because of Simic's spare, understated language, so typical of *White,* which imagines a resolution then lists possible causes. Instead of being a human bride, White appears like the kind of animal featured in zodiacal bestiaries. The lines about wanting to be tied to this beast's tail at first seem festive, perhaps alluding to bows or decorations tied onto the tail of a prize animal. But the tone of the poem is uncertain, and quickly shifts from the calm gravity of the opening lines. The ending verges on being comically exaggerated humility, yet the preceding lines about a "chill" and a "knife" suggest hidden fears about any alliance with such an alien, possibly even bestial, force. The poet may be trying to crack a joke because he is afraid of what may come.

Later poems in the first section of *White* confirm the poet's premonitions: the shapes that the poet imagines White to take gradually become more and more frightening. In the fourth poem, for example, she is a "Hard-faced" old woman running a badly aired inner-city grocery who intimidates the poet in his guise as a young boy buying a cupcake (6).[3] In the fifth and seventh poems she appears in somewhat more merciful guises, as a "kind nurse" who can show the poet the "place of salves" (7) and as a mother who sings the child-poet an unsettling lullaby about an insomniac shepherd in the Arctic Circle:

> And he can't get any sleep
> Over lost sheep.
>
> And he's got a flute
> Which says Bo-Peep.
>
> Which says Poor boy,
> Take care of your snow-sheep.
>
> (9)

But both of these masks aren't really assumed by White so much as they are by the poet; as the opening of the fifth poem makes clear ("That your gaze / Be merciful . . ."), these poems function more as invocations or prayers than as descriptions of events that have actually occurred.

In the last two poems of the first sequence, suggestions of violence return. The poet's language implies that his invocations have failed; the transformation he sought seems here more like an execution or a religious martyr's mortification of the flesh than a rebirth. White has become a kind of Our Lady of Pain, a nurse who may offer people salves but who created their wounds in the first place:

> Woe, woes, it sings from the bough.
> Our Lady, etc. . . .

You had me hoodwinked.
I see your brand new claws.

Praying, what do I betray
By desiring your purity?

There are old men and women,
All bandaged up, waiting

At the spiked, wrought-iron gate
Of the Great Eye and Ear Infirmary.

(11)

By the next poem, the last one in the first sequence, this incarnation of White has become neutered, not feminine, and wounds the psyche indifferently, blindly:

We hear holy nothing

Blindfolding itself.
It touched you once, twice,

And tore like stitch
Out of a new wound.

(12)

The hushed expectancy and the infinitive verbs of the first poem in the sequence gradually vanish as the poet immerses himself in his various dreams of what White might be like when she answers his summons. Now, at the end of the first sequence, Simic speaks in the past tense, as if his wounding has already happened. (It hasn't; it's just the eloquence of his vision.) In the course of ten poems to White, his dream of a newborn self ("Touch what I can / Of the quick") has turned into a nightmare in which that point of contact with White is far more painful than he ever expected.

The first sequence of *White* ends at this point, as the poet tries to heal his damaged confidence. We are thus taught to read the gap between the first and second ten-poem sections of *White* as a *wound,* a textual space rendering rending. In fact, the shifts of tone that sometimes occur between lines or between poems in the sequences may be read this way as well, so that they are seen as aporia, moments of loss and doubt that the poet's lines cannot stitch whole. They are moments of equivocation within an invocation, and make the tone of Simic's poems, despite their relatively simple diction, fiendishly difficult to define.

The poet's second sequence of ten poems in *White* uses many of the same personae for both himself and White. We see the poet as a young child, aspiring bridegroom, and hermit scholar, and White appears as an old widow, a bride, an animal, a maternal figure comforting orphans, and a daemonic muse. The second sequence, however, seems to evolve in ways that reverse the pattern of the first. If the first sequence began soberly then evolved into the terrifying vision of Our Lady of Pain, the second begins full of black humor but gradually modulates its voice to that of a young child praying and singing softly, "Now I lay me down to sleep." The second sequence in *White* thus slowly folds back the unfolding of the first, so that at the end the poet is back to where he began, hushed, prayerful, and alone. Perhaps this represents the poet's only possible way of imagining how to heal the wounds in the body of his work.

In the second sequence's first poem, the poet imagines White's questions, then gives his own wily answers; they parry White's thrusts and become almost slapstick versions of the tortures imagined with such horror in the last poem of the first sequence:

> What are you up to son of a gun?
> I roast on my heart's dark side.
>
> What do you use as a skewer sweetheart?
> I use my own crooked backbone.
>
> What do you salt yourself with loverboy?
> I grind the words out of my spittle.
>
> And how will you know when you're done chump?
> When the half-moons on my fingernails set.
>
> With what knife will you carve yourself smartass?
> The one I hide in my tongue's black boot.
>
> (14)

Alternatively, we may read this as the *poet's* queries, followed by White's responses. Either way, the poet here is a sort of spiritual artful dodger, a Huck Finn on the mean streets of Chicago or

New York able to evade any disaster that White may send his way. The next two poems also combine the call-and-response structure of traditional ballads, blues lyrics, and street-game rhymes with contemporary punk patois. But the poet now laughs at himself more easily, and preempts White's challenges even before they can be asked:

> Well, you can't call me a wrestler
> If my own dead weight has me pinned down.
>
> . . .
>
> Well, you can't call me smart,
> When the rain's falling my cup's in the cupboard.
>
> Nor can you call me a saint,
> If I didn't err, there wouldn't be these smudges.
>
> . . .
>
> The flea I was standing on, jumped.
> One has to manage as best as one can.
>
> I think my head went out for a walk.
> One has to manage as best as one can.
>
> (15–16)

"One has to manage as best as one can" is a superb deadpan line. One can well imagine Buster Keaton saying it to himself in his most desperate moments, as when the landscape keeps changing under him in the scene when he climbs into a film in *Sherlock, Jr.*

As the poems of the second sequence progress, the age of the poet seems to vary greatly, but the modulation in the sequence's overall tone from brash to tender becomes dear. The seventh poem in the sequence is another variation on an imagined marriage between the poet and White that merges the language of a child's geometry lesson with that of a marriage ceremony. The implication is that the marriage, if ever consummated, will be difficult to sustain, for the partners are as at odds with each other as a child's fragile body and the eternal purity of geometric truths.

Do you take this circle
Bounded by a single curved line?

I take this breath
That it cannot capture.

Then you may kiss the spot
Where her bridal train last rustled.

(20)

Once again the bride in white vanishes just on the threshold of the poet's ceremony.

In other prominent poems in the second half of the sequence the poet reappears in his familiar guise of the orphan. In the sixth poem, for example, he is confronted yet again by White in the form of an old woman: "She offered him / A tiny sugar cube / / In the hand so wizened / All the lines said: fate" (19). In the eighth and tenth poems, the poet seems like a child talking to himself, perhaps with a maternal figure nearby. We are back to the hushed, prayerful persona that opened the first sequence. The eighth poem is a haunting lullaby for an insomniac somewhat like the earlier song about Bo Peep; clouds and snowflakes form shapes then blow them away, and details from a child's imagination are disconcertingly placed against a vast, indifferent backdrop:

Winter can come now,
The earth narrow to a ditch—

And the sky with its castles and stone lions
Above the empty plains.

The snow can fall . . .
What other perennials would you plant,

My prodigals, my explorers,
Tossing and turning in the dark

For those remote, finely honed bees,
The December stars?

(21)

Speaking in the plural, the poet here appears to be addressing not just the child within him but also all his many selves. Each is an explorer, a prodigal returning to where he started from, and each searches for a lost pastoral world where human beings will feel as at home in the universe as bees in a flowering meadow. Though the poet's tossing and turning continues, his mood is calm and confident as he imagines the future. This lyric is my personal favorite in *White,* perhaps because it reminds me of other works that have the scale of a zodiac and the intimacy of a lullaby, such as René Char's poems to Orion.[4]

The poet's last poem in *White*—his final "summoning," as he calls it (23)—recalls the steadfast, serious tone of his very first poem. There is "Solitude—as in the beginning," Simic says, "And fear—that dead letter office. / And doubt—that Chinese shadow play." He still cannot be sure that his prayers will summon White, or that they will give him any hint of what she will be like or how she will treat him if she does arrive. As in the first poem, he speaks and then waits, lingering on the threshold connecting this world and the spirit world. Mixed in with this humble voice, however, is a hint of the urchin who strutted and mocked both White and himself at the beginning of the second sequence of poems. He not only seems positive that White's presence will be maternal; he also imagines her creating him in her own image and then—she is a poet's muse, after all—giving birth to him through her mouth: "A zero burped by a bigger zero— / It's an awful licking I got." However White may beat me, he puns, her "lickings" will also be maternal, like that of a lioness licking clean her cub after boxing his ears. The lyric then closes with the same humble expectancy with which it began: the poet is not a tough talker but an orphan in bed, awake, alone and softly praying for a comforting dream to appear:

> Does anyone still say a prayer
> Before going to bed?
>
> White sleeplessness.
> No one knows its weight.

Simic ends *White* with a masterstroke: after summoning White many times, he evades his own personae and in the two-part section "What the White Had to Say" allows White to take over his voice and have the last word. If this is self-effacement, it is also victory, for his muse has at last crossed over the threshold from whiteness and had her words appear in black ink on the page. In the two twenty-line monologues which are spoken by

White (pp. 26–27), she appears in guises that readers of the earlier sections will readily recognize. At times she is both mother and lover, a pastoral force engendering and caring for the poet's many selves:

> Poems are made of our lusty wedding nights,
> The joy of words as they are written.
> The ear that got up at four in the morning
> To hear the grass grow inside a word.

Elsewhere in her monologues she boasts to the poet that she contains many selves he will never realize. She forever remains partially undisclosed, the White that got away:

> Cleverly you've invented name after name for me,
> Mixed the riddles, garbled the proverbs,
> Shook your loaded dice in a tin cup,
> But I do not answer back even to your curses,
> For I am nearer to you than your breath.[5]

Just as he'd feared, the poet's muse here rises up in all her daemonic power, ever elusive and always dangerous. She can rip apart all his earlier selves, all the previous orderings of his life into poems that he fondly calls the "body" of his work, and she can evade all his future figures of speech attempting to figure her forth.

> Because I am the bullet
> That has gone through everyone already,
> I thought of you long before you thought of me.
> Each one of you still keeps a blood-stained handkerchief
> In which to swaddle me, but it stays empty . . .

The previous twenty poems in *White* were all written using five tidy couplets and, generally, end-stopped lines. But the twin concluding poems by White herself are a torrential stream of run-on sentences, enjambed lines, mixed metaphors, changing voices, and seemingly formless paragraphs—pure energy vaporizing the poet's well-wrought urns. Moreover, if White in the early lyrics generally was given her personae one by one, in her own section of *White* she shifts her masks much more rapidly, merging and mocking the poet's own descriptions of her. These simultaneous states of being are appropriate for such a pale muse, even though Simic's mixed voices and metaphors do make it difficult for the reader at first to become oriented and able to discern a unified presence in these last two poems. But that is as it should be; accommodating oneself to White's sublime fluidity is one of the demands she makes of us. All her masks of bride, benevolent widow, animal, Gorgon/Medusa, and Eumenides pass rapidly by us, and, feigning closeness with the poet, she parodies his earlier pretensions to being a hermit scholar ("Out of poverty / To begin again . . ."):

> One sun shines on us both through a crack in the roof.
> A spoon brings me through the window at dawn.
> A plate shows me off to the four walls
> While with my tail I swing at the flies.
> But there's no tail and the flies are your thoughts.

By the end of White's first poem, she has so taken over the poet's voice that his inhalation of her foreignness—his inspiration—is compared to drowning:

> Steadily, patiently I lift your arms.
> I arrange them in the posture of someone drowning,
> And yet the sea in which you are sinking,
> And even this night above it, is myself.

In the second poem by White, she tempers her invasion of the poet somewhat. Her tone is tender and elegiac, and she seems sincerely to speak of herself as the poet's equal, dropping her accusatory use of the second person and adopting the first person plural, so that she becomes a fellow orphan or an animal under the poet's care:

> One gaunt shadowy mother wiped our asses,
> The same old orphanage taught us loneliness.
> Street-organ full of blue notes,
> I am the monkey dancing to your grinding . . .

White's monologue and *White* itself ends with the poet nestled close to White's side, secure and finally able to stop his tossing and turning. It is as if the poet at the very last moment of the poem has finally earned the right to touch her. Appropriately, the last lines are hushed, as if White's words were a lullaby sung by one orphan to another, and the poet's many incarnations as scholar, suitor, and frightened child are at last discarded, leaving unbounded peace, steady breathing, and a dream of children's games celebrating infinite transformation. The new self that the poet prayed for, like a new tooth, seems effortlessly on its way:

> Time slopes. We are falling head over heels
> At the speed of night. That milk tooth
> You left under the pillow, it's grinning.

Helen Vendler once argued that Simic is a strong poet plagued by poems with weak endings that merely complete a "known shape" (358). If this assertion sounds odd to a reader familiar with the dramatic accelerations and new twists in the concluding lines of poems such as "The Forest," "Breasts," "Charon's Cosmology," "Shirt," or "Prodigy," it will thoroughly perplex the reader of *White,* for rarely has a modern sequence of poems ended with such an apocalyptic fusion of tumult and calm—a whirlwind summoning and blending the persons, places, and things of the poet's vision. To measure their dramatic power, the two lyrics that make up "What the White Had to Say" ought to be allowed to stand (or whirl) in the mind's eye next to the final sections of Yeats's "1919" and Stevens's "Auroras of Autumn," both of which offer similarly climactic moments of revelation and erasure.

II.

> O give me the clue! (it lurks in the night here somewhere;)
>
> . . .
>
> O how joys, dreads, convolutions, human shapes, and all shapes,
> spring as from graves around me!
> O phantoms! you cover all the land and all the sea!
> O I cannot see in the dimness whether you smile or frown upon
> me. . . .
>
> (Whitman, "Out of the Cradle Endlessly Rocking,"
> (615 [1867 version])

The closing passages of *White,* particularly Simic's reference to White as a "gaunt shadowy mother," may remind some readers of the "old one" swathed in sweet garments who rocks the cradle in Whitman's "Out of the Cradle Endlessly Rocking" (1859).

This relation of *White* to Walt Whitman is worth considering more closely.

The music of Whitman's poem imitates first the mockingbird's lament for the loss of its mate and then the sinister susurrus of the sea, the "fierce old mother" incessantly moaning the word "death." Together, the songs of bird and sea cause the poet to understand for the first time that he will die. Soon after he overhears the bird pleading for its lost mate to appear against the background of the white breakers ("What is that little black thing I see there in the white?"), he himself is looking out to sea and beholding his own twin, a swimmer, and his "white arms out in the breakers." At first, the boy hopes that this figure's arms are "tirelessly tossing"; his vision is as much a wish fulfillment as the mockingbird's. But by the poem's end he admits that the secret the sea has shown him is a "drowned" one. Intuitively, he understands that the swimmer could not survive: it was his childhood self struggling against the undertow of his new knowledge that he is not immortal. The adult poet, moreover, understands that the sea has nursed him on this bitter wisdom and given him his voice. It is as if the child's sudden experience of death compelled him to fill the void he felt with song—as if by pouring out words and music he could somehow will into being the vanished sense of wholeness he once knew:

> For I, that was a child, my tongue's use sleeping, now I have heard
>   you,
> Now in a moment I know what I am for, I awake,
>
> . . .
>
> A thousand warbling echoes have started to life within me . . .
>
> . . .
>
> My own songs awaked from that hour. . . .
>
> (213–14)

But if the experience of loss destroys the child's illusion that all is permanent (thus rendering him a spiritual orphan from the things of this world), paradoxically such experience also supports the child's new, more mature self. Images which first reminded the poet of his secure childhood (such as "Pour down your warmth, great sun! / While we bask we have two together, / / Two together!") are by the end of the poem used to describe the experience of division, not wholeness. The poet's knowledge of death is a kind of grim but benevolent foster-parent, personified as an old crone "swathed in sweet garments" who bends her wrinkled face toward the child's, whispering in his ear, rocking his cradle, "pouring down" upon him her hoarse hissing, her bitter understanding that we are all orphans on this earth.

Simic's muse of Whiteness is also a half-benevolent, half terrifying foster-mother, and his child-poet an orphan. The first and second parts of *White* have as their epigraph a line from "Out of the Cradle" which implies that the poet's songs, like those of Whitman's mockingbird, are inspired by loss: "What is that little black thing I see there in the white?" To make the connection between his poem and Whitman's even clearer, Simic in 1980 published a revision of a central line in White's monologue, altering it from "I am the emptiness that tucks you in like a dove's nest" to "I am the emptiness that tucks you in like a mockingbird's nest." In "Out of the Cradle" this nurturing figure modulated in the middle of the poem from the mockingbird to the sea-mother. Remembering this transformation, Simic has White in her monologues describe herself as both a mockingbird and an ocean: as a mockingbird she tucks the poet in at night, and as the sea she is the water "in which you are sinking." There are other parallels between "Out of the Cradle" and *White*. Both Whitman and Simic describe the death of the poet's earlier self, and both end their works with an ambiguous moment of rebirth. Whitman is "awaked" and sings of birth yet stares into what passes for a death's-head, the face of the old crone, while Simic "falls" asleep but finds a new self rising within him: "Time slopes. We are falling head over heels / At the speed of night. That milk tooth / You left under the pillow, it's grinning." Simic's milk tooth here seems both sinister and heartening: it grins like a skull, suggesting the self that has died, but it also reminds us that a child's milk teeth are replaced by his adult ones, including his "wisdom" teeth.

Simic's reference to the "milk tooth" may also allude to other famous lines by Whitman about coming of age, the notorious section in "The Sleepers" in which he described a child's passage into adulthood by referring to teething:

> [I] am curious to know where my feet stand—and what is this
> flooding me,
> childhood or manhood—and the hunger that crosses the bridge
> between.

The cloth laps a first sweet eating and drinking,
Laps life-swelling yolks—laps of ear of rose-corn, milky and just
ripened;
The white teeth stay, and the boss tooth advances in darkness . . . .
(651 [1855 version])

The sudden changes of the body during the end of childhood are no less frightening to a child than the advancing stages of the mind's own transformations as one self yields to another. The boss tooth of the boy's manhood—his sexuality, his knowledge of evil and of death—ruthlessly expels his childhood self. This change is a prelude to the continual remaking of the self that is exemplified in "The Sleepers" and that Whitman wants the adult psyche to undergo each night during dreaming. Similarly, in *White* Simic uses references to drowning, falling, and teething to depict not just the passage from childhood to adulthood but also the passage he as an adult wants to make from one self to another.

Simic's *White* should also be read as a meditation on another form of drowning and rebirth—the influence (literally, the in-flowing) of a previous writer's voice upon his own. Such a preoccupation with poetic predecessors is appropriate to *White,* for any poem about the poet's urge to be reborn must also be a poem about his or her origins. Simic seeks a new, "white," unknown voice to inhabit him, yet as his desire for such an event increases so too does his knowledge of how thoroughly both his new and his old voices resound with those of his predecessors, particularly Whitman's. Indeed, like the child in "Out of the Cradle," he paradoxically comes of age and discovers his own voice only after he loses his illusions of wholeness and admits for the first time the terrifying insurge of an alien, foster-voice whose music is not his own. *White* is Simic's collection of strategies for summoning forth his muse. But when she appears, one of her masks is that of "White-man," Whitman.[6]

Simic alludes most clearly to this necessary inflooding in the penultimate poem of the poet's second sequence. With puns on the phrases "getting through" and "going through," he refers both to the process of transformation itself, the new self passing through (or flooding) the old self, and to the poet's stricken understanding of the process as it happens. That is, the spirit which teaches him about death and transformation must "get through" to the poet's obtuse old self, which Simic here portrays as a sort of cantankerous old man indignant at the fact that he can't be around forever. White's forces, however, are irresistible; they have all the power of an army of ants dismantling a body, and force the speaker to joke grimly about his own decomposition:

> Had to get through me elsewhere.
> Woe to bone
>
> That stood in their way.
> Woe to each morsel of flesh.
>
> White ants
> In a white anthill.
>
> The rustle of their many feet
> Scurrying—tiptoeing too.
>
> Gravedigger ants.
> Village-idiot ants.
>
> (22)

White's concluding monologues also tease the defensive poet by playing upon the phrase "getting through." The poet, like the old man, or an innocent child, stubbornly believes that his voice and his self are of his own making. But White is disdainful and imperious. "I am the bullet that has gone through everyone," she chants mockingly at the beginning of each of her two speeches, using "everyone" to refer to the poet's menagerie of selves. Then she forces him to locate the source of all of his powers of self-creation *outside* of himself: "I thought of you long before you thought of me." It is a moment of sheer terror; the fragile levees defining the poet's self are inundated and swept away. Like the child in "Out of the Cradle," the poet in *White* loses his illusions of independence and is flooded by a foreign presence; he learns how frail his "own" voice is, and that it is loaned to him, not his to keep. The poet had prayed for such a gift of a new voice repeatedly throughout his sections of *White,* but even his worst fears of what White might do to him had an involuntary arrogance to them, as shown by his references to himself as a heroic martyr in her presence. He still believed that he could "summon" White as if she were a genie and bid her to give him a new self on demand. During White's monologues, however, he learns that even his pretensions to summoning her were under her control. She may give him a new self or drown his old self and leave it at that. This is the grim undercurrent of White's monologues, songs whose melodious hissing is kin to that of the old crone who rocks the cradle in Whitman's poem. By the end of White's poems, however, her tone becomes more benign, even motherly, though an edge of her original anger remains. Her influx lifts or floats a new self to the poet even as it drowns the old one; she seems both a mother in mourning arranging the limbs of her lost child and a mother who rocks a newborn one—Simic's newborn poetic self—in her arms: "Steadily, patiently, I lift your arms . . . / . . . the sea in which you are sinking, / And even this night above it, is myself."

A similar death and transfiguration occurs when Whitman's voice invades Simic's. At first it is Simic's undoing: when in *White* he finds his own voice immersed in the dangerous, powerful rhythms of Whitman's, he can only pray that his fate will not be that of the "white" swimmer in "Out of the Cradle." But after enduring the successive infloodings of White, Simic has earned the right to discover the new voice that he asked for rising slowly but buoyantly within him. This voice is recognizably his own, although the drone of Whitman's sea-mother can still be heard beneath it.

Such an emergence in the last lines of *White* even as the poet's old self "falls" asleep and is whirled away shows that Simic, like Whitman, takes up Emerson's oracular challenge to the American poet in *Nature:*

> These are examples of Reason's momentary grasp of the scepter; the exertions of a power which exists not in time or space, but an instantaneous instreaming causing power. The difference between the actual and the ideal force of man is happily figured by the schoolmen, in saying, that the knowledge of man is an evening knowledge, *vespertina cognito,* but that of God is a morning knowledge, *matutina cognito.* (54)

In *White,* Simic confronts "evening knowledge," what Emerson would later call "Fate": the knowledge of powerlessness, limitations, death, an instantaneous in-streaming of a force foreign to himself. But he has managed to stay afloat, and thus may have revealed to him what Emerson calls "morning knowledge," the "ideal" force of man—and the poet—which seeks to be broken and reborn again and again. Paradoxically, Simic tries to free himself from history by immersing himself within an American literary tradition that denies history and affirms only "morning knowledge," the poet's inalienable right (as Emerson said in *Nature)* to discover an original relation to the universe (21). Simic assays the dangerous crossing from "evening knowledge" to "morning knowledge" each time he begins a poem in *White;* he seeks to discard his earlier, time-bound selves and return to a place lit by the milk-white light of dawn. But none of the poet's twenty poems in *White* complete that return successfully. White does not appear except hypothetically, and the poet is left in twenty different states of "evening knowledge"—hopefulness, despair, terror, and anger. In "What the White Had to Say," however, the "White" muse representing the American oracular poetic tradition finally descends upon Simic and claims him, and *White* ends with the poet just about to receive the morning-new self and voice for which he has prayed so long.

III.

> Only for the sake of the hopeless ones have we been given hope.
> —Walter Benjamin, *Illuminations* (17)

In 1977 Simic published a short essay—really a collection of paragraphs, a notecard prolegomenon—entitled "Composition"; it bears on the quest to recover "purity" in *White.* Simic noted that the poet's search is a search for origins, an epic journey leading backward in time rather than forward in space. He hoped that this desire to discover primordial voices beneath our historical ones sought the secret strength of poetry and the source of its perpetual renewal. The "difficulty" of modern poetry from Imagism to Surrealism is that it has invested all its energies to permit that ancestral and archetypal thought to become audible in its purity. *(Uncertain Certainty,* 112)

Simic's many masks in *White* and in his early Braziller volumes accordingly tend to possess the archetypal qualities that Yeats associated with masks. Simic's early personae are unlike Browning's, which speak with single, everyday voices, and unlike Pound's and Eliot's, which speak with the many voices of a historical period. They are more kin to the songs sung by the orphans and beggars in Rilke's *Büch der Bilder* or any of Yeats's volumes; they employ the ahistorical, ancestral voices of *the* orphan, *the* vagabond, *the* rogue, *the* stepmother. Simic's use of such generic psychic personae is complemented by his pervasive interest in imitating riddles, incantations, and charms, all primary sources for lyric poetry, and folkloric formulae and notated incident, all kernels of narrative. What originally attracted him to such works is that they seemed outside of time, or so steeped in it they felt eternal.

Intriguingly, however, the personae in Simic's work in the late 1970's and early 1980's appear to have evolved away from the strongly archetypal to a mode that mixes such universal correspondences with much more autobiographical and historical detail. "Forest," for instance, opens Simic's first Braziller volume and strikes its keynote; its hero is somewhat like a blend of Prospero and Whitman, with the former's rough magic ("my roots and streams / Will stitch their chill into the heart of man") and the latter's stentorian confidence ("Ladies and gentlemen, you will hear a star / Dead a million years, in the throat of a bird"). Simic's language stresses the archetypal qualities of all the poem's events—all "man" is involved, time is measured in eons rather than in forty-hour weeks, and the knowledge the poem teaches is ancient, even prehistorical:

> There'll be plenty of time
> When an acorn grows out of your ear
> To accustom yourself to my ways,
> To carve yourself a hermit's toothpick.
>
> (3)

In "Forest," identity dependent upon a particular place, time and society gives way to a primordial self, as if the dark forest of man's collective unconscious were reclaiming the collapsing cities of modern personality. Simic's volumes *Charon's Cosmology* and *Classic Ballroom Dances,* both finished when he was also reworking *White,* represent an apparent turning-point. Such prehistoric forces remain ever-present, but paradoxically they seem all the more compelling because they are *less* confidently inherited; several of the poems are filled with more personal and historical references than Simic has ever included, and their protagonists' escape from history, when it occurs, is more provisional, more tentative.

In "Furniture Mover" for example, the speaker longs to escape from the burden of carrying his possessions, his body and his self. He wants to arrive at a future destination in his life ahead of time or, rather, ahead of Time, ahead of his history. The tone of the poem is also much like that of *White,* hushed and prayer-like but with muted comic asides. The tragicomic battle of the speaker's soul and his furniture mover is at a standoff; he wants to leave behind his physical, historical self (represented by the furniture mover), but he always arrives in the future just one step too late:

oh
Mr. Furniture Mover
on my knees

let me come
for once
early
to where it's vacant

you still
on the stairs
wheezing
between floors
(*Classic Ballroom Dances* 41–42)

The speakers in Simic's earlier poems tended to be archetypal presences, as in "Forest"; magicians or fortune-tellers interpreting the mysteries of such presences, as in "Needle" from *Dismantling the Silence,* which begins, "Watch out for the needle, / She's the scent of a plant / The root of which is far and hidden"; or heroic voyagers who escape history entirely, as in "Explorers," which ends with each of the explorers greeting a newly discovered world: "You are all / That has eluded me. / / May this be my country" (64, 67). Such oracular confidence is generally absent in *Classic Ballroom Dances,* where the tone is grayer, the events suggest historical as well as mythic incidents, and the characters tend to be not those who have escaped history but those who have been disfigured by it—orphans, war refugees, beggars, lunatics, widows and widowers, a pair of "ancient lovers" in the volume's title poem, on the "dancefloor of the Union Hall, / where they also hold charity raffles / On rainy Monday nights of an eternal November" (52). Such figures had been in Simic's work from the start, but never had their presence loomed so large or been described in such detail. If part of Simic wanted to escape from history, another part of him had learned that the poet has the responsibility of the furniture mover to remember—to carry—as much as he or she can bear.[7]

Two of Simic's other new collections from the 1980's, *Austeri-*

ties and *Unending Blues,* develop this new direction even more thoroughly, as does the important essay Simic published in *Ironwood* in 1984, entitled "Notes on Poetry and History." This essay reverses several of the premises of earlier pieces such as "Composition"; in it, Simic emphasizes how a poet must confront "the irrationality of history":

> We are orphans of ideologies. Everyone who made history in this century in our name believed that the massacre of the innocents was permissible for the sake of the future. Our savagery differs from that of the previous centuries in that we kill almost exclusively to prove some theory of history. The idea is that one must be merciless for the sake of the coming happiness. The problem is that there are always some who stand in the way, who refuse to accept the inevitable. The gallows and penal colonies erected for these people have been justified by the loftiest ideals. We live in the shadow of these intellectual slaughterhouses. The poet who forgets that is living in fool's paradise. (*Uncertain Certainty* 125)

The shadow of these slaughterhouses lengthens across Simic's most recent volumes, even as the shades of the prisonhouse increasingly occupied Wordsworth's mind after they made their appearance in the midst of his "Immortality Ode" of 1804. (Interestingly enough, Wordsworth's poem also has an ancestor to Whitman's crone, a "homely Nurse" who does all she can "To make her Foster-child, her Inmate Man, / Forget the glories he hath known" [11.81–83].) Such shadows make the moments of tenderness and peace in Simic's recent collections all the more poignant.

Another way to think of these developments in Simic's work is to compare them to the blues, with stress on how deeply Simic feels this art form reflects the historical circumstances of its creation. In a recent interview, Simic paid tribute to the "incredible verbal invention" of blues lyrics:

> What one would call "jive," but also eroticism, the tragic sense of life. If the blues were French, we'd be studying it at Yale. As it is, hardly anyone knows my heroes, people like Cripple Clarence Lofton, Frankie Jaxon, or Bessie Jackson, who also called herself Lucille Bogan. They are our Villons.
>
> Anyway, blues taught me a number of things. How to tell

a story quickly, economically. The value of gaps, ellipses, and most importantly, the virtues of simplicity and accessibility. (*Uncertain Certainty* 69–70)

All the poems in Simic's volumes after 1977 may be thought of as being filled with blue or "bent" notes—notes bent away from perfection by the pressure of history and mortality.

Over the years Simic has also stressed a very different source of inspiration, his reading in philosophy, including Heidegger (such as "The Origin of the Work of Art") and Husserl. It is not clear how much of the work of another German thinker, Walter Benjamin, Simic has read, but there are at least three reasons why Benjamin's writings prove invaluable for a reader seeking to understand the new direction Simic's work has taken since *White,* and I would like to end this essay by sketching them.

First, Benjamin would surely have endorsed Simic's comment that we are all "orphans of ideologies"; he was deeply suspicious of all forms of utopian idealism, including Marxism. For this reason Benjamin remained skeptical of the Hegelian strain in German philosophy in the 1930s, even though he was friends with and had been influenced by several of its most important figures, including Theodor Adorno.[8] Benjamin's skepticism about designs for ensuring "progress" in history is superbly captured in his late essay "Theses on the Philosophy of History," when he comments on a Paul Klee work he owned:

> A Klee painting named "Angelus Novus" shows an angel looking as though he is about to move away from something he is fixedly contemplating. His eyes are staring, his mouth is open, his wings are spread. This is how one pictures the angel of history. His face is turned toward the past. Where we perceive a chain of events, he sees one single catastrophe which keeps piling wreckage upon wreckage and hurls it in front of his feet. The angel would like to stay, awaken the dead, and make whole what has been smashed. But a storm is blowing from Paradise; it has got caught in his wings with such violence that the angel can no longer close them. This storm irresistibly propels him into the future to which his back is turned, while the pile of debris before him grows skyward. This storm is what we call progress. (*Illuminations* 257–58)

Such a passage could be an epigram for all of Simic's poems about history, not to mention the fact that there is an uncanny correspondence between such a merciless Angel of revelation and White.

Second, like Simic Benjamin was fascinated with junk- and rag-dealers, orphans, and derelicts—*chiffonniers* or *Lumpensammlers,* as he called them. They were his types for the artist amidst the ruins of modernity, collecting and transfiguring commonplace objects, the refuse of history. In Benjamin's words, describing his great final collage project, the *Passagenwerk,*

> Method of this work: literary montage. I need say nothing. Only show. I won't steal anything valuable or appropriate any witty turns of phrase. But the trivia, the trash: this, I don't want to take stock of, but let it come into its own in the only way possible: use it. ("N [Theoretics of Knowledge; Theory of Progress]")

This strikes me as a kind of *ars poetica* for collage poems of Simic's like "Classic Ballroom Dances" or "Baby Pictures of Famous Dictators," both from *Classic Ballroom Dances.* Such a connection between Benjamin's ragpicker persona and Simic's is further strengthened when we learn that Simic has mentioned that his recent poems about the nightmare of history are a response in part to some of his earliest memories, of scavenging for war souvenirs among the rubble and corpses in Belgrade, Yugoslavia, in 1944–45 (*Uncertain Certainty* 68–69).

Third, difficult collage poems such as "Baby Pictures of Famous Dictators" or "History" (the latter from *Unending Blues)* cannot be understood without a knowledge of how to interpret fragments and lists, and Benjamin is our greatest modern theoretician of these forms. The texture of a poem like "Baby Pictures . . ." is that of a montage, and many of its images are hallucinatory and Bosch-like. To use a Benjaminian word, they are "phantasmagorias," flickering collections of images stressing not only the contradiction between utopian ideals and their aftermath, but also their fantastical and artificial, even comical, nature. In his "Theses on the Philosophy of History," Benjamin approvingly quotes Baudelaire on this subject, from his "Salon of 1859":

> "I long for the return of the dioramas whose enormous, crude magic subjects me to the spell of a useful illusion. I prefer looking at the backdrop paintings of the stage where I find my favorite dreams treated with consummate skill and tragic concision. Those things, so completely false, are for that very

reason much closer to the truth, whereas the majority of our landscape painters are liars, precisely because they fail to lie." (*Illuminations* 191)

"Baby Pictures of Famous Dictators" has just such a Baudelairean and Benjaminian sense of the lies of history, recording its broken panorama of illusion and suffering with spleen, black humor, and "tragic concision":

> The epoch of a streetcar drawn by horses;
> The organ-grinder and his monkey.
> Women with parasols. Little kids in rowboats
> Photographed against a cardboard backdrop depicting an idyllic
> sunset
> At the fairgrounds where they all went to see
> The two-headed calf, the bearded
> Fat lady who dances the dance of seven veils.
>
> And the great famine raging through India . . .
> Fortune-telling white rats pulling a card out of a shoebox
> While Edison worries over the lightbulb,
> And the first model of the sewing machine
> Is delivered in a pushcart
> To a modest white-fenced home in the suburbs . . .
>
> (*Classic Ballroom Dances* 22)

This kind of poem is essentially a collection of debris or souvenirs, leavings or Baudelairean "dejections" culled from history's "archives of debauchery, the stockpile of waste" (Benjamin, quoted by Wohlfarth 151). And like all of Simic's best poems, including *White,* it gives us a sense that the poem on the page must ultimately be understood as a ruin, a pile of fragments from an ideal form no longer attainable.[9]

White is indispensable for helping us account for the growing presence of such irony and such historical detail in Simic's work. For in *White* (unlike *Dismantling the Silence)* the poet's desire to transcend history is eventually subverted; the "white" muse of purity and "morning knowledge" is also what I have called Whitman's crone or Benjamin's ragpicker, a muse of tragedy and fallen experience. *White* will become a permanent part of American oracular poetic tradition because it is a powerful poem about a quest to leave irony behind and to return to oracular assertion. But it also turns upon itself and becomes simultaneously an ironic *critique* of an oracular poet's belief that he or she may transcend time and disown the grim absolutes of "evening knowledge." At first glance, perhaps, *White* seems different from Simic's more recent ironic lyrics, for it appears patently to be a poem in which the poet sheds his old self and ends in free fall, free from space and time and safe in White's embrace. But that moment of free fall cannot last. The last lines of the poem about the milk tooth that the poet has placed under his pillow while he dreams imply that he is poised at the moment of transformation, just about to recross the boundary separating eternity from time to accept the new, time-bound, and necessarily disfigured self that White will give him.

Thus although *White* is a successful quest to return to White's embrace, its ending foretells another beginning when that embrace is broken and the child-poet is exiled and falls into time, selfhood, particular lyric forms, and ink marks on the page. It is apparent that the drama of summoning White has been enacted again and again, and that Simic's poetry collections gather with increasingly ironic detail the various mortal selves that White left the poet each time she descended upon him, passed through him, and then vanished. Guided by his female muse, Simic at the end of *White is* in the same position as the child in "Out of the Cradle Endlessly Rocking"—just on the verge of a tragic awakening. The pain and loss caused by such an orphaning will inspire all his songs: "For I, that was a child, my tongue's use sleeping, now I have heard you, / Now in a moment I know what I am for, I awake. . . . "

If Simic's volumes from *Dismantling the Silence* onward contain portraits of the selves that his muse has awakened within him, in *White* he gives us a behind-the-scenes glimpse into what it is like to summon one's psychic forces and then watch them invade, form shapes, and displace each other. In doing so, Simic has created a poem whose intimate immensity gives it a right to be called an epic in scale if not in length. Unlike previous epics, *White* does not incorporate large chunks of narrative; instead, it rewrites narrative in the key of the lyric, with each of its poems compacting its story within the confines of the spot of time, rarely more than a few moments, in which the lyric traditionally takes place. *White* also has the requisite epic subject, the story of the struggle to return home, and it uses the traditional epic mode of characterization, employing larger-than-life archetypal personae for its protagonists. Presenting the struggle between a poet and his predecessors, and between "evening knowledge" and "morning knowledge," the experience of time and the appetite for that power which frees one from time, *White is* a long ur-lyric, a thumbnail or miniature epic about the painful birth of the lyric itself.

NOTES

1. All quotations from Simic's volumes will be cited parenthetically in the text, while full bibliographic information about them may be found in the Works Cited listings at the end of the essay. For all citations from *White* I use the 1980 revised edition, except where specified. Simic's revisions of the poem included changing selected lines, transposing a few lyrics, and cuffing some others to replace them with new poems.

2. For more information on the history of *White*'s composition and other matters, see the George Starbuck interview with Simic in *Uncertain Certainty,* pp. 27–45; the interview is dated 1975. Also relevant is the first published discussion of *White,* by James Carpenter.

3. This lyric was originally in the second ten-poem sequence, but was moved to its present position in the first sequence in 1980.

4. The best of these are included in Franz Wright's fine volume *No Siege Is Absolute: Versions of René Char.*

5. The 1980 text has "Shook you loaded dice." But since White is addressing the poet in this passage, surely "you" is a misprint for "your."

6. Harold Bloom's well-known theory of poetic influence was being developed, interestingly enough, during the same decade that Simic was writing *White. The Anxiety of Influence is* obviously relevant to this discussion, but I have found Bloom's *Kaballah and Criticism* perhaps even more suggestive for thinking about White as the muse of inspiration and revision.

7. For two earlier articles on the matter of Simic's evolution, see David Young's and David Walker's essays.

8. The best introduction to Benjamin's work is Michael W. Jennings' recent book, which includes discussion of Benjamin's differences with Adorno and other members of what would become known as the "Frankfurt" school of social criticism, most of whom left Germany with the rise of Hitler. Heidegger was not a member of the Frankfurt school, and stayed in Germany. Recently, Heidegger's association with the Nazis has provoked some reassessment of his thought: see Thomas Sheehan's article.

9. For further discussion of this concept of the fragment, see Jennings, Chapter Five; Bloom, *Kaballah and Criticism;* and Philippe Lacoue-Labarthe and Jean-Luc Nancy, *The Literary Absolute: The Theory of Literature in German Romanticism.*

WORKS CITED

Benjamin, Walter. *Illuminations*. Ed. Hannah Arendt. New York: Schocken, 1969.

———. "N [Theoretics of Knowledge; Theory of Progress]." Trans. Leigh Hafrey and Richard Sieburth. *The Philosophical Forum* 15.1–2 (1983–84): 1–40.

Bloom, Harold. *Anxiety of Influence: A Theory of Poetry*. New York: Oxford, 1973.

———. *Kaballah and Criticism*. New York: Continuum, 1975.

Carpenter, James. "Charles Simic: *White*." *Ironwood* 4.1–2 (1976): 72–84.

Emerson, Ralph Waldo. *Selections from Ralph Waldo Emerson*. Ed. Stephen E. Whicher. New York: Houghton Mifflin, 1957.

Jennings, Michael W. *Dialectical Images: Walter Benjamin's Theory of Literary Criticism*. New York: Cornell University Press, 1987.

Lacoue-Labarthe, Philippe, and Jean-Luc Nancy. *The Literary Absolute: The Theory of Literature in German Romanticism*. Trans. Philip Barnard and Cheryl Lester. Albany, N.Y.: SUNY Press, 1988.

Popa, Vasko. *Homage to the Lame Wolf: Selected Poems, 1956–1970*. Trans. Charles Simic. Oberlin, Ohio: Field Translation Series, 1979.

Sheehan, Thomas. "Heidegger and the Nazis." *The New York Review of Books* 35.10 (June 16,1988): 38–47.

Simic, Charles, and Mark Strand, eds. *Another Republic: 17 European and South American Writers*. New York: Ecco, 1976.

Simic, Charles. *Austerities*. New York: Braziller, 1982.

———. *Charon's Cosmology*. New York: Braziller, 1977.

———. *Classic Ballroom Dances*. New York: Braziller, 1980.

———. *Dismantling the Silence*. New York: Braziller, 1971.

———. *Return to a Place Lit by a Glass of Milk*. New York: Braziller, 1974.

———. *Selected Poems: 1963–1983*. New York: Braziller, 1985.

———. *The Uncertain Certainty: Interviews, Essays, and Notes on Poetry*. Ann Arbor: University of Michigan Press, 1985.

———. *Unending Blues*. New York: Harcourt Brace Jovanovich, 1986.

———. *White*. Durango, CO: Logbridge-Rhodes, 1980.

———. *White*. New York: New Rivers Press, 1972.

Vendler, Helen. *Part of Nature, Part of Us*. Cambridge: Harvard University Press, 1980.

Walker, David. "O What Solitude: The Recent Poetry of Charles Simic." *Ironwood* 4.1–2 (1976): 61–67.

Whitman, Walt. *Leaves of Grass: The Inclusive Edition*. Ed. Emory Holloway. Garden City, N.Y.: Doubleday, 1926.

Wohlfarth, Irving. "Et Cetera? The Historian as Chiffonnier." *New German Critique* 39 (1986):143–68. Special issue on Walter Benjamin.

Wright, Franz. *No Siege Is Absolute: Versions of René Char*. Providence, R.I.: Lost Roads, 1984.

Young, David. "Review of *Classic Ballroom Dances*." *Field* 24 (1981): 83–88.

GEORGE HITCHCOCK

Charles Simic's *Return to a Place Lit by a Glass of Milk*

Charles Simic is certainly one of the most gifted and influential poets of his generation (he was born in 1938, in Belgrade, and came to this country shortly after the War). He has attempted—and in his best poems largely succeeded in—a return to a language of the utmost simplicity, an alphabet of things, yet things where the human emotions are never for long absent. He invokes the primitive human myths, the folk memories and the structures of fables, which our conscious minds have too often forgotten.

"I want to simplify; I want to return to and communicate some basic human content," he said in a recent interview *(Skywriting,* vol. 1, no. 2). For readers who may not yet have come across his poetry let me give an example or two (from his earlier books) of where this simplification leads:

EVENING

The snail gives off stillness.
The weed is blessed.
At the end of a long day
The man finds joy, the water peace.

Let all be simple. Let all stand still
Without a final direction.
That which brings you into the world
To take you away at death
Is one and the same;
The shadow long and pointy
Is its church.

From "A Gathering of Poets," review of *Return to a Place Lit by a Glass of Milk. Western Humanities Review* 28 (autumn 1974).

At night some understand what the grass says.
The grass knows a word or two.
It is not much. It repeats the same word
Again and again, but not too loudly.

And later from the same collection:

Bones

My roof is covered with pigeon bones.
I do not disturb them. I leave them
Where they are, warm
In their beds of feathers.

At night I think I hear the bones,
The little skulls cracking against the tin,
For the wind is blowing softly, so softly,
As if a cricket were singing inside a tulip.

What is joy to me is grief to others.
I feel grief all around my house
Like a ring of beasts circling a camp fire
Before dawn.

Very fine poetry, I submit, with an elemental verity which escapes many of our more sophisticated and self-conscious poets. Its strength lies not only in the universal character of the experience and imagery, but in the quality of the poet's life which it expresses—a life of simplicity, never far from the verities of labor, poverty and suffering, a life in which we believe and respect, as we do not believe and respect the lives of all too many of our current crop of poets.

From this point of view, Simic's latest book *(Return to a Place Lit by a Glass of Milk;* Braziller, $5.95 cloth, $2.95 paper) largely seems to me to be marking time. There are many excellent poems and there is certainly no slackening in the language but what I miss is the emotional urgency one feels in the earlier poems. Simic is a poet who, like Antaeus, gains strength from the earth which nurtures the laborer and immigrant, and as he proceeds into aerier climes some of the magic of his poetry becomes dispelled into mere games, riddles and pseudo-proverbs. At the same time his indebtedness—to Zbigniev Herbert and Vasko Popa, *inter alia*—becomes a little more obvious. His tradition is that of peasant poetry, with strong Middle European roots, and the transition to a status as an urbanized American teacher is fraught with its own peculiar perils: what began as strengths have a tendency to become mannerisms. After all, there are only so many homiletic proverbs one can rewrite, and even the ballad and child's verse forms Simic frequently uses for his variations have an inexorable law of diminishing returns.

DAVID IGNATOW

Charles Simic's *Charon's Cosmology*

The poems in Charles Simic's latest book show, for one thing, that it is possible to write intensely personal poetry without openly placing oneself at the center. In certain poems, though, he allows us to believe that he is writing to us directly. In *Charon's Cosmology,* his seventh book, Mr. Simic does not write in a face-to-face confrontation with his subject and yet the effect is direct and immediate, though they are obviously of another dimension. His poems echo and re-echo in the mind, as of memories of lives, impulses and cataclysms long since buried within us. Here is an example:

THE PRISONER

He is thinking of us.
These leaves, their lazy rustle
That made us sleepy after lunch
So we had to lie down.

He considers my hand on her breast,
Her closed eyelids, her moist lips
Against my forehead, and the shadows of trees
Hovering on the ceiling.

It's been so long. He has trouble
Deciding what else is there.
And all along the suspicion
That we do not exist.

Here with a few strokes he draws us into a complex of perceptions and feelings that have been lying beneath the surface of our conventional defenses, to be penetrated by just this act of revelation, awakening us once more to an awareness of our true lives.

From "Three Poets" by David Ignatow, *New York Times Book Review,* 5 March 1978.

Mr. Simic achieves his successes with the use of symbolist and at times surrealist techniques, but beyond the mere triumph of method lies something far more urgent for him, as can be sensed in "The Prisoner." He is under siege of an anxiety that expresses itself in a highly tangential manner. We all walk around with hints and allusions that flash upon us to a life we rush past in our hurry to bury ourselves in a routine away from fear. Mr. Simic's anxiety is real for us, but his way of handling it is to reveal it to himself completely and, consequently, reveal it also to us. Mr. Simic finds his release in contemplation and in writing of it. This is by now the classical approach among contemporary poets, but he does it differently. In fact, he is quite explicit about its connection with a received religion, as expressed in the last lines of "The Cure":

> They say of St. John of the Cross
> That he would sit,
> Just the way I'm sitting now
> In a small dark place,
> And through a window
> Gaze at a distant landscape.

The meaning of this passage is inescapable: that the association is with suffering contained and made sacred through contemplation and, for Mr. Simic, in the act of writing about it. It is his solution to the mystery of living that all of us confront. That he does it often brilliantly is to our benefit as well.

ROBERT SHAW

Life among the Cockroaches: Charles Simic's *Classic Ballroom Dances* and *White (A New Version)*

For one who vividly remembers Simic's early appearances in little magazines some fifteen years ago, it is startling to encounter him not as a new but as an established poet. But there he now stands, panting a little on that problematic ledge, mid-career, a foothold that proves sticky for some poets, slippery for others, and uncomfortable for all.

The poet's lack of ease is caused in part by the erratic demands of readers—or at least of those readers who make demands known by writing reviews. "X has yet to find his own voice," complains the critic, reviewing a first book. Three books later, the same critic writes, "X's poems have all been sounding alike for some time now. . . . With so many younger poets imitating him, does he have to imitate himself?" A poet gets punished for not having a voice, and if he has one, he gets punished for using it.

It is too simple (and simply wrong) to say that poets tailor their styles to gratify their critics. But critical demands, even if they do not force a poet to alter his or her style in a specified way, encourage him to change in whatever way he will. An American myth of progress, a pioneer faith in Manifest Destiny, still shapes the preconceptions of many critics and poets in our literature. The absence of change, of visible movement, suggest failure. We expect each collection of poems to advance beyond its predecessor. Paradoxically, we often harbor with our demand for development and novelty, a conflicting desire for continuity, a wish to hear once more a voice we recognize. Hard to please, we want Simic to change, but not so much that his poems sound like those of someone else.

On the whole, Simic seems to have met such pressures in a measured and discerning way. He confidently begins *Classic*

From "Life among the Cockroaches" by Robert Shaw, *New Boston Review* (March–April 1981).

Ballroom Dances with a "Table of Delectable Contents," that shows not only his love for lists, but also his delightful mixture of insouciance and metaphysical seriousness:

> *Of the genealogy and great antiquity of the invisible*
> *Why can't we see the end of our nose.*
> *The invisible's account of the way in which it escaped from the visible.*
> *How the invisible spends its time when it rains. . . .*

And so on, including this item: "*Of his life among the cockroaches, and of what he saw and learned among the ineffables.*" Simic clearly means to proceed with the program of his earlier poetry—to search for a spiritual significance in physical objects. The eerie confrontation in "Shirt" is a typical example:

> To get into it
> As it lies
> Crumpled on the floor
> Without disturbing a single crease
>
> Respectful
> Of the way I threw it down
> Last night
> The way it happened to land
>
> Almost managing
> The impossible contortions
> Doubling back now
> Through the knotted sleeve

Simic discovered early that even the most common objects—a spoon, a needle, a stone—assume an unsettling but beguiling strangeness when they are regarded with the poet's imaginative fixity. Indeed, the most striking perception of his early poems was that inanimate objects pursue a life of their own and present, at times, a dark parody of human existence. Thus, the humble fork "resembles a bird's foot / Worn around the cannibal's neck."

> As you hold it in your hand,
> As you stab with it into a piece of meat,
> It is possible to imagine the rest of the bird:
> Its head which like your fist
> Is large, bald, beakless and blind.

He imagines taking up residence inside a stone:

> . . . within, it must be cool and quiet
> Even though a cow steps on it full weight,
> Even though a child throws it in a river;
> The stone sinks, slow, unperturbed
> To the river bottom
> Where the fishes come to knock on it
> And listen.

The imaginative spirit of such poems is at the same time alienating and embracing. Even as Simic recognizes the strangeness of objects in their separate existence, he strains to assimilate them to his own experience. Or, making the more arduous effort in the opposite direction, he enters a foreign sphere of being and makes himself at home, for example, within a stone.

Simic has a beautiful two-line poem called "The Wind":

> Touching me, you touch
> The country that has exiled you.

This is his vision: a man lives in apparent intimacy with the world surrounding him—touching and being touched by it—and yet all the while knowing himself to be an exile, a stranger who can at best only pretend to be at home here. Either the poet or the wind could be the speaker, and still the point would be the same.

The theme of exile is commonplace in this century's literature. Many authors use it simply as metaphor, but for Simic the experience is real: born in Yugoslavia in 1938, he was brought to this country as a child and today the exile's consciousness still colors his language as well as his view of existence. Having mastered a second language, Simic is especially aware of the power of words, and of the limits which words grope to overcome. His diction is resolutely plain: as with the everyday objects he writes about, he uncovers unexpected depth in apparently commonplace language. He chooses unremarkable words with remarkable deliberateness and sets them sturdily side by side in arrangements that seem somehow inevitable. Like any good poet, he understands the uses of silence; his poems stop when they ought to, after saying what can be said.

Understandably, Simic's very success in his accustomed modes seems to have made him wary of merely repeating himself. This anxiety may account for some of the less characteristic and, I feel, less successful pieces in this new book. Simic's new handling of comic effects, for example, is unreliable. He has a genuine, rather bleak sense of humor, best expressed in a grimly succinct poem like "Primer," which tells of a little boy who got dirty playing in the ashes and then went in for dinner:

> Little lump of ashes, they said,
> Here's another lump of ashes for dinner,
>
> To make you sleepy,
> And make you grow.

But when Simic tries to broaden his comic tone, he produces an unconvincing kind of surrealist slapstick, as in "Great Infirmities":

> Everyone has only one leg.
> So difficult to get around,
> So difficult to climb the stairs
> Without a cane or crutch to our name.
>
> And only one arm. Impossible contortions
> Just to embrace the one you love . . .

A more promising experiment is the poem "Prodigy"—unusual in being, apparently, an actual childhood memory. Simic recalls learning to play chess in 1944 in a small house near a Roman graveyard ("Planes and tanks / shook its windowpanes").

> I'm told but do not believe
> that that summer I witnessed
> men hung from telephone poles.

The chess game, of course, becomes a symbol—of the patterns of conflict, danger and escape that make up life—but the poem otherwise treats personal experience directly, without the mediation of myth. It would be interesting to see more from Simic in this autobiographical vein; this is at once vivid and different.

Simic's willingness to balance change and continuity in his career is most clearly demonstrated by his new version of *White,* a book-length poem first published in 1972. Although Simic has honed his phrasing, rearranged sections, and added some new material, the poem remains recognizable to those who knew it before. The changes are unobtrusive—fine adjustments rather than wholesale tinkering—and young poets daunted by the necessity of rewriting could learn a lot by setting the two versions of *White* side by side. Here is a section of the 1972 version:

> Well you can't call me a wrestler
> If my own musk has me pinned down.
>
> Well you can't call me a cook
> If the pot's got me under its cover.
>
> Well you can't call me a king
> If the flies hang their hats in my mouth.
>
> Well you can't call me a windbag
> If I don't move, the light wouldn't have reached here.

Here is the same section revised:

> Well, you can't call me a wrestler
> If my own dead weight has me pinned down.
>
> Well, you can't call me a cook
> If the pot's got me under its cover.
>
> Well, you can't call me a king
> If the flies hang their hats in my mouth.
>
> Well, you can't call me smart
> When the rain's falling my cup's in the cupboard.
>
> Nor can you call me a saint,
> If I didn't err, there wouldn't be these smudges.

The changes, especially in the first and final couplets, are slight but telling. Simic has given logic to his metaphor by replacing the inconsequence of "musk" with "dead weight." The rewriting of the final two lines allows them to follow the rhetorical pattern of the preceding series, rather than going off in a randomly different direction. Simic saw that "windbag" wasn't right—either as diction or in placement. The new last lines are a fitting culmination; they unify the section and replace a puzzling lapse in tone and inner logic.

The poem itself is Simic's longest, most difficult, but most rewarding work. White, from which all colors of the spectrum are derived, evidently represents the source in or beyond the unconscious mind from which all poetic images are drawn. In keeping with the established themes of Simic's poetry, White appears through the poem in enigmatic flashes, suggesting an invisible order of being impinging what is visible. It represents the mystery which the poet seeks to evoke even while knowing that it exists beyond the reach of elucidation. The poem begins:

> Out of poverty
> To begin again:
> With the color of the bride
> And that of blindness,
> Touch what I can
> Of the quick,
> Speak and then wait,
> As if this light
> Will continue to linger
> On the threshold.

In this poem the creation of something, however imperfect, out of pristine nothingness, Simic is remarkably successful at drawing the reader into his own creative moment. Reading these black words set on a white page, we seem to be with the poet in the very act of writing to hear the words uttered out of a potent surrounding silence:

> We haven't gone far . . .
> Fear lives there too.
> Five ears of my fingertips
> Against the white page.
> What do you hear?
> We hear holy nothing
> Blindfolding itself.
> It touched you once, twice,
> And tore like a stitch
> Out of a new wound.

In his willingness to rework an already successful poem, Simic shows both courage and artistic integrity. The new *White* is a carefully meditated effort to change his work constructively—not disowning what he has done, but bringing to his original insights a deepened skill and self-knowledge.

DAVID YOUNG

Charles Simic's *Classic Ballroom Dances*

Last summer, in a composite review for *The Washington Post,* I found myself complaining about the tendency of many male poets to be the victims of their own egotism, placing themselves at the center of their poems as existential heroes and asking us to underwrite both their self-pity and self-esteem. The problem is by no means exclusive to men—among the poets who have set poor examples we must number Anne Sexton as well as Robert Lowell, John Berryman, and Robert Penn Warren—but I especially noticed it among the men in a large group of books I was sorting through in search of something to praise, and that's the form my complaint took. Had I had the new collection of Charles Simic before me, things would have been different; I would have been able to point to two poets of my generation who, in very different ways, have resolved the problem of excessive self-preoccupation in their poetry. There are a number of other reasons for celebrating these poets, of course, and I shall try to enumerate some of them, but I want to begin my account of Simic by noting his success at resolving the crisis of subjectivity that has weakened so much recent American poetry. How much that success is deliberate and how much it is the happy result of temperament and sheer talent would be difficult to say; what is clear is that both these poets, now in their forties, have found ways of handling subject, voice, and vision that make them impressive poets and better models than some of the poets who have preceded them.

There can be few serious readers of poetry who have failed to discover what this poet has to offer. The new collection, *Classic Ballroom Dances* contributes to the steady enlarging of Simic's world and canon in ways that are sometimes familiar, sometimes unexpected. Take for example the title poem:

From a review of *Classic Ballroom Dances* by David Young, *Field* 24 (spring 1981).

Classic Ballroom Dances

Grandmothers who wring the necks
Of chickens; old nuns
With names like Theresa, Marianne,
Who pull schoolboys by the ear;

The intricate steps of pickpockets
Working the crowd of the curious
At the scene of an accident; the slow shuffle
Of the evangelist with a sandwich-board;

The hesitation of the early morning customer
Peeking through the window-grille
Of a pawnshop; the weave of a little kid
Who is walking to school with eyes closed;

And the ancient lovers, cheek to cheek,
On the dancefloor of the Union Hall,
Where they also hold charity raffles
On rainy Monday nights of an eternal November.

The title seemed to point away from the ordinary; the poem leads us back to it, but then we begin to admire the poem as an artifact. Art turns to life and back again, with elegant sleight-of-hand. The wit and inventiveness that inform this delightful catalogue have been constants in Simic's work from the beginning. The music here is perhaps a little richer (e.g., the way "accident," "evangelist," and "sandwich" connect amidst a sizzle of sibilance, a soft-shoe) and the movement a little more unpredictable: the poem dances deftly among the "dances" it is discovering. Stylistically, there is less of the overt comparison Simic has always been so adept at ("An apron . . . The blood on it smeared into a map"), and even more trust in the simple power of juxtaposition, cheek to cheek. The images are sometimes of the archetypal sort from which Simic has created a world of proverbial folk-wisdom and magical simplicity—the grandmother with her chicken, for example—but they are counterpointed by images from a much more mundane reality—the nuns and their names, the charity raffles on rainy nights—that the earlier work did not tend to include. Simic is like a magician who is able to work more and more things into his act, and following his progress is exhilarating.

As to the matter of subjectivity I raised earlier, we find the poet present in this poem only as inventor and presenter. He does not comment on the world of the poem other than by his choices for its furnishings, and he does not refer to his own experience or emotions at all. Yet if we try to describe the tone of the poem, we realize how much his presence means, for he is both the cool and witty observer of a parade of human folly and the tender cataloguer of human sadness and isolation. His apparent absence (compared to those poets who center the poem on their suffering and/or sensitive response to experience) turns out, to my mind, to be a most responsible presence, morally as well as aesthetically.

There are poems in this collection, however, where the use of the first person and the kind of experience invoked make us feel we are dealing more directly with the poet. "Empire of Dreams" is such a poem; "Prodigy" is another:

> I grew up bent over
> a chessboard.
>
> I loved the word *endgame.*
>
> All my cousins looked worried.
>
> It was a small house
> near a Roman graveyard.
> Planes and tanks
> shook its windowpanes.
>
> A retired professor of astronomy
> taught me how to play.
>
> That must have been in 1944.
>
> In the set we were using,
> the paint had almost chipped off
> the black pieces.
>
> The white King was missing
> and had to be substituted for.
>
> I'm told but do not believe
> that that summer I witnessed
> men hung from telephone poles.

I remember my mother
blindfolding me a lot.

She had a way of tucking my head
suddenly under her overcoat.

In chess, too, the professor told me,
the masters play blindfolded,
the great ones on several boards
at the same time.

The very deliberate movement of this poem, its constant stopping and starting, seems to track the memory's discoveries, sudden bursts of brief recall. We recognize that the poem may draw on personal experience, but we also sense its suppression of personal emotion; the deadpan manner finally makes the emotional impact stronger, but it also serves to divert attention from personal experience and memory to the emerging pattern of chess game as refuge from (and mirror of) the world of tanks, planes, and executions, a world which also stretches out to include the history implied by a Roman graveyard and the realms studied by the professor of astronomy: several boards at once. The ending is wonderfully inconclusive, especially as it refers us back to the title: what kind of prodigy the boy is or will be is left open, and we duck out of his strange little world before we have answers. What we'll retain is a strong sense of how firmly the mundane details of chess set and wartime have been elevated into a stunning design. Again, it is Simic the artist rather than Simic the refugee or deprived child who remains, as what I've called a responsible presence.

There's a good deal of interesting experiment to be found in *Classic Ballroom Dances*. Some poems, like "Baby Pictures of Famous Dictators," "The Little Tear-Gland That Says," and "Begotten of the Spleen," go further into the sardonic, I think, than Simic or almost anyone else has been. They take the most nightmarish aspects of our century's history and juggle them with a kind of weird merriment:

The Virgin Mother walked barefoot
among the land mines . . .
St. Peter pushed a cart
loaded with flying carpets.
They weren't flying carpets.

They were bloody diapers.
It was a cock-fighting neighborhood.
The Magi stood on street corners
cleaning their nails with German bayonets.
("Begotten of the Spleen")

There's also a good deal of experimentation with movement in this collection. A poem called "The Stream" is strung out in erratic and fragmentary lines that attempt to characterize its subject; the sense of engagement that results is striking, and the interpenetration of self and world that this poem achieves constitutes a new mood and manner for Simic. Several of the poems —"Furniture Mover," "Elegy," and "The Tomb of Stéphane Mallarmé"—are written in a short-line style (one to five words to a line, average between two and three) with a margin that snakes in and out, again a new departure for this poet:

in this starless
summer night
windy and cold

at the table
brought out
hours ago
under a huge ash tree

two chairs
two ambiguous figures
each one relying
on the other . . .
("Elegy")

For me these poems are only intermittently successful. Too often they get so abstract and attenuated that they seem to drift away like smoke. But I admire Simic's way of striking out in new directions, his absence of artistic complacency.

As an artist develops and acquires increasing technical mastery, there's a danger that the means will become the end, the symbols and patterns be worshipped for their own sakes, the craft replace the vision. When this happens, the poet becomes a parodist of his or her own earlier work, and the vitality and tension begin to drain out of the poems. Simic has skirted this danger by letting recent history more and more overtly into his mythic world, cross-ventilating it, and by his experiments with form and movement. At the same time, he hasn't abandoned the terse, understated, witty mode he is master of. The poem I'm about to cite is unmistakably Simic's: it bears the stamp of his artistic personality at every point. Whether or not you could say it's from this volume isn't so clear, but you don't, reading *Classic Ballroom Dances,* find yourself saying, "Oh, that's in the earlier manner." The poem feels completely right in its context. In its swift, sharp strokes, its unerring placements, its grim wit and invigorating imagery, it is characteristic of this original and uncompromising writer at his best:

HARSH CLIMATE

The brain itself in its skull
Is very cold
According to
Albertus Magnus.

Something like a stretch of tundra
On the scale of the universe.
Galactic wind.
Lofty icebergs in the distance.

Polar night.
A large ocean liner caught in the ice.
A few lights still burning on the deck.
Silence and fierce cold.

The reader gets a chance to be creative here, filling out the suggestions and supplying the emotions. Somebody recently called those little bitten-off sentences a mannerism of contemporary poetry. So what? They're splendid. The economy of this poem ought to make readers rejoice, not grumble. It's a large metaphor but a miniature novel. It's a Luminist landscape and a metaphysical kick in the pants. It makes most poets look like garrulous fools. We should be grateful to have Charles Simic working in our midst. Especially when we see how easily he has mastered the relation of the artist to the work of art. He's your partner in *Classic Ballroom Dances*—indeed, he's the bandleader, the band, and the whole damn ballroom—but he also knows how to let you step out on your own.

PETER STITT

Imagination in the Ascendant: Charles Simic's *Austerities*

Curiously, it may be through one of his least strong, least characteristic poems that we can best define the métier of the Charles Simic of *Austerities*. In "The Great Horned Owl," a "Grand Seigneur" appears in the poet's backyard. Simic shows him "my belt, / How I had to / Tighten it lately / To the final hole." The owl is not impressed; he "Studies the empty woodshed, / The old red Chevy on blocks. / Alas! He's got to be going." We can easily imagine what Robert Penn Warren, Donald Hall, Dave Smith, Mary Oliver, or a dozen others would do with this subject; it would be a visit from a god, a serious, symbolical moment. None of them would prance before the bird like a clown, however, showing it how thin they've become lately. Simic's interest is not out there, on the bird; it is with his own performance, the song and dance of his own internal Grand Seigneur, the imagination.

Much has been made by critics of the folk influence which was so pervasive in Simic's earlier work, his preoccupation with "preverbal, pre-conceptual consciousness," with "childhood, folklore, eroticism, food, animals, and plants" (to quote an anonymous reviewer in *Virginia Quarterly Review*). All this seems well behind Simic now; the poems in *Austerities* are preeminently verbal performances, conceptual and sophisticated, allusive to a wide range of western thought and literature. There are overt references here to Kepler, Newton (twice), Parmenides, "Pharaonic avenues," Homer; the speaker's wife is said to be "Pascal's own / Prize abyssologist / In marriage"; he and she take a walk and see "young hoods on the street corners" who "all looked like they'd read Darwin and that madman Pavlov, / And were about to ask us for a light"; and a dissertation on "East European Cooking" begins: "While Marquis De Sade has himself buggered, / O just around the time the Turks / Were roasting

From "Imagination in the Ascendant" by Peter Stitt, *Poetry* 143 (October 1983).

my ancestors on a spit, / Goethe wrote 'The Sorrows of Young Werther.' " Veiled allusions abound as well, as the references to Frost in "Crows" ("The absolutely necessary / Way in which they shook snow . . ."), at least two to Whitman, another to Pound, demonstrate. In short, Simic is a post-modernist par excellence, heir to Eliot (in ironic literary allusiveness) and Stevens (in commitment to a world of imagination).

Austerities is a masterfully entertaining book, even at its most somber. Simic is famous for his handling of human cruelty, which he keeps at bitter and witty distance through the use of irony. "Rough Outline" is typical of his best:

> The famous torturer takes a walk
> Whom does he see standing there in the snow
> A pretty girl in a wedding dress
> What are you doing out there all alone in the cold
>
> You're the famous torturer much feared
> I beg you to spare my love
> Who is in your darkest prison cell
> I wish to marry him etc.
>
> I will not give back your bridegroom
> He must be tortured tonight
> By me personally
> You can come along and help him lament his fate
>
> She remained where she was
> The night was cold and very long
> Down by the slaughterhouse a dog-like creature howled
> Then the snow started to fall again

This is both serious and not serious, which, of course, makes it all the more serious. It is a tone and situation we are familiar with, and the author indicates his own similar familiarity through the use of "etc.," as well as the generally sketchy form. This kind of thing shows best in such short poems, each a sort of jazzy intermezzo. Thus a book of poems of such pieces never becomes a symphony, or even a *Rigoletto;* rather, a series of short concerti, or an album of popular songs. If the book is at all disappointing, it is as a whole; the parts which make it up are a complete, and rarely a shallow, delight.

LIAM RECTOR

Charles Simic's *Selected Poems*

Charles Simic's *Selected Poems* has recently appeared and triumphantly illustrates what such a book can offer the old admirer, the new fan. It includes selections from all the Braziller books published from 1967 to 1982, as well as a revised version of *White,* published in 1972 by New Rivers, and *Weather Report for Utopia and Vicinity,* a collection of previously unpublished work published in 1983 by Station Hill Press.

About halfway through the book we find these lines, from "The Lesson":

It occurs to me now
that all these years
I have been
the idiot pupil
of a practical joker.

Diligently
and with foolish reverence
I wrote down
what I took to be
his wise pronouncements
concerning
my life on earth . . .

Simic's *Selected* is in many ways just this: the village idiot (with the tone of the pupil) has listened to an immense practical joke which contained a mock-foolish wisdom. It's a considerable and considered wisdom indeed, one often taking on the voice of "An abstract street / on which an equally abstract intelligence / forever advances, doubting / the sound of its own footsteps." Simic's legendary gallows humor gallops like a riderless horse throughout this book, and its somberness, wisdom, and insane laughs are everywhere present:

From "Poetry Chronicle" by Liam Rector, *Hudson Review* 39 (autumn 1986).

I can't get any peace around here:
The bread on its artificial limbs,
A headless doll in a wheelchair,
And my mother, mind you, using
Two knives for crutches as she squats to pee.
("A Landscape with Crutches")

A bedbug who suffers, who has doubts
About his existence. The miraculous
Laughing dove. A thousand-year-old turtle
Playing billiards. A chicken who
Cuts his own throat, who bleeds.

The trainer with his sugar-cubes,
With his chair and whip. The evenings
When they all huddle in a cage,
Smoking cheap cigars, lazily
Marking the cards in the new deck.
("Animal Acts")

Simic's poetry is a kind of philosophical insomnia, one wherein the present is noted and remembered but soon floats off into the formulas and imaginings of history and the unlikeliness of the future . . . The imagination in these poems, which I think takes as its source *innocence,* is continually taking its first look at a first world, reacting with both awe and horror, wisdom and austerity. This imagination has done a great deal to animate the supposedly inanimate, in poems like "Fork," "My Shoes," "Ax," "Brooms," and many others which now figure a kind of "surrealism" for their time; but in addition, and this the *Selected* makes painfully obvious, Simic's work has about it a purity, an originality unmatched by many of his contemporaries.

White, a book-length poem, is a welcome inclusion in its re-edited form. A helpful and hilarious discussion of that poem, with George Starbuck, is included in *The Uncertain Certainty,* a collection of interviews, essays, and notes on Simic's poetry, by Simic himself, recently published in The University of Michigan's "Poets on Poetry" series. It's a useful companion volume to the *Selected,* and collects many of the few prose pieces Simic has written and published. One would hope there will be more of this from Simic. His essay, "Negative Capability and Its Children," is an important *entrée* into his work and into the whole of contemporary poetry. As Robert McDowell said in his recent review of the Michigan series (*The Hudson Review,* Autumn 1985), "the mum generation was always talking," and these interviews and scattered prose pieces are all we have from some of the most powerful poets of our day. The shadow of the New Criticism and "The Age of Criticism" was a long one, one which I think eventually discouraged analysis and prose elucidation in the generation immediately following it, and we're all a little poorer for that, inevitable though it now seems to have been.

BRIAN C. AVERY

Unconcealed Truth: Charles Simic's *Unending Blues*

Unending Blues, Charles Simic's eleventh book of poems, seeks to reveal truth, as does all his poetry. For Simic, truth is not obvious and eternal but is gathered only through continual seeking. In his essay "Notes on Poetry and History," Simic borrows a definition of truth: "For the Greek Protagoras truth meant the unconcealment of what is present" (*Uncertain Certainty* 128). In *Unending Blues,* Simic attacks calcified interpretations of meaning by questioning the process of representation and presentation as a means to reveal this truth.

Strangely enough, a common charge leveled against Simic's poetry is that it is parable-like. Such a misunderstanding may not pose a serious problem for other poets, but for Simic, authorial intention serves as a crucial means to understanding. In a 1984 interview with Simic, Sherod Santos raised the issue: "I notice in reading reviews of your books that critics at times have a tendency to read your poems as parables. Is that the result of your working beyond the framework of realism?" Simic's three short sentences serve as more of a correction than an answer: "I don't know. I don't write parables. If I say 'rats in diapers' that's to be taken literally" (*Uncertain Certainty* 78). Such an answer seems glib, until one extricates what Simic means by the literal. If one accepts the parable as a type of allegory, then Simic is simply resisting allegory.

According to Angus Fletcher, allegory exists to present a meaning; its superficial meaning functions only to inspire or create a meaning apart from the literal.

> Whenever a literary work is dominated by its theme, it is likely to be called an allegory, on the grounds that thematic content is not usually so free of logical control that it could be there by accident. . . . [With allegory] the secondary meaning arises immediately from the primary surface of literal narration or drama, and constitutes the raison d'être of the primary

> surface. Allegorical stories exist, as it were, to put secondary meanings into orbit around them; the primary meaning is then valued for its satellites. (*Allegory* 220–21)

It follows, then, that if Simic resists allegory, his poetry cannot be interpreted according to these orbiting secondary meanings. "We have actual allegory when a poet explicitly indicates the relationship of his images to examples and precepts, and so tries to indicate how a commentary on him should proceed," writes Northrop Frye in a passage that Fletcher uses to augment his own definition of allegory (90).

Simic's comments to Santos indicate that he is unwilling to have his poetry read as allegory, and he is also unwilling to *write* poetry that can be construed as allegory. Three years after the publication of *Unending Blues,* Simic published "Notes on Philosophy and Poetry," in which he proclaims his interest in philosophy as well as his often failed attempts to put his thinking into poetry. In this essay, Simic writes:

> There is a major misunderstanding in literary criticism as to how ideas get into poems. The poets, supposedly, proceed in one of these two ways: they either state their ideas directly or they find equivalents for them. What is usually called philosophical poetry seems to be either a poetry of heightened eloquence or some variety of symbolism. In each case, the assumption is that the poet knows beforehand what he or she wishes to say and the writing of the poem is the search for the most effective means of gussying up these ideas. (*Wonderful Words, Silent Truth* 62)

This attitude toward thinking creates, according to Simic, poetry that merely repeats what has been previously thought and stated. "There would be no hope that poetry could have any relation to truth," he writes (64), and there would be "no poetic thinking." This poetic thinking, here defined negatively, is not a repeating, but an uncovering; truth is not re-presented in poetry but is discovered over the course of the poem. With allegory, the poet does not discover but preaches, for the poet consciously puts both a primary meaning and a secondary meaning into the work of art, with the secondary meanings floating around and accessed through an examination of the initial meaning. How Simic's poems mean depends upon his resistance to allegory;

Simic does not re-present the truth as much as he tries to discover it.

Nor does Simic merely want to offer a poetry that is mimetic. In Simic's view, refusing to assign a secondary meaning and hoping to represent reality through mimesis is also inauthentic. Fletcher distinguishes allegory from mimesis by pointing out that mimetic art yields a host of characters who act according to their own character, or according to how a character or object would act realistically. Allegory and mimesis both represent: mimesis represents perceived experience, while allegory represents the author's prescribed set of ideas. A mimetic rendering of reality does not purport to provide meaning beyond the realistic scene or the actions of characters, and it hopes to provide an equivalence of the poem's scenes and characters. But as Simic explains in an interview, instead of attempting "an acceptable equation," following the "echoes and resonances" of an event's language provides a more interesting and authentic poetry, a poetry that thinks (*Uncertain Certainty* 61).

However, Simic presents a dialogue in *Unending Blues* between these modes to develop what he elsewhere calls the "literal." "December," the book's first poem, is also its simplest and shortest. Its brevity invites the reader to assign a meaning that is left unsaid, and thus Simic tempts the reader into an allegorical mode.

> It snows
> and still the derelicts
> go
> carrying sandwich boards—
>
> one proclaiming
> the end of the world
> the other
> the rates of the local barbershop

Both of the men in this winter scene wear signs and thus proclaim messages and even meanings. The signs the poet gives to them (namely, the title "derelicts") make them interchangeable with each other, while indicating and even evaluating their social standing; each could be made to wear the other's sign, significantly undercutting their messages. And the signs read each other: by itself, the board "proclaiming / the end of the world" should be terrifying, but its relationship to the board bearing "the rates of the local barbershop" reminds us that such eschatological messages have been proclaimed with laughable regularity. However, the truth of the apocalyptic sign is summoned when one reads the barbershop sign as a symbol of the problems that an industrialist society produces: exploitative labor practices and objectifying advertising, to name only two that show up in the eight short lines of this poem.

This quick reading of "December" suggests that Simic intended such a response. But the extent to which Simic *intended* this reading remains arguable. To determine whether or not Simic intends this poem to be read allegorically moves the argument to hair-splitting determinations of the extent of authorial intention; how explicit the poet has to be to indicate a poet's commentary, for instance. As Paul Smith states, an allegorist must define the correspondence between the primary and secondary needs of the system: "Such an authority—all that is ever really essential to allegory—is the fixed state of allegory's discourse: A fixity of its underlying reference is vital for its accurate functioning," though in the absence of such an explicit authority, the reader can "establish a serviceable but *ad hoc* typology for the text" (107). Thus, as Smith suggests, as long as the *reader* can establish this fixity of reference, the reader can produce a representative reading, despite the author's intentions.

Thus, Simic needs to create a poem that operates in a complete condition of uncertainty. Both the reader and the poet find themselves in the midst of what Simic calls (in his essay "Composition") the "mixture of deliberate and involuntary."

> One is continually torn between the desire to let things be and the desire to assert oneself. The peculiar intensity and weight the words have in a good poem are probably due to this split, and the turmoil it causes in the psyche. In any case, the great wish is to make visible, to let the spirit of the occasion manifest itself. A poem which would be a threshold between worlds, where the poet is simply the ceremonial doorman. (*Uncertain Certainty* 112)

To create this threshold, Simic must "present" the images, the details, and the historical phenomena of his poems without "representing" them through a system of equivalence. That is to say, Simic is an agnostic of allegory. Poetry must be allowed to think, and it thinks through its literalness: to let the words—

rather than the poet—say what they are saying. A phrase like "rats in diapers" is not intended to be mimetic in that it is not supposed to be representative of anything, other than what the language says. As Simic himself asserts,

> I believe with Stevens that the real must always be the base. First the soil enriched with cowshit, and then the rose with its thorns and its scent. The parable wants to talk only about the scent and doesn't care how the rest comes out. The issue is always how to be faithful to all the parts. (Letter to the author, 4 October 1988)

If a phrase—or, in the case of "rats in diapers," an image—is to be taken literally, it may first be perceived mimetically, but ultimately it is meant to open up and discover new meanings that hint at truth. One can assign abstractions that are represented by the two sandwich boards in "December" to produce a fairly convincing allegorical reading. However, in the volume's second poem, "The Marvels of the City," an allegorical reading becomes too complicated because it seems overdetermined upon an initial reading. The poem's first two stanzas show a speaker who travels through variously named city streets.

> I went down the tree-lined street of false gods
> The cobbled street of two wise monkeys
> The street of roasted nightingales
> The small twisted street of the insomniacs
> The street of those who feather their beds
>
> That's right—the street of the dog's metaphysics
> The dark alley of the Emperor's favorite barber
> With its fountain and stone lion
> The closed shutters on the street of the hundred-year-old harlot
> The flag-bedecked courthouses and banks
> On the square of the betrayed revolution

However, while the reader may have trouble assigning meaning to each item of the surreal catalog of streets, one can see a correspondence with the poet's act in general. The poet's wandering almost automatically reifies Simic's abstraction of following language rather than seeking an equivalence. In addition, the poet walks among streets and locations whose names seem to represent contradictions, failures, or oxymorons: "false gods," "wise monkeys," "roasted nightingales," the century-old prostitute who apparently has business this evening, and the "betrayed revolution" that continues to be celebrated. As the poem continues, the poet arrives at "the tavern at the sign of the Pig and Seraphim." Inside, he sits among its patrons and reports their conversation.

> Erudite salamanders sipping wine of arctic vintage
> Hamlet's wine the wine of stargazers
> Loveless couples the wine of idiot savants.
>
> We are solely of the mind said one
> Beyond Good and Evil said another
> But the waiters black hair growing out of their ears
> Just took our orders and said nothing

As the waiters stand back, silently acknowledging and even responding to the wishes of the drinkers, they seem to represent the authentic use of language. Thus, by contrasting them to the drinking thinkers, the poet seems to be fixing a meaning. After wandering within this marvelous city, searching for ontological truth, the poet discovers that the truth is held by those who silently enable the others' pointless speech.

Thus, if Simic has offered the message of the need to listen in silence to language rather than merely repeat what others have previously thought, he seems to have re-presented it through allegory rather than presenting it through a kind of discovery. While his individual characters do not seem to construct much more than drunken philosophical ramblings ("everybody is a philosopher after a couple glasses of wine," he says in an interview [*Uncertain Certainty* 24]), the structural representation suggests a symbolic reading. The single "erudite salamander" who summons the title of Nietzsche's work seems to strengthen the idea that Simic is merely writing a poem that operates through a process of representation.

Simic has presented his first two poems in the volume as failures, which run the risk of lapsing into the allegorical. Ultimately, he has not failed, however, for both poems serve to present the drama between the allegorical urging of both poet and reader and the need for the literal, where true discovery takes place. Ambiguity, then, is the open threshold from which discovery takes place. Discovery and presentation, in their opposition to equivalence and representation, create a midst that the poet must seek out in order to reveal the truth from the midst itself. One may chose between the equally believable placards in "December," or one can choose to side with the drunken philosophers or the silent waiters. As Simic explains in his essay "Negative Capability and Its Children," the poem in this midst is "a kind of magnet for complex historical, literary and psychological forces, as well as a way of maintaining oneself in the face of that multiplicity" (*Uncertain Certainty* 83).

Thus, one of the contributing factors to the poet's inability to use language to represent reality is history's inability to represent a coherent and logical story of the past. "I don't believe in history anymore," says Simic in his interview with Sherod Santos. "I don't believe in history as a road to utopia and the accompanying idea that the present is a kind of fertilizer, in human terms, for that future flower garden" (*Uncertain Certainty* 74–75). Simic claims he has nothing to replace this doubt of both the Christian and Marxist models of history. However, in "Notes on Poetry and History," he proclaims, "One must, in spite of everything, give faithful testimony of our predicament so that a true history of our age might be written." That means a poetic vision that does not foster a vision of progress but one of uncertainty: "In place of history's 'distance,' I want to experience the vulnerability of those participating in tragic events" (*Uncertain Certainty* 126).

Once again, Simic has placed his poetry in a dramatic context, and he emphasizes this drama's form as well as content by calling attention to the sense of tragedy. In "Toward Nightfall," he sets up a tension between the existence of these tragic events and the inability to explain what makes them "tragic."

> The weight of tragic events
> On everyone's back,
> Just as tragedy
> In the proper Greek sense
> Was thought impossible
> To compose in our day.

The machinery of tragic fortune, which would include the trappings of fate, divine order, and historical teleology, apparently does not exist in this age of ambiguity. However, like history, there is nothing to replace it with, and its absence in this poem presents itself with events that are still described as tragic without the assurance of the system that instilled the sense of tragedy in human existence in the first place.

The poem describes the dramatic apparatus of "scaffolds, / Makeshift stages," and their accompanying "puny figures" who are compared to "small indistinct animals / Caught in the headlights / Crossing the road way ahead ." But as the poet describes the condition from a somewhat cosmic perspective, he places the reader (or another representative human) within the scene itself,

> In the gray twilight
> That went on hesitating
> On the verge of a huge
> Starless autumn night.
> One could've been in
> The back of an open truck
> Hunkering because of
> The speed and chill.

Therefore, rather than continuing an abstract discussion of the human condition, the poet seeks to demonstrate the condition of the "one." Instead of discussing history's inconsequential figures as doomed road kill, the poet places them on the stage; the shift has been made to the "everyone," away from tragedy and "the tragic events" themselves.

In fact, no tragic event is ever specifically revealed, while the possibility of one's being in this condition is strengthened as the phrase "One could've been" is repeated. "One could've been walking" along the same road, apparently, frightened by "the many troubling shapes / The bare trees made." "One" is the one abstraction that makes the poem most open and possible, and therefore it most poignantly demonstrates the condition of ambiguity. Any reader acts as "one" in this drama.

> One could've been in
> One of those dying mill towns
> Inside a small dim grocery
> When the news broke.
> One would've drawn near the radio
> With the one many months pregnant
> Who serves there at that hour.

"The news" is never revealed, leaving any actual events ambiguous. Thus, Simic suggests no one specific event is necessary to make one feel this overwhelming weight; it is their accumulation that gives one a sense of fright. The poet asks,

Was there a smell of
Spilled blood in the air,
Or was it that other,
Much finer scent—of fear,
The fear of approaching death
One met on the empty street?

One will never know, apparently, as Simic leaves the question suspended, only adding the final vignette of "six factory girls" walking arm in arm "as if they'd been drinking." One could've been one of them, says the poet, as she excuses herself, feeling out of sorts "For no reason, very pale." She climbs into bed with her clothes still on, trembling.

It's just a bad chill,
She keeps telling herself
Not having seen the papers
Which the landlord has the dog
Bring in from the front porch.

The old man never learned
To read so well, and so
Reads on in that half-whisper,
And in that half-light
Verging on the dark,
About the day's tragedies
Which supposedly are not
Tragedies in the absence of
Figures endowed with
Classic nobility of soul.

The "one" is open and remains ambiguous, as is "the event"; one apparently does not even need to know about it to be affected by it. Without mourning its passing, Simic suggests that classical tragedy is no longer possible because of this variability. The possibility of anyone's suffering puts "the weight of tragic events" on "everyone's back." Print and electronic media present all events as equal and immediate data, while our entertainment (seen in the "monsters on movie posters" that are displayed for the factory girls) serves only to entertain and not analyze.

This variability of both victim and "historical event" is developed most noticeably in the poem "History." The banal presentation of the players in this small drama and the ironic tone of the poet suggest that Simic has again presented an outline of interchangeable and even redundant events, but the title seems clearly to ask readers to see the poem as a representation of the abstraction called "History."

> Men and women with kick-me signs on their backs.
> Let's suppose he was sad and she was upset.
> They got over it. The spring day bore a semblance to what they
>   hoped.
> Then came History. He was arrested and shot.
>
> Did they speak in heroic couplets as he's dragged away looking
>   over his shoulder?
> A few words for that park statue with pigeons on it?
> More likely she wipes her eyes and nose with a sleeve,
> Asks for a stiff drink, takes her place in the breadline.
>
> Then the children die of hunger, one by one.
> Of course, there are too many such cases for anyone to be
>   underlining them with a red pencil.
> Plus, the propensity of widows to flaunt their widowhood:
> Coarse pubic hair, much-bitten breasts.

The poet's focus is not on the historical events (which remain too general to refer to a specific place or time) but on how historical events are used in the name of History. Through a simple witness, the poet reveals the unfortunately commonplace horror of the events themselves; "there are too many such cases for anyone to be underlining them with a red pencil," he comments. But as he discusses the widow in a plural and sexual context, he seems to have assumed the voice of those whose insouciance has caused these events. From the perspective of History, such events happen too often to take notice, even justifying the loss of many innocent lives to the machinery of history.

This space, then, that Simic opens—between "the spring day" and History, between the heroic and the realistic, between the poet's reporting of the process of history and the assumption of the Historian's voice—presents ambiguity. Simic is chiefly interested in that threshold, forcing the reader to traverse the direction of thought that the poem takes. The final stanza presents truths from similarly disparate sources.

> History loves to see women cry, she whispers.
> Their death makes Art, he shouts, naked.
> How pretty are the coffins and instruments of torture
> In the Museum on the day of free admission to the public!

The "he" who shouts the platitude about death and "Art" seems to reveal a vignette introduced in the previous stanza. The widow is now sexually exploited for her own survival. Or the man is the voice that the poet presents earlier, the insouciant historian who sees History as fodder for representative Art, to be used to propel or oppress the masses. The loss of quotation marks within this poem allows the speakers of such statements to remain ambiguous. Are the last two lines any less authoritative if they are pronounced by the omniscient poet or by the naked Artist, for instance?

Thus, these unascribed and even competing voices serve to comment on each other, forcing the reader to ask *where* history is located: in the execution, the orphans dying of hunger, the statue, the glittering coffins, or elsewhere. "History," says Simic in "Reading Philosophy at Night,"

> is antireductive. Nothing tidy about it. Chaos! Bedlam! Hopeless tangle! My own history and the history of this century like a child and his blind mother on the street. She mumbles, talks to herself, sings and wails as she leads the way across some busy intersection. You'd think the sole meaning of history is to stand truth happily on its head! (*Wonderful Words* 60)

By contrast, poetry (along with philosophy) expresses "that need to get [Being] down to the essentials, to say the unsayable and let the truth of Being shine through" (60). To demonstrate what he means—and that truth is not found through representational pronouncements—Simic tells a story of a class field trip he took as a boy to a war museum in Yugoslavia. The museum contained mainly photographs that the children had to examine, portraying hangings, executioners, naked corpses, and a man whose throat was about to be slit. "The killer sat on the man's chest with a knife in his hand. He seemed pleased to be photographed. The victim's eyes I don't remember. A few men stood around gawking. There were clouds in the sky" (58). This last detail is important to Simic's point:

> There were always clouds, blades of grass, tree stumps, bushes, and rocks no one was paying any attention to. In one photograph the earth was covered with snow. A miserable, teeth-chattering January morning and someone making someone else's life even more miserable. (58)

Simic points to the variability of daily existence, out of which the historians foolishly attempt to reduce to a single lesson. The poet, too, focuses on the same specific elements, but in Simic's perspective, the poet presents the thing itself—the literal thing that has been made strange in the presence of human atrocity, and the atrocity made strange in its proximity to the commonplace. In each case, the poet reveals the essence of the recorded events more authentically than the historian.

Obviously, Simic is not interested in making attractive "coffins and instruments of torture." What Simic *does* want to include in his poetry is less certain, other than "faithful testimony of our predicament so that a true history of our age might be written." In other words, Simic's openness will allow that "true history" to be written, even as he may not yet be writing that history himself. Thus, in the first part of *Unending Blues,* he has presented allegories that expose their own inauthenticity because they are allegories. In part 2, Simic presents what seem to be allegories of history, but they reveal their own inauthentic presentation so that the reader has no choice but to see representation as problematic. "Department of Public Monuments" proposes, "If Justice and Liberty / Can be raised to pedestals," so should History.

> It could be that fat woman
> In faded overalls
> Outside a house trailer
> On a muddy road to some place called Pittsfield or Babylon.

She does not remain on pedestal, however, as the poet describes how she prepares her chickens for slaughter while her "dogs rattle their chains."

This figure—which certainly seems to operate allegorically—is joined by a man and a boy in "Outside a Dirtroad Trailer." However, the poem opens with a knowing reference to the mode of allegory that has already come into question within this volume.

O exegetes, somber hermeneuts,
Ingenious untanglers of ambiguities,
A bald little man was washing
The dainty feet of a very fat woman.

In a chair under a soaring shade tree,
She kept giggling and shaking her huge breasts.
There was also a boy with glasses
Engrossed in a book of serious appearance.

One black sock drying on the line,
A parked hearse with trash cans in back,
And a large flag hanging limp from the pole
On a day as yet unproclaimed as a holiday.

The poet mocks those who would attempt to make sense of this scene through the means of representation, and he continues to goad them through the "appearance" of the book, the ambiguous flag, and the "day as yet unproclaimed as a holiday." Whether or not the giggling, buxom woman is the figure of History, Simic does not offer her as a marker for history, but opens up the issue of how to read history. To Simic, to make history out of everyday details and events requires an adherence to uncertainty, and therefore arbitrariness.

Simic's understanding of chance seems to derive from his debt to surrealism. From "the spontaneous association of two very distinct realities," one is able to grasp their relationship only through mental play, as he writes in "Negative Capability and Its Children." Therefore,

> The goal in surrealism as in symbolism is a texture of greatest possible suggestiveness, a profusion of images whose meaning is unknown and unparaphrasable through a prior system of signification. The surrealist poet offers the imaginary as the new definition of reality, or more accurately, he equates the imaginary with a truth of psychological order. Here, the separation between intuition and what is real is abolished. Everything is arbitrary except metaphor, which detects the essential kinship of all things. (*Uncertain Certainty* 88–89)

In several poems, then, Simic offers extended similes without any referents, providing a radical experiment where metaphors can attempt to detect a common being. Early in the volume,

"Implements of Augury" begins, "Something like an empty chair and table / In a fortune-teller's storefront." From this landscape, the poet describes "The Madame herself withdrawn from view," the street, and then the city's churches, hospitals, prisons, and government institutions, "All equally deserted now." "Ever So Tragic" does state its tenor, but only in one word, which the poem then develops only through a series of images: "Heart—as in Latin popsongs / Blaring from the poolhall radio." As I have pointed out, in "Toward Nightfall" the word "like," which compares the "puny figures" on "makeshift stages" to "small indistinct animals / Caught in the headlights," leads the poem in its strange directions. These poems open their meaning through ambiguity. They mean to name something, but something that cannot be named without being destroyed, and thus, the "something" can only be named by approximation, by referring to the image by use of the simile. This inability to name fully whatever it is the similes are trying to approximate leaves their meaning open-ended. Simic is allowing their metaphoric quality to suggest their ambiguity: unlike the myth of equivalence that mimesis or allegory inspires, metaphors demonstrate the impossibility of exactly naming a thing, and therefore allow what is only possible to operate in its place.[1]

Perhaps as the best example of how Simic seems to use metaphors to suggest a surreal logic, one can examine "Trees in the Open Country," the last poem in part 2. The poem also opens with a simile ambiguously tied to the title.

> Like those who were eyewitnesses
> To an enormity
> And have since remained downcast
> At the very spot,
>
> Their shadows gradually lengthening
> Into what look like canes, badly charred,
> No choice but to lean on them eventually,
> Together, and in a kind of reverie.

As one long simile (and one long four-stanza sentence), this poem presents steadfast points that one must adhere to in a wide-open landscape. The fading light and lengthening canes suggest increasing debilitation and uncertainty; with the shadow-canes, one has "no choice but to lean on them eventually," like the temptation for equivalence that Simic tries to resist. But the trees themselves, as parables for those who remain steadfast, cannot be pinned down specifically, for they are witnesses only to "*an* enormity," suggesting both any number of historical enormities within our century as well as the condition of ambiguity itself that these enormities have created.

The trees may serve to represent, but the poet has chosen that moment just before the trees fade into obscurity to ask what these trees could represent. The eyewitness trees not only lean toward but upon darkness. Therefore, they depend upon uncertainty, much like the poet and reader who must choose to read the poem's image according to uncertainty, either leaving the metaphor's references forever conditional, or relying upon equivalence as the only and inauthentic means of knowing. In the last two stanzas, that conditionality increases, as the trees wait in silence. And the "you" the poet addresses—perhaps himself, perhaps a simple open reference to a "one" addressed in the last stanza—may still be listening to the trees, the poet, or the tenorless simile in order to make sense of its openness.

> Awaiting the first solitary quip
> From the maddeningly occulted birds,
> Night birds bestirring themselves at last—
> If you are still listening,
>
> One has the impression the world
> Is adamant on a matter of great importance,
> And then—it isn't anymore . . .
> Unless it's now the leaves' turn to reply? (Simic's ellipsis)

Amid a possible reference to the former nightingale's pronouncement of "it," the "world" itself may speak "adamant on a matter of great importance." The poet tries to remove himself as much as possible from the equation of determining his own path for the poem and let the world itself speak before it changes its mind, or before the impression of its speaking passes.

Rather than following a calculative equivalence that one imposes on a metaphor (where the metaphor's vehicle serves a tenor only to make the tenor less abstract), this poem shows how one must let the metaphor speak for itself. In this case, the eyewitnesses (this metaphor's vehicle) suggest the act of attention that the reader (the "you" and the "one") must observe in the act of revealing. The poem performs a kind of self-reflection. The trees are like eyewitnesses, which are like the poet and reader, who need to witness the making-present of the metaphor. The vehicle illuminates itself, more than its tenor, as the poem does not merely describe "trees in open country," but suggests something that the trees suggest. At the poem's end, the trees have not yet spoken, indicating a need to remain silent and be open in this metaphoric way to what (and even *if*) the trees are saying.

Simic's view of metaphor, then, suggests that approximation can open the ability of an authentic discovering of truth. The use of metaphor allows for poetic thinking, even making poetry (with its insistence on metaphor) the natural choice for revealing the world's truth. Rather than allegory's attempt at renaming, the poet can hope only to approximate—to get close to the truth while still remaining distant. The arbitrary arrival at one's need to eyewitness suggested in "Trees in the Open Country" demonstrates the surprise that both poet and reader can find when attempting to take the world's phenomena and let it help make sense of the age. When opposed to allegory, Simic's idea of metaphor works more authentically by first making strange or distant the things of this world, rather than trying immediately to bring them close. Thus, as a system that uses chance occurrence to reveal connections, it works most authentically to makes sense of an uncertain age and world. By detecting "the essential kinship" of arbitrary things, Simic's use of metaphor allows his poetry to avoid serving history; instead of renaming an already established symbolic system to represent predetermined meanings, Simic allows those meanings to remain open and reveal their own truth.

While Simic never imposes a moral obligation on poets to reveal truth in this authentic manner, he does say that poets seem to be able to make more sense of this age of uncertainty than other artists. In his interview with Simic, Bruce Weigl asks how Simic reconciles the larger forms of history (especially the twentieth century) with "the more exclusive forms" of art. "In other words, why write poems in the late twentieth century?" Simic answers by referring to Martin Heidegger.

> Already Hölderlin asked the question: ". . . and what are poets good for in a destitute time?" And Heidegger replies: "In the age of the world's night, the abyss of the world must be experienced and endured. But for this it is necessary that there be those who reach into the abyss." I continue to believe that poetry says more about the psychic life of an age than any

> other art. Poetry is a place where all the fundamental questions are asked about the human condition. As for our age, the world has never been a more complex place. God is dead, we say, but our TV preachers talk to him all the time. Such contradictions are everywhere. Our situation is impossible and, therefore, ideal for philosophers and poets. (7)[2]

The place of metaphor in poetry (and, Simic adds, philosophy) detects the essential kinship in an otherwise arbitrary existence. Poetry asks questions and reveals the truth about the contradictions of our age, rather than deny those contradictions or simplify its complexities.

Thus, Simic's poetry primarily demonstrates this age of contradictions by signifying a loss of future-driven system. But out of that loss, the poet finds an ability to remain calm, to experience *and* endure the impossible situation of this century. In the last part of *Unending Blues,* Simic's poet seems to reach a kind of peace in the midst of uncertainty that Simic has painted. Without history, divinity, or even allegory to help one make sense of the world, the poet turns to art as a means of changing uncertainty into its more positive connotation of possibility. In "Painters of Angels and Seraphim," the first poem of part 3, the poet falls asleep in a rowboat "After a long lunch of roast lamb / And many glasses of heavy red wine." Overhead, the willow branches "went on fussing . . . As if to make my shade even deeper." The poem's final stanza questions a state of existence beyond the material.

> I woke once to pull my shirt off,
> And once when I heard my name
> Called by a woman, distant and worried,
> Since it was past sundown,
> The water reflecting the dark hills,
> And the sky of that chill blue
> That used to signify a state of grace.

The water reflects the sky, but that simple mirroring draws attention to the sky's inability to represent a "state of grace." The sensualist poet seems calm in the absence of that state; the poet does not even allude to the backdrop of history in this poem. In "Reading Philosophy at Night," Simic claims that this sort of attention to momentary consciousness within the midst of chaos is how poetry allows itself to reduce, to create "epiphanies of hinting in a few words at complex matters" (60). He illuminates this sense of poetry in typical metaphoric fashion.

> Like imperturbable Buster Keaton alone with the woman he loves on an ocean liner set adrift on the stormy sea. Or an even better example: Again drifting over an endless ocean, he comes across a billboard, actually a target for battleship practice. Keaton climbs it, takes out his fishing rod and bait, and fishes peacefully. That's what great poetry is. A superb serenity in the face of chaos. Wise enough to play the fool. (*Wonderful Words* 60–61)

Simic begins this image with a reference to Keaton's love; throughout *Unending Blues,* Simic's poet will occasionally happen upon love as a value left even in destitute times. Despite the book's title, when the poet mentions love, it always appears as a presence and not an absence. Unlike Willie Dixon's characterization, "One day a man can have the blues because his wife or girlfriend left him, and the next day he can have the blues because she came back," Simic's "blues" signify something other than missing or misguided love. In "Painters of Angels and Seraphim," for instance, the woman remains distant, but by calling the poet's name, she briefly shows a kind of concern. Earlier in the volume, the poems' indication of love seems to grow. In "William and Cynthia," the couple visits "the Museum / Of Dead Ideas and Emotions." Yet Cynthia's fear at "monstrous ideas in glass cases, / Naked emotions on stone pedestals / In classically provocative poses" shows that at least her own emotions seem rather healthy. To indicate a greater seat of compassion, Simic often uses the image of the heart, as in "Ever So Tragic," the poem that follows "William and Cynthia." This extended simile begins with the single word "Heart," comparing it to "Latin popsongs" that blare from a poolhall's jukebox. The poet describes a scene between a man and a woman, but with overtones that speak of our age of uncertainty.

> The air had thickened, the evening air.
> He took off his white shirt.
> The heart, one could mark it
> With lipstick on a bare chest,
> The way firing-squad commanders mark it.

The lipstick and firing squad seems to suggest love in the age of atrocity, much like William and Cynthia's relationship that continues at some level within the historically driven and passionless museum.

In part 2, the poem "In the Alley" addresses a tattooist drawing a bird of paradise on a sailor's chest on a snow-filled night among "the great towers of Banking and Industry." As the poet comments on "the spread wings, the wide-open beak / Triumphant—where the heart was!" it is almost as if the heart has been replaced by the exotic bird. Later, in "To Helen," the poet addresses his wife in perhaps the most matter-of-fact tone in the volume: "Tomorrow I'm having my bones photographed / With my heart in its spiked branches," he says. While the tree is "ill-shapen and alone in a field" whose crab apples make one regret, the heart becomes a nest. In each of these poems, the heart becomes a symbol that remains compassionate in the face of obscurity and regret.

Simic's poems, then, suggest that love survives the chaos inherent in our age; it enters the metaphors that disclose the truth of things in our age and leaves without having been transformed to the hatred that generates the century's acts of atrocity. Therefore, Simic's blues signify something other than the poet's need for love. As "Painters of Angels and Seraphim" states, blue no longer signifies "a state of grace"; instead, Simic's "blues" signify the absence of such a state. And, within that condition of ambiguity, surrealism—with its use of metaphors and chance—works well to reveal the truth of the age. The blues operate with surrealism, says Simic. Sherod Santos asks Simic if he sees surrealism "as a literary equivalent to jazz." Simic does not disagree, but adds that he believes there is more surrealism in blues: "What one would call 'jive,' but also eroticism, the tragic sense of life. If the blues were French, we'd be studying it at Yale" (*Uncertain Certainty* 69–70). Simic claims that his interest in blues as an art form "taught me a number of things. How to tell a story quickly, economically. The value of gaps, ellipses, and most importantly, the virtues of simplicity and accessibility" (70). The metaphoric distance, where approximation creates a more authentic poetry than equivalence would, not only is valuable in its own right, but allows Simic to compress stories into four lines and to use simple yet suggestive language that opens meanings.

Simic also comments on blues in general in his essay, "No Cure for the Blues." Curiously enough, he recognizes that "the chief preoccupation of much country and urban blues is the relationship between men and women" (*Unemployed Fortune-Teller* 47) despite his own inclination for other subject matter in his blues. However, more in common between his own poetry and blues is "The comic seriousness of these songs [that] understands the coexistence of misfortune and laughter. It is in that joyful irreverence and freedom that one must seek their truth" (47). Simic joins with others who have made the same claims about the blues; for example, Ralph Ellison says blues "speak to us simultaneously of the tragic and the comic aspects of the human condition" (256).

Simic feels that the confluence of the tragic and comic is unique to the twentieth century's ambiguity, creating a tension that can only be "resolved" through the logic of metaphor. Rather than classical operations of comedy that seem to be "a temporary interruption of harmony," the modern age's ambiguity results from humor being present always.

> I think in the twentieth century humor has become ontological. It's a permanent disruption, it's a world view, a philosophy of life. Everything is equally tragic and comic in the long run, but for the two to occur at the same time as in our century, that's really curious. Also, I don't know what the definition of humor is, but it seems to me that if you could find a good definition it would pretty much resemble that of modern poetry: the irrational element plus the attitude. Because the person, the victim of a joke as well as the person who cracks a joke—they both sense themselves defeated. Yet, probably in humor, too, there is a kind of yearning for harmony, some kind of metaphysical synthesis. In other words, a basically poetic way of gobbling the world. (*Uncertain Certainty* 19)

When Simic describes this "poetic way" of gobbling existence, he seems to be recasting his use of metaphor and poetic thinking. Like metaphor, humor can also detect the kinship of things as it employs imaginative leaps of logic that makes the commonplace strange. Metaphor, then, is an attempt at harmony, in the midst of defeat that claims any harmony is not possible.

"Without a Sough of Wind," the volume's last poem, condenses many of the book's themes into a single sentence six stanzas long. The twentieth century looms large in this poem, but against this impending feeling, Simic's poet proposes a highly illogic thing—love—as the hint of meaning in this condition.

Against the backdrop
Of a twilight world
In which one has done so little
For one's soul

She hangs a skirt
On the doorknob
She puts a foot on the chair
To take off a black stocking

And it's good to have eyes
Just then for the familiar
Large swinging breasts
And the cleft of her ass

Before the recital
Of the long day's
Woes and forebodings
In the warm evening

With the drone of insects
On the window screen
And the lit dial of a radio
Providing what light there is

Its sound turned much too low
To make out the words
Of what could be
A silly old love song.

In offering "a silly old love song" as a replacement for the evening news, the poem runs the risk of being a vapid platitude, while the near-excessive descriptions of the woman's body remove the poem out of romance into earthy familiarity. The poet does sense defeat ("one has done so little / For one's soul"), but the momentary pause in the company of what is "good" postpones the day's "woes and forebodings," allowing the poet to be conscious of his fortunate place in the century. The words of the love song cannot be heard, but they seem to impose themselves conspicuously on the poet's attention more than the likelier recital of woes and forebodings, or the certain ambiguity of the twilight world. The poet calls attention to signs that are both increasingly ambiguous but also increasingly affirmative. He is therefore able to end the volume with hope that remains authentic in its possibility, despite the certainty that the condition that this hope springs out of is a certain ambiguity that appears unending.

In a review of *Unending Blues,* Peter Stitt claims that the final poems in the volume help to erase the earlier suffering that had been developed:

> It seems impossible not to conclude that Simic has arranged the poems in the book so that they will end up contradicting his title. Though blues they may often be, these certainly are not blues unending. A tone of affection enters, lightly sounded midway through the book, and grows in power and range until it drowns out all wailing by the end. (203)

While Stitt's praise of Simic's unusual end draws attention to the volume's solace, the force of the upbeat finale occurs in other matters as well. In the final poem especially, the tragic wailing is drowned out only for a moment. The day's woes and forebodings threaten to consume the speaker once this moment of affection passes. The poet has found momentary solitude, escaping both unending uncertainty and tragic blues. But if suffering will return, the poet has hope that these moments of solace will occur again as well.

Much of that solace will return through the poetry. *Unending Blues* stands not only as a fine collection of poems but as a real attempt to search for the truth that is hidden in our existence. Through his use of poetic thinking, Simic has employed a means to explore truth rather than merely repeat it. Despite the inescapable tragedy of our age, Simic also has discovered the value of the familiar to raise us above the incessant suffering inherent to any age. But once the reader peeks within its fascinating interior, it will startle, illuminate, and delight, all in the same moment of consciousness.

NOTES

1. Simic's own comments on these poems, in a letter to me (6 May 1988), verify this thesis: "As for '[Implements of] Augury' and 'Toward Nightfall'—the idea is, that these scenes hint at meanings. They are indeed like something . . . except it's hard for the speaker to say just what? Their nature, their flavor depends on something else. Their reality depends on their conditional existence. It's like saying, I've seen this

before . . . I've just entered the realm of archetypes—old meanings and their aura, etc. Something like that!" (Simic's ellipses).

2. Simic is quoting from Heidegger's revised lecture, "What Are Poets For?" (*Poetry, Language, Thought* 92).

WORKS CITED

Dixon, Willie. Liner notes. *The Real Folk Blues.* By Howlin' Wolf. Chess MCA, 1987.

Ellison, Ralph. *Shadow and Act.* New York: Random House, 1953.

Fletcher, Angus. *Allegory: The Theory of a Symbolic Mode.* Ithaca, N.Y.: Cornell University Press, 1964.

Frye, Northrop. *Anatomy of Criticism: Four Essays.* Princeton: Princeton University Press, 1957.

Heidegger, Martin. *Poetry, Language, Thought.* Trans. Albert Hofstadter. New York: Harper and Row, 1971.

Simic, Charles. "The Metaphysician in the Dark: An Interview with Bruce Weigl." *American Poetry Review,* September–October 1991, 5–13. Reprinted in this volume.

———. *The Uncertain Certainty: Interviews, Essays, and Notes on Poetry.* Ann Arbor: University of Michigan Press, 1985.

———. *The Unemployed Fortune-Teller: Essays and Memoirs.* Ann Arbor: University of Michigan Press, 1994.

———. *Unending Blues.* San Diego: Harcourt Brace, 1986.

———. *Wonderful Words, Silent Truth: Essays on Poetry and a Memoir.* Ann Arbor: University of Michigan Press, 1990.

Smith, Paul. "The Will to Allegory in Postmodernism." *Dalhousie Review* 62, no. 1 (spring 1982): 105–21.

Stitt, Peter. "The Whirlpool of Image and Narrative Flow." *Georgia Review* 41, no. 1 (spring 1987): 192–208.

CHRISTOPHER BUCKLEY

Sounds That Could Have Been Singing: Charles Simic's *The World Doesn't End*

A quote from Fats Waller, "Let's waltz the Rumba," serves as an epigraph for Charles Simic's 1989 Pulitzer Prize–winning collection of poetry, *The World Doesn't End.* While there is humor in this allusion, a hint of jazz and unpredictability readers have come to know as part of Simic's work, the use of the quote is not flip or casual; the line from Waller is purposeful. Simic is signaling us how he intends this book of poems to be read; he is describing the texture and technique for this collection, which for the most part is written in prose poem form. He's saying, "Let's do it a little differently now, jazz it up, change the face a bit, show some different moves; let's adjust the look and feel, the texture; let's explore this artifice, but let's keep the rhythm, the soul, the nostalgia and imagination—so better to reveal the world—but nevertheless, let's dance."

I want to say from the outset that *The World Doesn't End* is a very consciously structured book, that the poetic form was chosen—as all forms should be—to best contain and amplify the subjects and themes. Simic has published many books, including a *Selected Poems, 1963–1983* (1985) and a "Revised and Expanded" *Selected* in 1990 (both from George Braziller), and all of those poems employ a more traditional poetic line. Simic chooses the prose poem for this book, as it best provides a form for the voice and material that go back to his essential poetic roots—the European or Eastern European folk tale.

Before I take up the efficacy of the prose poem form vis-à-vis the folk tale texture and the experience of the poet, and before I talk about the three-part strategy of the book with its section-closing, traditionally lined poems, I want to spend a little space addressing the carping of the few critics and poets objecting to a book of prose poems being awarded the Pulitzer Prize. I won't speculate as to the motivations of the one or two who complained, but it does seem, at this point in time, a little unnecessary to justify the prose poem—or any poetic form for that matter—as legitimate. Time and history have already done this; nevertheless, for the record . . . .

There is a spate of handbooks on prosody and poetic form available today. A random selection will reveal the prose poem as one of many poetic forms available to a poet. Lewis Turco includes it in his *The Book of Forms,* Michael Benedikt edited *The Prose Poem: An International Anthology,* George Myers Jr. edited *Epiphanies: The Prose Poem Now,* and one could go on.[1] However, the most helpful listing, I think, is in *The Longman Dictionary of Poetic Terms* edited by Jack Myers and Michael Simms.[2] Myers and Simms are thorough in their listings, and the entry on the prose poem covers three pages; their initial definition is comprehensive and makes the point that the prose poem is an historic form and one that employs essential elements of poetry:

> a form of poetry in prose format that contains the devices and modes of perception of lined-out poetry. The real roots of the prose poem go back as far as the origins of poetry itself since the line break is a relatively recent invention—neither the ancient Greeks nor the Anglo-Saxons in their original manuscripts employed line endings. But the earliest forms of the prose poem, as a separate genre, appear in the Old Testament, early folk tales, fables, and parables which used allusion, symbol, and imagery in a less diluted form than is usually found in prose. (244)

There is also reference to the prose poem in early Chinese poetry and of course the use of the prose poem by the French Symbolists Baudelaire, Rimbaud, Mallarmé, and Valéry. In addition to elements of poetry mentioned above, Myers and Simms go on to make an important point about rhythm in the prose poem.

> There is a great deal of internal rhythmical and syntactical movement in the poem which takes up the slackness in formal tension that is the inevitable result of not using line endings . . . there is sometimes the repetition and counter-point that we usually associate with poetry. But if a steady and predictable rhythm were to be used in a prose poem, the natural fluidity of the form would be stultified and the work would seem wooden. (245)

Obvious to any reader of *The World Doesn't End* is the rhythm of Simic's voice, the rhythm of the phrasing and imagery; a rhythm, I would venture to say, that contains more music than much recent poetry written in lines. One might suspect that the carping about line breaks or their absence in a book of poetry that received the Pulitzer Prize might not be the entire agenda of the people complaining. The most essential elements of poetry, rhythm, imagery, essential subject, and vision, are everywhere in this book. Again I would like to quote from Myers and Simms, who quote from Michael Benedikt's book on the prose poem.

> "There is an intense use of virtually all the devices of poetry, which includes the intense use of devices of verse. The sole exception to access to the possibilities, rather than set priorities of verse is, we should say, the line break." (245)

To argue that poetry is only "verse" and that *The World Doesn't End* is not poetry and therefore should not have received the Pulitzer Prize seems more than a little absurd and does not serve the interests of poetry in the larger sense—one of the aims of an award, one would think.

If you listen carefully to these poems, you will hear the familiar rhythms and concision of Simic's poetry and will visualize the images. These poems contain his direct statements, declarative openings, compression of narrative, and fabulous imagery. The elimination of line breaks, the elimination of the "appearance" and artifice of more traditional poetry, allows another artifice to take over, one that, on the surface and in appearance, allows more initial credibility; for these poems, by and large, contain the somewhat surreal observations of an incredible world, and the prose poem provides a "fluidity" and matter-of-fact forward movement through images and events that otherwise might well have the reader pausing.

Simic has chosen a form that best works as a coefficient of his subject and vision. Myers and Simms have pointed out that often the prose poem is "witty, skeptical, or self-consciously playful," and I am sure that this was also a consideration of Simic when choosing this form. The form, like the folk tale, gives the illusion of reporting-witnessing something strange and wondrous; it thus accommodates Simic's observation of the world, a witnessing of incidents from his childhood and his past that are incredible, even surreal, by everyday standards. As in much of his previous work, Simic lies to mix humor with the deadly serious, to reinforce the real emotional center with the surreal detail or image. Simic speaks to this predilection in his poetry in his interview with Bruce Weigl.

> Yes, yes! the tragic and comic under the same roof. They'll accompany the most tongue-in-cheek verses with a mournful tune, or vice versa: the words are tragic but the tune is a dance. I love that! A lot of folk music does that, though not in every culture. I know people get upset when there's too much mixing of the two. They want either one or the other. Mixing tragedy and comedy is a great transgression in their view. Serious art is very serious. Well, I don't think it needs to be.[3]

The appearance of prose, then, allows the reader to enter these fantastic events with more credibility, a little more anchored, apparently in the "prosaic" world. The "tale," as one of our oldest forms of literature, has always presented the mythical element, the heroic, the larger-than-life. Simms and Myers are helpful when they define the folk tale as "a verse of prose narrative celebrating a historical event, hero, belief or mode of behavior." And X. J. Kennedy offers that a tale "is a story, usually short, that sets forth strange and wonderful events in a more or less bare summary, without detailed character-drawing" (161).[4] The prose poem form, then, is the perfect one to contain and amplify events that often sound as steeped in mythology and wondrous imagery as any folk tale. Both tale and the prose poem offer dramatic closure—something happens in a sequence of actions that will resolve or conclude the tension set forth in character, action, or the witnessing of the speaker.

Simic grew up reading folk tales, and the events—strange, wonderful, and tragic—set forth in *The World Doesn't End* are often drawn from a period of the poet's life during which the world was exactly that—strange, wonderful, and tragic. In his essay "Serbian Heroic Ballads,"[5] Simic recounts how at ten years of age he began to read Serbian folk poems and read them so often that even today he can remember and recite favorite passages from the ballads. In these ballads, Simic tells us, the mythical is always present, but so is the real. The Serbs sing of the tragic sense of life but make that into a something he calls "heroic spite." The "Kosovo Cycle" sings of the defeat of the Serbs at the hands of the Turks. Some of this texture, this attitude, can be found in *The World Doesn't End;* here is a salient passage from that essay.

> The poet of the Kosovo Cycle rebels against the very idea of historical triumph. Defeat, he appears to be saying, is wiser than victory. The great anti-heros of these poems experience a moment of tragic consciousness. They see the alternatives with all their moral implications. (111)

For the folk poet of these poems, true nobility and heroism come from the consciousness of the difficult choice. They say the old Greeks had a hand in this. Very possibly. The world from which these poems came didn't change that much from the days of the Greek dramatists.

And so it is no wonder, writing of his early years during the war, the astonishing things he saw, that Simic chooses apparently wondrous and incongruous images, or that the witnessing voice is the voice of the folk tale, the texture of strange history. That the form used is the prose poem is logical and appropriate for the way it blends the fabulous imager, the heroic and the incredible, with a voice that reports "truly" what the speaker has seen and how that might be resolved or has taken place in such a world as ours.

In his essay "In The Beginning," Simic provides a straightforward account of growing up in Belgrade during and immediately after the German occupation of that city;[6] page to page, event to event, and image to image, we read an actual but also surreal document—surreal especially in the sense that his experience is happening to a boy between the ages of three and ten, that these are the formative days for interpreting the world there presented—the deaths, the wounded in the streets, the suspension of all usual social order such as school and parental supervision, the people hung from telephone poles—all this is an introduction to a world that lacks coherence. Add to this the problem of immigration: moving to stay ahead of the war and bad economics. In his interview with Bruce Weigl (and in the poems in this book, and in many other poems) Simic describes being an immigrant. One can see that particular influence on his vision and his technique: "You learn not to take things for granted. 'Where are we going to immigrate to next?' My father used to ask me. He was only half joking. Life is unpredictable. Anything can happen. . . . That's the historical and autobiographical context of my poetry." And so history—actual, invented, or interpreted—is important to Simic, important to the poems in this collection as they take on that texture of the folk tale that reports a history that is strange and wonderful and often reclaimed from a deep historical past. The prose poem, its apparent lack of artifice, then, best serves this conceit by offering up the dramatic, even seemingly without adornment or embellishment. Appearing plain and more factual, it is the most appropriate vehicle for the elliptical or surreal imagination or dramatic outcome—it even more easily admits the imagination, which will try to yield some emotional response and focus on the events in a fluid fashion. In the interview with Weigl, Simic tells us that "the experience of immigration did compel me to ask and continue to ask certain questions about the twentieth century history." And a bit later he adds,

> "Form is the extension of content" said Creeley, and Levertov changed it to "form is the revelation of content." I agree with them. So it's [form] not *an invention*—something out of nothing—but a discovery of what is already there. In my experience (content) myth lurks, and so does history. Poetry is the archeology of the self. The bits and pieces one keeps digging up belong to the world—everybody's world. It's a paradox that has always amused me. Just when you think you're most subjective, you meet everybody else.

Simic is a careful poet. He is highly conscious of form and content. For *The World Doesn't End* he knows the prose poem to be the best form for this particular history. In the Weigl interview he says: "I always felt poetry is made half-way between speech and song. It's a question of nuances, of course, and it depends on how you hear the poem. Do you want it spoken, declaimed, intoned, or sung? . . . Think of prose poems! There's no question there's such a thing. I think the distinction I made before applies. Prose poems are spoken in a certain way, not sung." And so in this book Simic makes use of the prose poem form, which departs slightly from other traditional forms, which realistically contains some strange and wonderful music, which mixes things up just enough to convey the poet's view of his history—a truly emotional, imaginative, and mythical history—and which, as Simic says in a poem from the book's third section, gives us "sounds that could have been singing."

The World Doesn't End is divided into three sections, each with a slightly different voice and seen from the perspective of a slightly different vision. Part 1 presents views from the perspective of childhood, a personal history of sorts, but one without the usual autobiographical detail and chronological progression. Part 2 includes poems spoken by a slightly more mature speaker; more politics, philosophy, and mythic material enter the book through these poems. Part 3 provides an absurdist history of the world, more current, more introspective than the first two parts.

The poem that introduces the landscape of Simic's strange world also initiates Simic's historical journey.

> My mother was a braid of black smoke.
> She bore me swaddled over the burning cities.
> The sky was a vast and windy place for a child to play.
> We met many others who were just like us. They were trying to put on their overcoats with arms made of smoke.
> The high heavens were full of little shrunken deaf ears instead of stars.[7]

Told from the point of view of a child growing up in Belgrade during World War II, this prose poem makes almost literal sense despite the fantastic images. The emotional truth anchors the poem, the translation of what it felt like to be there into images taken from the scene at the time—hence the mother is a braid of black smoke, the sky of smoke over the burning cities is all there is, the only place for a child of imagination to escape to or in. No bright outlook, no one listening—deaf ears instead of stars, so it must have seemed to that child, so it must seem now to one remembering that time and place. So we have a history, an eyewitness account in declarative sentences in a form that does not call attention to itself, that provides a voice that does not then isolate images or ask for pity. In the best sense of the folk tale, it reports the strange and wondrous without fanfare—"So it was, and so it came to pass. . . ." And yet we have the concision and imagery we want from poetry, the startling image that provides closure, the rhythm that makes us aware of a particular voice, one just edged with music, enough to keep us listening and engaged. The "fluidity" that Myers and Simms point out in their dictionary of terms would be lost outside the prose form, as would the credibility of the images, presented in such a summary fashion as in the tale. The prose poem form allows the voice to control what it presents, and though the images are often fantastic on first reading, the texture of firsthand experience, which comes through the prose form, enables the reader to sense and identify the realism lurking beneath the surface.

At this point, it's important to acknowledge and add a point Peter Stitt made in his review of Simic's *Selected Poems*. Stitt maintains, quite correctly, that "Far from being a surrealist, . . . Charles Simic is in fact one of the most fierce—though almost one of the most indirect—realists writing today."[8] Stitt was one of the first to connect the apparently surreal or unanchored images in Simic's writing to the realistic experience of growing up in Europe during World War II, and also to point out the mythological and conceptual "realism" of Simic's imagery. He quotes lines from Simic's poem "Prodigy": "I'm told but do not believe / that that summer I witnessed / men hung from telephone poles" and comments thusly, "It isn't that this did not happen or that Simic was not there to see it; rather, he says, his mother 'had a way of tucking my head / suddenly under her overcoat.' "

Stitt goes on to show the fabulistic/folk tale narrative roots in Simic's work to that point. In discussing "Empire of Dreams," Stitt points out that the poem's allusive narrative structure is generally typical and descriptive of Simic's "indirect practice." "The poem has a narrative structure, though the meaning of its action, like the meaning of its details, is more suggestive than exact. Thus the poem is vaguely allegorical and resembles a fable." In *The World Doesn't End,* this again is typical of Simic's texture and method, and it becomes even more amplified and more apparent in the prose poem format.

In part 1, Simic is careful to establish the child's voice before moving on to other histories, careful to start with a more ostensibly realistic perception before moving to the more fabulistic. There are a number of poems in the first section about the poet's mother, and the following poem reveals one very "unreal" side of the war—a tender memory of how his mother tried to go about her life in spite of the pressing realities:

> It's a store that specializes in antique porcelain. She goes around it with a finger on her lips. Tsss! We must be quiet when we come near the tea cups. Not a breath allowed near the sugar bowls. A teeny grain of dust has fallen on a wafer-thin saucer. She makes an "oh" with her owlet-mouth. On her feet she wears soft, thickly padded slippers around which mice scurry.

This is arguably a "real" portrait of the poet's mother, an accurate and precise moment that becomes emblematic of her character. Here are the serene virtues of tea, the quiet life of a middle-class woman about to break to pieces amid the war. The very next poem includes his mother and grandmother, ironing and sewing, and though there are apparently surreal images in the beginning and in the folk tale–style ending, the ending image must indeed have seemed emotionally true and accurate to a child there and then.

> "You will ruin your eyes, Henrietta, in such bad light," her mother warns. And she's right! Never since the beginning of the world has there been so little light. Our winter afternoons have been known at times to last a hundred years.

A mild exaggeration compared to other images, to other tales, but one presented in the same calm and exact voice as the rest of these poems, one establishing the objective, firsthand, and yet mythic tone and vision for the book.

In a poem beginning "I am the last Napoleonic Soldier," Simic presents a very real vision of a ghost, an emblem of earlier and perhaps all wars, a spirit still wandering the earth. This soldier, this ghost, is still retreating from Moscow, and he speaks as the Germans and the Russians are going various ways down the road at the end of World War II—the armies change, but nothing else changes in two hundred years. Again, a talelike image ends the poem, a strange and wondrous detail: "I have a ceremonial saber. I use it to cut my hair, which is four feet long."

In the next poem, the child speaker reports an even more fantastic event.

> He held the Beast of the Apocalypse by its tail, the stupid kid! Oh beards on fire, our doom appeared sealed. The buildings were tottering; the computer screens were as dark as our grandmother's cupboards. We were too frightened to plead. Another century gone to hell—and for what? Just because some people don't know how to bring their children up!

Here again it is not hard to imagine a child watching the war: a soldier or patriot with a machine gun, a mortar, bombs falling.

Part I includes more purely mythic poems that manage, however, to still hint at modern war.

> The city had fallen. We came to the window of a house drawn by a madman. The setting sun shone on a few abandoned machines of futility. "I remember," someone said, "how in ancient times one could turn a wolf into a human and then lecture it to one's heart content."

A scene from World War II, highly suggestive of any war—the fallen city, the abandoned machines, ruined houses—and connected to the mythic and to the history of the world with one fabulous and despairing image of the wolf, implying one might have a better chance reasoning with the wolf than with human beings.

Part 1 ends, as do the other two parts, with a short, lined poem, a coda, a kind of punctuation for the section:

> The roaches look like
> Comic rustics
> In serious dramas.

When we consider the long history of wars, all the armies marshaled across the countries, all the high drama settled with the dust, this image may well present to us a sense of irony and folly. In it, we may see reflected the history of government and the histories of people who lived and died in their wars—the aftermath of wars (roaches) and then again a substantial portion of humankind reflected in them, its seriousness and comic gestures in costumes/uniforms/conventions/beliefs. And though lined, this poem makes fablelike use of insects and has a palpable connection to the texture of war.

The speaker throughout part 1 is a child and simultaneously the grown poet who goes and has gone through the world with a child's heart, without cynicism, willing to believe what he sees and how he sees it, and ready to behold that which is strange, accept it at face value, and therein see a personal connection to history in the largest sense. This speaker is guileless, somewhat gullible, and inquisitive; he is one who engages us with fantastic tales and visions and compels us with a poignant history in a voice that sings a mythic history.

The speaker of the poems in part 2 represents a maturation of the point of view seen in part 1. Poems here are more philosophical, thematically and allusively. The prose poem accommodates the concerns and textures of these poems—allowing the direct address some of the poems rely upon—and provides, via the folk tale linkage, a dramatic instead of lyric closure. Many of these poems comment upon the absurd and/or ironic conventions of society; and some point out the callousness and blindness of society to the individual—whether an ancient society or a contemporary one, as in the following poem:

> A poem about sitting on a New York rooftop on a chill autumn evening, drinking red wine, surrounded by tall buildings, the little kids running dangerously to the edge, the beautiful girl everyone's secretly in love with sitting by herself. She will die young but we don't know that yet. She has a hole in her black stocking, big toe showing, toe painted red. . . . And the sky-scrapers . . . in the failing light . . . like new Chaldeans, pythonesses, Cassandras . . . because of their many blind windows.

Some poems in this part have a slightly autobiographical origin, as in the second half of the poem beginning "Everything's foreseeable."

> My grandmother sweeping the sidewalk knows that. She says there's no god, only an eye here and there that sees clearly. The neighbors are too busy watching TV to burn her as a witch.

A truly ironic view on the sad state of contemporary society as well upon society in earlier times—Puritan clearly, perhaps even ancient—and Simic again brings the past, pulls history, into perspective in the present.

Other poems in part 2 are more conceptual and more openly hostile and politically specific. One offers a possible allegory for the place of poets and philosophers in society as they seek patronage.

> He calls one dog Rimbaud and the other Hölderlin. . . . Tonight they will light tall candles and drink wine. Later, they'll open the door for the dogs to come in and eat the scraps under the table. "Entrez, mes enfants!" he'll shout into the night, bowing deeply from the waist.

In the following poem Simic dramatizes the anger of the anarchist/revolutionary, or perhaps even of the poet or philosopher:

A dog with a soul, you've got that? You apes with heads of Socrates, false priests' altar boys, retired professors of evil! I imagine cities so I can get lost in them. I meet other dogs with souls when I'm not lighting firecrackers in heads that are about to doze off.

Blood-and-guts firecrackers. In the dark to see, you ass-scratchers! In the dark to see.

The prose form allows also for direct address, as in an epistolary poem, and in so doing so allows the speaker to make connections that might otherwise seem pretentious or sentimental. When Simic does not rely on dramatic closure, he uses the imagistic; even in a straightforward narrative he manages to maintain an element at least textually connected to the folk tale. In the following poem, he ends with the image of a spider that directs the movement of the poem to a strange and luminous image that objectifies the feeling and lonely situation of subject and speaker and so preserves the poem from any overbearing concern for the speaker. He addresses Nietzsche.

Dear Friedrich, the world's still false, cruel and beautiful.

Earlier tonight, I watched the Chinese laundry-man, who doesn't read or write our language, turn the pages of a book left behind by a customer in a hurry. That made me happy. I wanted it to be a dreambook, or a volume of foolishly sentimental verses, but I didn't look closely.

It's almost midnight now, and his light is still on. He has a daughter who brings him dinner, who wears short skirts and walks with long strides. She's late, very late, so he has stopped ironing and watches the street.

If not for the two of us, there'd be only spiders hanging their webs between the street lights and the dark trees.

Such dreams, such empires are dreamed like this, Simic seems to be saying—whether by the laundryman, the poet, or the philosopher, and perhaps he is also saying that in reality, our daydreams and our desires add up to little more than dark and almost invisible webs of thought. Yet there is great pathos here in the immediate, personal tone, in the direct address to Nietzsche, one who would know about this situation, has thought it over seriously. Simic offers a philosophical poem, addressed to a philosopher, presented without pretension or abstraction. The direct address and the recounting of incident in the prose form enables the poem to escape sentimentality and self-pity by keeping the incident or the narrative moving forward and by rendering it in an objective manner.

Most poems in this section end with a dramatic closure and report strange and fantastic images and events in the tradition of the folk tale. Reading one of these about a hanged man who steps down from the scaffold and walks to the tavern to order a beer for himself and one for his head, I am reminded of the W. S. Merwin translation of an Amazon Indian tale about a severed head that became the moon. Simic offers up a poem in the tradition of the tale, and it affirms how many strange things happen in the world.

In other poems in part 2, Simic uses the prose poem form to present a succinct scene so exactly written that it works as many of William Carlos Williams's poems do: rendering detail of such a perfectly representative moment that dramatic closure is unnecessary; the understated image and observations provide complete poetic movement and epiphany without elaboration.

> The ideal spectator who lives only for art, hands folded behind his back. A blank canvas appropriately entitled "Blank" before him. It's exactly 11 A.M. in the provincial museum. One can hear the rumbling stomach of the uniformed guard, who has the face of someone drowned by moon-light.

So credible and so real in a proverbial sense, and yet so precisely drawn in detail, this poem takes on mythic proportions. One senses that this has gone on in the distant past and will somehow always go on like this: the dead and disinterested influencing our best artistic and social efforts, themselves becoming emblems of what we have let the world become in the twentieth century. The dark texture of such a tale is certainly Eastern European, if not Kafkaesque. The dispassionate observation of the prose poem nevertheless leaves us with a chilling emotional effect with regard to what our world, our art might come to.

Part 2 also ends with a short, lined poem, "Gospel," which functions as a coda to the section. In terms of the speaker's personal history, we have moved from the childhood of part 1 to a "middle" voice in part 2. The literal translation of "good news" in this poem does not quite ring true; the religious overtones, however, do lead us via the voice of the poem to metaphysical doubt—"Half-way to nowhere."

> Half-way to nowhere—
>
> I thought I heard
> Church bells ringing,
> The blind man on the corner
> Call out my name.

Nevertheless, the speaker is interpreting experience and finds at least some connection to the world as his name is called out. And still the poem has that mood of a tale—the journey, church bells, the proverbial blind man—in the sense of the larger history of the world, the details are timeless.

Part 3 progresses further in terms of the chronological development of the voice; the speaker is more mature and is recounting less firsthand experience in favor of a more absurdist history of the world, a world still fabulous and mythic, yet more contemporary and in some senses, more personal. These are not, however, autobiographical poems in the strictest sense. Asking Simic about the apparent autobiographical quality of poems in *Unending Blues,* Weigl received this response:

> They *sound* more autobiographical. They're certainly based on things I did, but I'm far more interested in the fiction. The "I" is many fictions. The object is always "truth," but not the literal one. . . . I'm more interested in history than in autobiography.

Witnesses to the events of the world in the first half of this final section continue to emanate from the strange land of the tale: police dogs dressed as children, a Minotaur, ghost ships and Hamlets; yet a more current and absurdist element enters in them all as well. As if to balance these disparate elements, a more overtly autobiographical mode is initiated by the poet. The speaker is at a downtown restaurant, a potted palm speaks to a mirror, a fat man on the street asks his transvestite lover to return: the astonishing events of the mythic past no more astonishing than the present and still rendered in firsthand observation, the objective witnessing of the prose poem. Surreal and disjunctive events continue even in the poet's/speaker's home territory. In the following poem, the speaker is in New Hampshire and dealing with current mythology and fable.

> Lots of people around here have been taken for rides in UFOs. You wouldn't think that possible with all the pretty white churches in sight so well attended on Sundays.
>
> "The round square doesn't exist," says the teacher to the dull-witted boy. His mother was abducted only last night. All expectations to the contrary, she sits in the corner grinning to herself. The sky is vast and blue.
>
> "They're so small, they can sleep inside their own ears," says one eighty-year-old twin to the other.

The closure here is simply matter-of-fact, and some of this is possible to imagine as headlines on those grocery store tabloids.

Part 3 also includes a lovely autobiographical piece about the speaker's father, beginning "My father loved the strange books of André Breton." But this poem moves beyond the person to reveal the common myth of the immigrant to the United States: " 'I love America,' he'd tell us. We were going to make a million dollars manufacturing objects we had seen in dreams that night." Although this piece keeps the narrative moving forward via the prose form, there is also a wonderful lyric rhythm present. Also in this third part is a lovely and strange memory of earlier days and a woman friend who wanted to be a country singer, all in a poem that abandons itself not to narrative closure but to the energy and youthful madness of the times.

Very near the end of this section is a poem that I read as fable and allegory for God the Creator.

> He had mixed up the characters in the long novel he was writing. He forgot who they were and what they did. A dead woman reappeared when it was time for dinner. A door-to-door salesman emerged out of a backwoods trailer wearing Chinese robes. The day the murderer was supposed to be electrocuted, he was buying flowers for a certain Rita, who turned out to be a ten-year-old girl with thick glasses and braids. . . . And so it went.

> He never did anything for me, though. I kept growing older and grumpier, as I was supposed to, in a ratty little town which he always described as "dead" and "near nothing."

In an objective sense, this poem is an explanation—as many folk tales are—of the riddle of the world, of history. The poem also expresses a very contemporary existential notion: a view of God not that far from say the one John Fowles exposes in his novels. Fowles has said that if there were a God, his second act (after creation) would have been to disappear, that God loaded the dice for the game, then vanished. Simic seems sympathetic with this sensibility in his poem and in comments made in an essay on William Stafford contained in *Wonderful Words, Silent Truth*.

> One should speak of Stafford's disappearing acts. As in "Traveling through the Dark," he leaves us at most crucial moments. At the end of his great poems we are always alone, their fateful acts and consequences now our own to consider.
>
> Solitude as an absolute, the only one.
>
> The heavens above couldn't care less.
>
> The poet asks the philosopher in us to consider the world in its baffling presence.
>
> An American sphinx in the desert of our spirit. Let us keep asking her questions.

In Simic's allegorical poem of God the Creator, he continues to rely on the language of the tale—"And so it went," and he creates what then appears to be a fable for our times, one that explains, in a way, all time—of the rush of experience, of history; the tale appears to say that our existence in history is baffling; so many strange things take place there seems to be no one minding the shop, as it were.

The coda for part 3 is a two-line poem titled "My Secret Identity Is," which echoes Simic's comments about the world in the Stafford essay.

> The room is empty,
> And the window is open

There is no punctuation at the end of the poem. The speaker has vanished: a witness but not an apologist. The/his identity has escaped; the speaker will not give "the answer" to or against such crazy experience. His view, his witnessing of history, has been presented; connections over time have been made, and, beyond that, how does one explain the world? It is fabulous and mysterious; it has its own shifts and continuums despite our attempts to impose order, to interpret it to our own satisfaction or in our own image, which has often and traditionally suggested that the world cannot get along without us. Simic says it can, and that at best its music and its images should be a source of beauty and wonderment to us. In the Weigl interview, Simic speaks directly to this point in responding to an old statement of his about the impossibility of writing poems.

> The actual situation is this: "one superfluous human being," as they used to say in the 19th-century Russian Literature, in the midst of all and everything—the humankind, history, literature, the infinite universe—is attempting to talk back in a dozen or so lines of poetry. No wonder people say the poets are nuts! The world so big and the poem so teeny. And yet —it's been done! The history of literature is full of examples: The impossible is possible. Remember Dickinson's
>
> " . . . and I alone —
> A speck upon a Ball
> Went out upon Circumference —
> Beyond the Dip of Bell."
>
> And she didn't even know—although she suspected—the unimaginable hugeness of the known universe. . . . That's the part I love; it's "known" but it cannot be imagined. . . . Anyway, once I remember myself, once I savor the full implications of my predicament, words come out of the astonishment—the comic astonishment!

Simic wants to leave us with these words and these astonishments, the music and imagery of a world ongoing in its wonder but true as anything we know; a world that despite us, doesn't end.

NOTES

1. Lewis Turco, ed., *The Book of Forms* (New York: E. P. Dutton, 1968); Michael Benedikt, ed., *The Prose Poem: An International Anthology* (New York: Dell, 1976); George Myers Jr., ed. *Epiphanies: The Prose Poem Now* (Westerville, Ohio: Cumberland, 1967).

2. Jack Myers and Michael Simms, eds., *The Longman Dictionary of Poetic Terms* (White Plains, N.Y.: Longman, 1989).

3. Charles Simic, "The Metaphysician in the Dark: An Interview with Bruce Weigl," *American Poetry Review,* September–October 1991, 5–13; reprinted in this volume.

4. X. J. Kennedy, ed., *Literature,* 2d ed. (Boston: Little, Brown, 1979), 101.

5. Charles Simic, "Serbian Heroic Ballads," in *Wonderful Words, Silent Truth* (Ann Arbor: University of Michigan Press, 1990).

6. Charles Simic, "In the Beginning," in *Wonderful Words, Silent Truth.*

7. Charles Simic, *The World Doesn't End* (New York: Harvest/ Harcourt Brace Jovanovich, 1989).

8. Peter Stitt, "Staying at Home and Going Away," review of *Selected Poems,* by Charles Simic, *Georgia Review* 40 (summer 1986), 111.

THOMAS LUX

The Nature of the Pleasure: *The Book of Gods and Devils*

The Book of Gods and Devils, not counting some limited editions, is Charles Simic's tenth, and one of his very best, books.[1] It is not a departure for him. It is, in fact, one more book in a voice and style that he had more or less perfected by the time his first full-length collection, *Dismantling the Silence,* was published in 1971. The voice (and the hard-to-define term *voice,* with all of its denotations and connotations, is probably more relevant to Simic's than virtually any other contemporary poetry) is characterized by, among other things, almost relentless concrete imagery and metaphor. Let me immediately contradict that, however, by saying that if there is one thing different about this book it is the occasional use of abstractions and a few nods to its philosophical influences. His voice is also characterized by what I'll call semisurrealism, a surrealism less wrenched, less arbitrary than hard-core surrealism. Other primary characteristics include clarity, brevity, an ever poignant "atmosphere" (which some may call tone, but by which I mean something even more literal: the poems' weather, most often gray, the rain just about to turn to sleet; the day is Monday, the month November, etc.), and a wry, almost gleeful-in-the-face-of-doom sense of humor.

This humor is often the key, or one of the keys, for the poems' successes. For all the sadness, loss, and dismal human situations in the poems, Simic is often a very funny and, at times, joyful poet. It is a serious humor (one of Simic's books carries the epigram "There is nothing so serious as a joke"), a dark humor, but, unlike some humor that is *not* supposed to make you laugh, Simic's humor *is* supposed to make you laugh, out loud. His humor, and the way he skewers the darker side of his psyche with it, is an important element of his work.

When I read the poem called "A Letter" that begins "Dear Philosophers, I get sad when I think / Is it the same with you?" I laugh. Out loud. Each time I read it. The comic opening is followed by a nagging memory of an "old girlfriend," an image of "beds covered with identical gray blankets," another image of a woman being tortured, a mock-philosophical exchange with a friend named Bob, and then the statement "Bob's father was taking their dog for a walk." This line is hilarious in its understated banality. It is perfectly comically timed. It also seems almost in conscious mocking agreement with Paul Valéry's sentiment when he said he didn't write prose because he loathed the idea of putting on paper a sentence like "Madam put on her hat and walked out the door." It is immediately followed by a heartbreakingly simple line, "He moved with pain; the dog waited for him." Simic makes you laugh, then snatches the laugh from your throat. None of the above is contradictory, of course. Or it is this contradictory nature that makes it human.

Simic is by no means the only poet to employ this technique (James Tate and Russell Edson come to mind), but no one does it quite like Simic, with the same ability to put the reader inside, to make so palpable the emotional atmosphere of the poem. When this poem, for example, ends semiabstractly ("There was no one else in the park, / Only bare trees with an infinity of tragic shapes / To make thinking difficult."), the reader does not experience deflation but the opposite—the "infinity" and the "tragic" surround the image, a silhouette of such sharp grief, such *physical* thought that one is left almost breathless. It is in this way, over and over, that Simic uses his imagery and his metaphors as a drill into our psyches, and this is why I derive so much pleasure from his poems, why I am drawn to him book after book and to the same poems over and over again.

In one of the essays in *The Uncertain Certainty: Interviews, Essays, and Notes on Poetry,* Simic asserts that "the meaning of images depends on the company they are in."[2] Sounds simple enough. Simic knows how to make his images keep odd and right company with each other. This is how images get turned into metaphors. This too has a great deal to do with the nature of the pleasure—how the images rub against one another, disappear into each other, contradict (to create a new angle, a new spark) each other, how they build and loop, how they create then halt then restart a momentum of thought in the reader's mind that is also felt in the reader's body. This kind of energy of imagination and/or metaphor is what I'd like to focus on by reading closely one quite short and, as is usually the case with Simic, deceptively simple poem:

Heights of Folly

O crows circling over my head and cawing!
I admit to being, at times,
Suddenly, and without the slightest warning,
Exceedingly happy.

On a morning otherwise sunless,
Strolling arm in arm
Past some gallows-shaped trees
With my dear Helen,
Who is also a strange bird.

A feeling of being summoned
Urgently, but by a most gracious invitation
To breakfast on slices of watermelon
In the company of naked gods and goddesses
On a patch of last night's snow.

Since this poem begins with the somewhat archaic evocative "O," which nowadays is difficult to use for reasons other than hyperbole or comedy, and since the line is also exclamatory, Simic plants in the reader's unconscious the notion that this poem is going to have something to do with joy, delight, play. Birds circling one's head are meant to make the reader associate with vultures circling a dying man, so immediately we're being prepared for an emotional/physical tug between something playful and something dark. With one line Simic dramatizes a great deal of action. He follows this with a syntactically halting, huffing three-line sentence, stringing along the reader. Often, just when you feel his syntax is becoming a little flat, predictable, he will suddenly shift it. The reader—the reader's body and ear—responds. Simic is setting the reader up, in this case, for the weirdly epiphanic moments of happiness that he is going to describe in the next stanza.

The second stanza begins with typical Simic weather: sunless. The speaker, however, is strolling arm in arm, an image of comfort and familiarity that uses familiar language, which lulls the reader, setting the reader up again, preparing the unconscious for the "gallows-shaped trees" in the next line. This kind of juxtaposition, which he again switches in the next line with "With my dear Helen," continues to give the poem energy and momentum. He is also teasing "Helen," the reader, and himself with the stanza's last line. "Strange bird" is a wonderfully euphemistic phrase here, the connotations of which are gentle and playful. By saying she is "also" a strange bird, the speaker suggests that he too is a strange bird for being moved to happiness by seeing crows circling his head, for seeing trees as gallows shaped.

Many poets would have ended this poem here, content with its lyric tenderness, its humor, its muted joy. But not Simic: he takes it one more turn (this is a sonnet-length poem, and this turn comes just about where a sonnet turns after the octave) in describing, metaphorically, his moments of happiness with a string of almost contradictory diction: "summoned," "urgently," and then the mockingly gentle "most gracious invitation," again drawing out the sentence, pulling the reader along, making him or her feel anticipation, just as at the end of the first stanza. Again: so much action, so much going on with so few words. He now follows with a tremendously multisensory line—wet, colorful, tasty, cool—which in turn leads us into, makes almost inevitable, the hilarious and hyperbolically sensuous penultimate line. And where does this marvelous repast take place, where does one breakfast on watermelon (ambrosia!) with naked gods and goddesses? "On a patch of last night's snow." Of course. What giddy, wild, tender, ecstatic progression this poem makes! What a poem of celebration! And what a beautiful love poem it is, for surely "dear Helen," who is at the center of the poem, is as much the occasion for its joy as what is not, or cannot, be named.

Although this essay is ostensibly about, and the poems I've quote are from, *The Book of Gods and Devils,* there is a way in which it is also about Simic's achievement to date. This book, as I've already said, does not represent a departure for Simic, but a refinement, and although its cast, its hue, is a little darker (though "Heights of Folly" would be a notable exception), a little more abstract or philosophical than earlier books, it is spoken in the same voice that emerged so vividly in the mid-1960s, was published in a first major collection in 1971, and has been building steadily (I think it's fair to call Simic prolific: nine books, not counting a *Selected,* in twenty years) to an incredibly rich and beautiful body of work. These poems make me happy, even proud, to be human. May Charles Simic still be in early midcareer. And may he ceaseth not until death!

NOTES

1. Charles Simic, *The Book of Gods and Devils* (San Diego: Harcourt Brace, 1990).

2. Charles Simic, *The Uncertain Certainty: Interviews, Essays, and Notes on Poetry* (Ann Arbor: University of Michigan Press, 1985), 122.

HELEN VENDLER

Totemic Sifting: Charles Simic's *The Book of Gods and Devils, Hotel Insomnia,* and *Dime-Store Alchemy*

Charles Simic's riddling poems, for all that they reproduce many things about his century (its wars, its cities, its eccentrics, and so on) in the end chiefly reproduce the Simic sieve—a sorting machine that selects phenomena that suit Simic's totemic desire. There is no escape-hatch in a Simic poem: You enter it and are a prisoner within its uncompromising and irremediable world:

> The trembling finger of a woman
> Goes down the list of casualties
> On the evening of the first snow.
>
> The house is cold and the list is long.
>
> All our names are included.

This short poem, entitled "War," exhibits all the hallmarks of the Simic style: an apparently speakerless scene; an indefinite article establishing the vagueness of place and time—"a woman" somewhere, anywhere, in a wintry evening; then a menacing definite article focusing our gaze, in this instance on "the" list; then a late entrance of the personal pronoun engaging the speaker's life and ours. This coercive poem of war excludes everything else that might be going on in "real" wartime—people eating, drinking, going to school, manufacturing guns, etc.—in favor of a single emblem, the domestic Muse enumerating the many war dead, followed (as in emblem books) by a motto underneath: "All our

---

From "Totemic Sifting: Charles Simic's *The Book of Gods and Devils, Hotel Insomnia,* and *Dime-Store Alchemy*" by Helen Vendler, *Parnassus: Poetry in Review* 18, no. 2 and 19, no. 1 (1993).

names are included." The motto broadens the emblem from the war dead to all dead.

Simic's poems, even when they contain a narrative, can almost always be "folded back" into a visual cartoon accompanied by a caption. I say "cartoon" at this point rather than "emblem" because Simic is a master of the mixed style, with vulgarity cheek by jowl with sublimity. Simic's interesting memoir of his youth, "In the Beginning," included in his collection of essays called *Wonderful Words, Silent Truth* (1990), suggests that both the working-class origin of his joking and hard-drinking father and the middle-class origin of his musical mother exerted Oedipal claims on his sensibility. The poems abound in working-class litter, both rustic and urban: pigs, kitchens, newspapers, dishes, gum-machines, butchers, sneakers, condoms, grease; but they also exhibit the furniture of the maternally-espoused ideal realm—monarchs, clouds, angels, Madonnas, martyrs, palaces, and saints.

Simic's work demands that we cohabit with both classes, with pigs and angels alone. "To think clearly," he says in the poem of that name "What I need is a pig and an angel." Then the fate of the pig and the task of the angel are sketched in:

> the pig knows what's in store for him
> Give him hope, angel child,
> With that foreverness stuff.

This is where some will part company with Simic. "I don't mind admitting that I believe in god," he said in an interview almost twenty years ago (reprinted in *The Uncertain Certainty* [1985]), and although the injunction of the "angel child" has a good deal of irony attached, Simic cannot do without the presence of the angel. To describe the world as it is, without the backdrop of the ideal, is to be a collaborator in the world's injustice. As Simic says to his angel, "Don't go admiring yourself / In the butcher's knife / As if it were a whore's mirror." The butcher and the pig alone do not a poem make.

Simic's mockery is aimed at the pig, the angel, and himself; the sardonically comic side of his nature alternates with the remorselessly bleak. Life is a vulgar joke; life is tragedy. Perhaps for one who as a child saw World War II in Yugoslavia, life will always be overcast by horror; and yet for one who escaped destruction, life will also seemed charmed, lucky, privileged. Simic is not unaware of appetite, relish, and gusto. And yet it is the coercive nature of his writing as I have described it, that I find the deepest truth about him: "I have you trapped and you can't get out." Think how different from his the lyrics of Wordsworth or Keats are, always leading you from hill to vale, from bower to nook. In them, alternative universes abound, with elbow-room, leg-room, head-room; styles meander, migrate, elevate you high, and beckon you low. Attention tightens and slackens, lyric solos are followed by choral effects (as in the "Grecian Urn"). All of these fluidities disappear in Simic. An unbearable tension darkens the air. "No one is to be let off," says the punisher. No air. Few windows. No key. Minimal furniture. The bread is stale. The view is circumscribed.

I deduce that this was Simic's fundamental experience of the world for so many years that he was destined to immortalize himself by finding a form that reproduced it exactly:

> Outside, the same dark snowflake
> Seemed to be falling over and over again.
> You studied the cracked walls,
> The maplike water stain on the ceiling,
> Trying to fix in your mind its cities and rivers.
>
> ("The Immortal")

The persistence of the definite article marks this symbolic scene as an iconic one, to be exfoliated into poem after poem. Simic has been annoyed that critics have spoken of his works as "parables," saying, "I don't write parables. If I say 'rats in diapers,' that's to be taken literally" (*The Uncertain Certainty*). Simic's inclination is indeed to present deeply literal details, but they take on parabolic or emblematic significance because so much has been erased in order to isolate those details in a glaring beam of pitiless interrogation. The first poem in *Hotel Insomnia* reads, in its entirety, as follows:

> The Black Queen raised high
> In my father's angry hand.
>
> ("Evening Chess")

Like many other Simic poems, this one depends on a verbless sentence fragment, its past participle suspending forever the father's wrath. Everything else has been suppressed—the chessboard, the table, the mother, the brother, the father's face; we are not told the motive for, nor the object of, the father's anger. The largest suppression of all is that of the frightened little boy sitting opposite the angry father. Perhaps we are to understand that the parents are quarreling. Or perhaps the father is angry at his son. In any case, the cowering child, so fully implied and necessary to the scene, is effaced except in his personal pronouns, and the hand grows immense as it occupies the whole world of the poem. The poetics that generates such a poem, dependent on a single detail, is one of ruthless extirpation. What remains on the page is monumentalized, pregnant with signification, a cartoon "hand" that all by itself can be "angry."

The two books of poems under scrutiny here, while preserving Simic's coercive style, vary in content. *The Book of Gods and Devils* is often autobiographical, sometimes covertly (as is Simic's wont) but at other times overtly so. There is, for example, a touching glimpse of Simic's first reading of Shelley in a "dingy coffee shop" in New York: The poem alternates between urban wreckage—drunks, the homeless, broken umbrellas—and the visionary reaches of Shelley's social prophecies:

> How strange it all was . . . The world's raffle
> That dark October night . . .
> The yellowed volume of poetry
> With its Splendors and Glooms
> Which I studied by the light of storefronts:
> Drugstores and barbershops,
> Afraid of my small windowless room
> Cold as a tomb of an infant emperor.
>
> ("Shelley")

What distinguishes this excerpt, and makes it something more than a reminiscence of adolescent idealization juxtaposed with urban banality, is the presence of two startling phrases—"the world's raffle," and the "tomb of an infant emperor." Neither of these is at all expectable, and one halts in coming to them as before a surrealist effect. Neither is strictly speaking surreal; both can be pressed into sense. But the essential lawless nature of Simic's imagination, darting against his coercive structures, is continually escaping the very prisons he has himself built.

A comparable poem of adolescence ("Crepuscular with Nellie") chooses as its moment of escape the writer's unearthly sense of joy while listening to jazz at the Five Spot; there follows a jolting comedown at closing time, with "the prospect of the freeze outside," and the disappearance (no doubt because her partner found the jazz more interesting) of the Nellie of the title. But the autobiographical reach of *The Book of Gods and Devils* goes back further than adolescence. There are also reminiscences stemming from Simic's wartime childhood ("We played war during the war, / Margaret. Toy soldiers were in big demand"). One of the best of these, "The Wail," recounts, I believe, the arrest of Simic's father by the Gestapo, recalled in the memoir "In the Beginning":

> One night the Gestapo came to arrest my father. This time I was asleep and awoke suddenly to the bright lights. They were rummaging everywhere and making a lot of noise. My father was already dressed. He was saying something, probably cracking a joke. That was his style. No matter how bleak the situation, he'd find something funny to say. . . .
>
> I guess I went to sleep after they took him away. In any case, nothing much happened this time. He was released.
>
> (*Wonderful Words, Silent Truth*)

Here is "The Wail," complete, in which the atmosphere of that night is recreated. The child Simic, his brother, and their mother wait to see if the father will return:

As if there were nothing to live for . . .
As if there were . . . nothing.
In the fading light, our mother
Sat sewing with her head bowed.

Did her hand tremble? By the first faint
Hint of night coming, how all lay
Still, except for the memory of that voice:
Him whom the wild life hurried away . . .

Long stretches of silence in between.
Clock talking to a clock.
Dogs lying on their paws with ears cocked.
You and me afraid to breathe.

Finally, she went to peek. Someone covered
With a newspaper on the sidewalk.
Otherwise, no one about. The street empty.
The sky full of gypsy clouds.

Simic here shows us nothing followed by nothing; fading light, coming night; stillness, silence, suspended breath; fear, no one about in an empty street. This is the classic Simic; a landscape or a room full of vague menace, a sinister light hovering above a clustered huddle of victims. The wail as title and caption is the unheard melody of the scene.

Though there are "persons" serving as dramatis personae or addressees in some of these poems—the "Nellie" of the jazz bar, the "Margaret" of the toy soldiers, a "Martha" here, a "Lucille" there, these women, otherwise unidentified, seem to serve only as pretexts for a line—"Bite into [the tomatoes], Martha"; "Better to grab hold of that tree, Lucille"—and have none of the human power of the mother and her terrified children in "The Wail." I'm not clear about Simic's purpose in resorting to these women's names as vocatives of address; they seem inert, pointless, and in some odd way useless to the poem. Their colorful particularity seems an affront to Simic's bleached-out negations; but they may be his way of affirming the verbal color of life even in the absence of situational color.

In *The Book of Gods and Devils,* for all the fascination of the quasi-realistic scenes retrieved from Simic's childhood and youth, it is the poems of slightly surrealist malice that still seem to me Simic's best. I can give one example, for reasons of space: it is his Black Mass parody of the religious quest, called "With Eyes Veiled":

First they dream about it.
Then they go looking for it.
The cities are full of fragments.
Some even carry parcels.

Trust me. It's not there.
Perhaps in the opposite direction,
On some street you took by chance
Having grown tired of the search.

A dusty storefront waits for you
Full of religious paraphernalia
Made by the blind. The store
Padlocked. Night falling.

The blue and gold Madonna in the window
Smiles with her secret knowledge.
Exotic rings on her fat fingers.
A black stain where the child used to be.

This poem displays Simic's characteristic anticlimaxes of disappointment falling after line breaks: We see icons "Made by the blind. The store / Padlocked." This is deflationary, but worse is to come. The degradation of the Madonna into fallen woman, "exotic rings on her fat fingers," is followed by the macabre replacement of Innocence by "a black stain." The successive images here—each one worked, significant, memorable—are "locked into" their respective lines by their placement. Simic's alternation of full sentences and sentence-fragments mimics the acquisition of knowledge: An original main-clause existential statement ("A dusty storefront waits for you"; "The . . . Madonna smiles") is followed by one or more short "takes" of perceptual noun-phrase noting: a padlock; dusk or exotic rings; a black stain. Once one has felt the point of these placements, both the anticlimactic line-break ones and the "noticing" noun-phrase ones, the poem is by no means exhausted; the semantic freight of its "paraphernalia," the implications of words like "secret," "fat," and "stains," sends forth ripples of suggestion in ever-widening circles. The achieved Simic poem is itself often a "black stain" of innocence destroyed, and, like a stain, it spreads and deepens.

Hotel Insomnia, the volume following *The Book of Gods and Devils,* reminds us that Simic suffers from "lifelong insomnia" ("In the Beginning," *Wonderful Words, Silent Truth*). This book is more an evolving sequence than a collection of separate poems. What makes it a sequence is the inscribing, on every page without exception, of several words from the repeated epistemological master list forming a backdrop to the whole. These are the worlds comprising the master list, and the rough categories into which they fall:

Closure	Menace	Home	Body	People	Nature	City	Sub-human
evening	black	father	hand	old men	rain	hotel	fly
dark	scream(ing)	child	naked	murdered	fire	street	spider
shadow	red	table	eye	old woman	cloud	sidewalk	web
empty	match	mother	head	prisoner	moon	city	mice
sleep(less)	deaf	door	fist	fortuneteller	view	(dime-)store	pig
crow(ing)	blood(y)	wall	heart	poet	sky	window	dog
insomnia	flame	room	mouth	nun	flowers	building(ers)	
death	unhappy	mirror	hair	homeless	eternity	ceiling	
silent(ce)	candle	corner	breasts	preacher	time	prison(er)	
shuffle	strange	love	tongue	glove	light	school	
secret	cross	dream		shoe	wind	cage	
night	white	happy			morning	shop	
winter	list	house			sun(light)	shutter	
end	blind	book			sea	glass	
snow	long	window			leaves		
afternoon	fallen	bed			woods		
late	broken	coat			bird		
storm	chilly	name			quiet		
fate	dumb	roof			beautiful		
unknown	pale	watch			truth		
whisper	mute	scribble			infinite		
	strange(r)	pencil			life		
	greasy	memory			world		
	knife	wine			golden		
	chewing	boy			day		
	slaughter	toy			air		
	scream	kiss					
	spike	doll					
	funeral						

Like Trakl, Simic moves counters such as these into new configurations within each poem. Each poem becomes a new chess game, but the pieces are often invariant.

Here is "Romantic Sonnet," played with some twenty of the magic counters, which I have underlined:

> Evenings of sovereign clarity —
> Wine and bread on the table,
> Mother praying,
> Father naked in bed.

Was I that skinny boy stretched out
In the field behind the house,
His heart cut out with a toy knife?
Was I the crow hovering over him?

Happiness you are the bright red lining
Of the dark winter coat
Grief wears inside out.

This is about myself when I'm remembering,
And your long insomniac's nails,
O Time, I keep chewing and chewing.

After reading sixty-six pages in which words like these are heard again and again, chiming with and against each other, one has a comprehensive picture of the mind in which they keep tolling. Simic's world has aged. About one poem in three has something old in it—an old dog, a blind old woman, old snow, shoes grown old, a crippled old man, an old cemetery. In Simic's insomniac nights, the world shrivels, wrinkles, dwindles, both physically and metaphysically. The spider on the pale ceiling enlarges its sinister web, the meadows themselves become a theater of cruelty, children and pigs alike are led to slaughter, a nun carries morphine to the dying.

Even the poems recording a moment of happiness or appetite—"Country Lunch," for instance—are shadowed by foreboding: "A feast in the time of plague— / That's the way it feels today." *Hotel Insomnia* celebrates the "funeral of some lofty vision," according to "Miss Nostradamus," one of its seeresses, Muses, and fortunetellers. And the lofty visions go by, in cultural history, almost too fast to count. "Gods trying different costumes / . . . emerge[d] one by one / To serve you"; Hellenism, Christianity, and Materialism fuse in "Aphrodite with arms missing dressed as a nun / Waiting to take your order." It is in this sort of philosophical shorthand that Simic sketches the unnerving persistence of the past into the present.

My favorite poem at the moment in *Hotel Insomnia* is a tour de force called "Tragic Architecture." With the reverse prophecy of informed hindsight, Simic now knows which of his elementary school schoolmates grew up to go mad, to turn into a murderer, or to consent to being an executioner. The potential cruelty of all children is laconically remarked: "The janitor brought us mice to play with." The children have "hearts of stone." And though

Simic is a grown man on another continent, he is almost forever imprisoned in his past, a boy left behind, forgotten by Time. "Tragic Architecture" is a circular poem, framed by its past/present trees in the wind:

> School, prison, trees in the wind,
> I climbed your gloomy stairs,
> Stood in your farthest corners
> With my face to the wall.
>
> The murderer sat in the front row.
> A mad little Ophelia
> Wrote today's date on the blackboard.
> The executioner was my best friend.
> He already wore black.
> The janitor brought us mice to place with.
>
> In that room with its red sunsets—It was eternity's time to speak,
> So we listened
> As if our hearts were made of stone.
>
> All of this in ruins now.
> Cracked, peeling walls
> With every window broken.
> Not even a naked light bulb left
> For the prisoner forgotten in solitary,
> And the school boy left behind
> Watching the bare winter trees
> Lashed by the driving wind.

The achieved musical form of this poem—solitary sentence-quatrain of the "I"; inventory of schoolmates; sentence-quatrain of the "we"; inventory of memory done in the third person—is typical of Simic's studied arrangements. The more extended sentences serve for reverie; the short declarative sentences serve as bricks to build a world. The entire impossibility of jettisoning a wretched past is more starkly exhibited in Simic than in any psychological treatise. And yet he does not treat his past in a "confessional" way; the material, we may say, remains psychologically unanalyzed while being thoroughly poetically analyzed (by image, by placement, by narrative). Simic's stylistic arrangements of experience suggest that tragic memory has at least found its appropriate architectural form.

It is not surprising, given Simic's gnomic forms, that he found the boxes of Joseph Cornell, mysterious formal arrangements of synecdochic objects, peculiarly congenial. His homage to Cornell's art, *Dime-Store Alchemy* (1992), could have, as its motto, the closing sentence of one of its prose poems: "The clarity of one's vision is a work of art." Admirers of Cornell's constructions will be drawn to Simic's "versions" of the boxes illustrated here. One box, for instance, contains a standing doll obscured by a hedge of twigs taller than she is. Needless to say, there could be many "readings" of his silent form, and perhaps only Simic would give us this one:

> The chubby doll in a forest of twigs . . .
>   A spoiled little girl wearing a straw hat
> about to be burnt at the stake.

This prose poem might be better without its final line—"All this is vaguely erotic and sinister"—but Simic likes to scrawl mottoes under his emblems. It seems to me that we would have known the doll-scene, as he has described it, was both erotic and sinister without being told.

Dime-Store Alchemy offers more, though, than poetic versions of Cornell boxes. It is a book of art theory, full of obiter dicta on how to construct an art-work, a vehicle of reverie, an object that would enrich the imagination of the viewer and keep him or her company forever. There are reflections on toys, dreams, fetishes, symbolic objects: "Two sticks leaning against each other make a house"; Cornell's art of the scavenger is composed out of "the strangest trash imaginable"; it is an invitation to a labyrinth. The successive alternatives offered in the poem "Matchbox with a Fly in It" (deriving from Vasko Popa's "The Little Box," reprinted here by Simic) are as applicable to poems as to Cornell's art-boxes:

> Shadow box [phenomena]
> Music box [the Muses]
> Pill box [Apollo as healer]
> A box which contains a puzzle [poetry as enigma]
> A box with tiny drawers [stanzas; secret contents]
> Navigation box [a directive]
> Jewelry box [poem as ornamental]
> Sailor's box [vital supplies]
> Butterfly box [preserved specimens]

Box stuffed with souvenirs of a sea voyage [memory and
displacement]
Magic prison [the presentness of the past]
An empty box [art as illusion]

The reader of any Simic poem has to stop, not to "translate," as I've done in shorthand here, but to feel the individual pressure of each modifying phrase, and to construct the sequential interrelations of the whole. Perhaps the order of some of the phrases above could be shuffled, but the restriction and disillusion of the last two namings in "Matchbox with a Fly in It" makes us see them as unalterable parts of its closure. The fly of the title is mortality itself, found inside all boxes, no matter what their aspectral surface. Simic's fly, like Stevens' blackbird, inserts itself everywhere.

For Simic as for Cornell, "the city is a huge image machine," and Cornell's daily wandering through New York, picking up cast-off objects that he would transform into his profoundly meditated arrangements, match Simic's own observant walks through streets full of cinemas, penny arcades, stores, vending machines, newspapers, and mirrors. No other book by Simic transmits so strongly as *Dime-Store Alchemy* what New York must have meant to him when he first arrived from Europe—"A poetry slot machine offering a jackpot of incommensurable meanings activated by our imagination. Its mystic repertoire has many images."

Myself, I draw the line at words like "incommensurable" and "mystic," but that is perhaps my loss. I really do find poetry commensurable with life—not "mystic" (which for me would lessen its wonder) but rather entirely within the realm of human power, however rarely that power appears. De Chirico is quoted by Simic a few pages earlier, uttering a sentiment with which Simic explicitly agrees ("He's right"):

Every object has two aspects: one current one,
which we see nearly always and which is seen by men
in general; and the other, which is spectral and metaphysical and
seen only by rare individuals in moments of clairvoyance.

I could understand such a statement if it were put in terms of ascribed value. After all, a perfectly bad painting is to its maker a beloved object, as it is to some of its viewers (see, for example Bishop's "Poem," on the bad painting by her great-uncle); and even an unlovely house is someone's castle. Perhaps the ascription of value to any object is a form of "clairvoyance," because objects look different seen with the eye of love or the eye of poetic scrutiny. But de Chirico doesn't seem to be talking about this sort of invisible halo, which we can all confer on many objects. No, some other claim is being made here. The "rare individuals" that de Chirico and Simic have in mind are artists. But is there some aspect of objects seeable only by artists? And if so, is a reader or viewer then privileged to see this "spectral" aspect through the eyes of the artist? Artists make us see many aspects of being, but none of them seem to me either spectral or metaphysical, nor do I feel admitted to a form of clairvoyance, in the usual occult sense of that word. I am wary of vaguely mystical claims made for poetry and the other arts, as wary as I am of ethical and civic claims, and of truth claims. There are better ways of making good citizens, or lying down laws of ethics, or providing a defense of truth claims, than lyric poetry. Poems, like all human fabrications, from straw huts to theology, are made to our measure and by our measure, and are not above or beyond us. We do not need to ascribe more to art than we ascribe to unaided human powers elsewhere. Language and paint are not metaphysical and forms are not spectral. Patterning is a universal human act; and even when it is extended to the most complex and imaginative and individual patterning, it is still ours and of us, no more. The power of art, for me, is precisely that it does *not* belong to some rare spectral realm. As Steven's said of the poet, "As part of nature, he is part of us, / His rarities are ours."

Simic is still enough of a surrealist to want to claim some realm edgily outside of nature—in nonsense, in philosophy, in paintings like de Chirico's or in boxes like Cornell's. It probably seems like reductionism to him if a critic wants to describe, in knowable human terms, that edge of unreason, that irrational element of poetry (as Stevens called it). The weird angles and colors of de Chirico, his mute and looming forms, do indeed want to intimate a realm other than the known world, and the same is true for Cornell's tiny environments, which the eye enters into and lives within. Perhaps critics are of two kinds—those that rest in the strangeness of such environments and truly regard them as alternate forms of existence—"spectral and metaphysical" and more empirical critics who will not rest until they find the link between those environments and the human ones from which they spring. Like others, I prize Simic for his stanzas of the eerily inexplicable (manifested in his wonderfully varied means of menace and his formally laconic manner), but I would be very unhappy if the stylistic imagination in them were not intimately linked to recognizable human predicaments. The Language Poets have sometimes made common cause with Simic, and he with them; but where they are often merely clever, he is clever and horrifying and heartrending. He is also down-to-earth and mockingly skeptical, especially with respect to himself; he never forgets the dime-store when he is about his stylistic alchemy. He is certainly the best political poet, in a large sense, on the American scene; his written emblems outclass, in their stylishness, the heavy-handiness of most social poetry, while remaining more terrifying in their human implications than explicit political documentation. In his plainness of speech, he is of the line of Whitman and Williams, but in the cunning strategies of his forms, he has brought the allegorical subversiveness of Eastern European poetry into our native practice. The next generation of political poets will be on their mettle if their want to surpass him.

LISA SACK

Charles the Great: Charles Simic's *A Wedding in Hell*

Imagine a Charles Simic poem in a police lineup of contemporary American verse. Talk about an easy identification—his is the minimalist text, second from the left, with no fancy diction or convoluted constructions. Since the beginning of his career 30 years ago, Simic has understood the value of economy and the virtue of elision. Compact and deceptively simple, his poems fit, like tiny jewel boxes, in the palm of the hand.

Yet the world conjured by a Simic poem is anything but small. Consider "Where the Dreamy Wabash Flows," from *A Wedding in Hell,* his newest book. Originally published in *The New Yorker* as "Read Your Fate," the poem's new title is far more ironic, suggesting the gentle end of a 19th-century idyll lamented in the opening line: "A world's disappearing." The first two stanzas hardly dispel that illusion. Simic describes a "[l]ittle street" with one dog and a "lone child," a street that "hid" its "undressed lovers." But by the third stanza, he mangles any nostalgia we may have felt. This is no sentimental elegy for a romantic time gone by; the lovers have been carted off in an open truck:

> They were still embraced traveling
> On their sofa
>
> Over a darkening plain,
> Some unknown Kansas or Nebraska
> With a storm brewing.
> The woman opening a red umbrella

From "Charles the Great: Big Things Come in Small Poems, Charles Simic's *A Wedding in Hell*" by Lisa Sack, *Voice Literary Supplement* (November 1994).

In the truck. The boy
And the dog running after them,
As if after a rooster
With its head chopped off.

This poem has a palpable mystery that defies paraphrase, but I'll venture to say what makes it great. The simplicity of the language invites readers to enter and tap their own unconscious. Simic wastes no time: we are airborne and banking steeply into association with that couple. The image is at first funny, then more unsettling as the poem proceeds. How can we not think of the Holocaust come to America's heartland? Voyeurs, we run after the truck too, staring at the naked lovers as the savageries of our century come crashing into the poem.

Simic rarely writes without invoking them. Thumb through his *Selected Poems* (George Braziller, 1985) and you'll find violence on almost every page, beginning with "Butcher Shop." An insomniac "I" walking late at night peers into the window of a butcher shop at a hanging apron, "the blood on it smeared into a map / Of the great continents of blood . . ." As Simic says in "Notes on Poetry and History" in *The Uncertain Certainty* (University of Michigan, 1985), "We live in the shadow of . . . slaughterhouses. The poet who forgets that is living in fool's paradise." Simic himself never forgets, and with good reason. Born in Belgrade in 1938, he lived through the German occupation (the building across the street from his house was destroyed by bombs when he was three) and the Yugoslav Civil War before escaping to Paris, and then to the U.S. when he was 16.

Life during the Russian liberation, as Simic describes it in *Wonderful Words, Silent Truth* (University of Michigan, 1990) was an adventure: he remembers roving the city with his friends and taking ammo belts and helmets from the bodies of German soldiers. But the civil war was no carnival—neighbors were executed all too regularly.

Simic doesn't assault us with this personal history in his poems. A master of indirection, he selects and juxtaposes a few striking images—a red umbrella opening against a darkening plain, a lurching, headless rooster, an apron stained with blood—and lets them resonate. And as they do, the central paradox of Simic's work emerges, never so clearly articulated as in that 1971 poem "Butcher Shop":

There is a wooden block where bones are
broken,
Scraped clean—a river dried to its bed
Where I am fed,
Where deep in the night I hear a voice.

Out of a place of death comes life. Hunger ends; images feed imagination. In dark times, poetry is consolation.

Twenty-three years later, Charles Simic, author of 18 volumes of poetry and translator of eight, winner of a MacArthur Foundation Fellowship and a Pulitzer Prize, still grapples with history and searches for meaning in a world that slaughters innocence. His anonymous Everyman wanders alone, through an increasingly destitute urban landscape, scooping up found fragments and images, then transforming them into visions. But consolation doesn't come readily. In *A Wedding in Hell,* despair nearly crushes the playful skeptic's voice that once could witness tragedy and find its comic underbelly.

I'm not surprised. Since the outbreak of civil war in Bosnia and Herzegovina, Simic's poems have grown more anguished and direct. I could see the change coming when *Hotel Insomnia* (1992) was published. Some of the poems in that volume were written during the Gulf War; Simic responded to it, for the most part, obliquely—prisons, spiders, insomnia, and crucifixions run through the text—except for one short poem aptly titled "War":

The trembling finger of a woman
Goes down the list of casualties
On the evening of the first snow.

The house is cold and the list is long.

All our names are included.

The brutal fighting in Simic's birth country would surely trigger reactions even more highly charged, especially when images from the earlier civil war obsess him: "[E]very tragedy . . . continues. Is still current. Is still present. . . . It still goes on, as vivid as it ever was."

If we can judge by *A Wedding in Hell,* Simic must be living through an unending flashback. Corpses, like those he saw hanging from lampposts as a child, sprawl across the television as he watches, impotent and helpless, in "Dark TV Screen": "The memory of this day's evil / Like a meat stall covered with flies. / Soul—flown through the open window. / Heart chewed like a dog's ball. . . . O Cordelia, my name is Lear. My name is / Primo Levi. I sit naked between / The open window and the dark TV screen, / My hands and sex bathed in the fire of evening." Simic has unclothed his despair; he wants an answer, guidance, but none is forthcoming to the philosopher/jester who once said, "What a mess! I believe in images as vehicles of transcendence, but I don't believe in God!" On page after page, he wrestles with questions of faith, only to profess an "infinite horror" of a Lord who's "been a long time making up [His] mind, / . . . about these madmen / Running the world. . . ."

And the urban landscape, so often a provider of those transcendent images—particularly in *Dime-Store Alchemy,* Simic's quirky homage to Joseph Cornell, who made detritus found on New York City's streets into art—is now full of sinister company, a drab maze of broken windows that "[e]ven in the sunlight . . . looks evil." The poet still takes his insomniac walks through deserted streets, but instead of lit butcher shops, ". . . Everything seem[s] / Anciently abandoned, / Closed forever and impervious to argument." And the "I"/eye, so good at seeing the beauty in horror, and its comic absurdity, is now less sure of itself: "I . . . am only an incomprehensible / Bit of scribble / On some warehouse wall. . . ."

Flashes of the wily old skeptic do appear in the half dozen or so prose poems. The form suits Simic's surreal imagination; his 1989 book of prose poems, *The World Doesn't End* (Harvest/HBJ), which won him the Pulitzer, may be his best work. ("Thousands of old men with pants lowered sleeping in public rest rooms. You're exaggerating! You're raving! Thousands of Marias, of Magdelenas at their feet weeping.") Simic sounds like the great Shakespearean fools in these pieces—his motley ravings make us laugh even as they chill us with the accuracy of their observation. The writing in the prose poems of *A Wedding in Hell* is fresh; it steers clear of the clichés that occasionally enter the other poems ("heart wrenching dread," "A despair / Darker than all your darkest / Nights"). I especially like "Heroic Moment":

> I went bare-assed into the battle. The President
> himself heard of my insolence. I was given a
> flea-bitten mutt to ride. I rode in the company
> of crows with a red plastic pisspot on my head and
> a dollhouse knife between my teeth.

And the seven pastoral love poems that surface at the end of section two provide a welcome break for the reader. But despair isn't far behind, as Simic reminds us in "Happiness":

> Do not flatter yourself,
> It's just the open window,
> A bird singing,
> The bright sunlight.

One poem is unlike any I've ever read—if it had appeared in the lineup, I might not have recognized it as Simic's. "Via Del Tritone" juxtaposes no surreal images. It begins simply:

> In Rome, on the street of that name,
> I was walking alone in the sun
> In the noonday heat, when I saw a house
> With shutters closed, the sight of which
> Pained me so much, I could have
> Been born there and left inconsolably.

Simic goes on to describe the interior, as he imagines it, a garden with a palm tree, dark stairs leading to cool rooms with high ceilings. "'You found what you were looking for,' / I expected someone to whisper." Never, in his previous work, has Simic expressed the pain of his exile in such a straightforward way. His outsider's status was always an advantage, teaching him that life was unpredictable and that anything might happen, as the antic careening of his poetry suggests. In this poem his pain and loss blossom like the most fragile of tea roses. He hasn't found what he was looking for. How can you reclaim a childhood that never was? Simic, unlike Nabokov, has no Eden to recall. His are "false memories," phantasms of heat. And as the war rages on in the place where his childhood should have been, salvage becomes less possible. The poet's cries flutter up from the page: "Help me to find what I've lost, / If it was ever, however briefly, mine."

PART TWO *The Infinite Line*

Do you take this line
Stretching to infinity?
I take this chipped tooth
On which to cut it in half.

ROBERT B. SHAW

Charles Simic: An Appreciation

In the acknowledgments on the copyright page of Charles Simic's *Return to a Phase Lit by a Glass of Milk* the usual paragraph thanking the editors of little magazines concludes with this sentence: "I also wish to thank the John Simon Guggenheim Memorial Foundation for a grant which paid my rent and food while this book was being written." There is something engagingly down to earth about this. Where most writers would use some neutral term like "support," Simic specifies "rent and food." The preference which this sentence hints at for the plain phrase and the concrete image goes fantastically far in his poems. It is the paradox of his style that his determined concentration on the most common things makes reality strange and, even when terrifying, strangely inviting. The poems have an arresting substantiality about them so that it seems almost inadequate to absorb them merely by way of the eye. For the reader they become, in a queer way, objects of nourishment, as Simic wittily suggests by entitling a little poem "Mother Tongue":

> Sold by a butcher
> Wrapped in newspaper
> It travels in a bag
> Of the stooped widow
> Next to some onions and potatoes
>
> Toward a dark house
> Where a cat will
> Leap off the stove
> Purring
> At its entrance.

Simic's own mother tongue is not the English he writes in. Born in Yugoslavia in 1938, he was brought to the United States

---

From "Charles Simic: An Appreciation" by Robert B. Shaw, *New Republic*, 24 January 1976.

as a child and grew up in Chicago. His first two collections of verse, *What the Grass Says* (1967) and *Somewhere among Us a Stone Is Taking Notes* (1969), were published by Kayak Press. A larger and more accessible collection, including many of these early poems, is *Dismantling the Silence,* which inaugurated the Braziller Series of Poetry in 1971. Simic's most recent collection, also from Braziller, is *Return to a Place Lit by a Glass of Milk* (1974). A single long poem, *White,* was issued by New Rivers Press in 1972. Simic has translated extensively from French, Russian, and Yugoslav poetry; especially notable for the light they throw on his own work are his versions of the Yugoslav poets Ivan Lalic and Vasko Popa. The decade has been a productive one for Simic, and his work proves him one of the few truly considerable poets of his generation.

When his readers think of Simic they think first of brief poems with titles like "Knife," "Stone," "The Spoon," "My Shoes." In such pieces the poet's originality was quite early apparent. They are at once weighty and evasive, and describing them is about as easy as picking up blobs of mercury with mittens on. Here and afterwards Simic's habit has been to look so long and fixedly at common objects that they acquire haloes of strangeness, and become disquietingly animated. The pathetic fallacy, until recently a local effect that poets were cautioned to shun whenever possible, constitutes both a means and an end in these poems as they record one imagination's morbid romance with external reality. A knife is seen as "Father-confessor / Of the fat hen / On the red altar / Of its throat," and a fork "resembles a bird's foot / Worn around the cannibal's neck":

> As you hold it in your hand,
> As you stab with it into a piece of meat,
> It is possible to imagine the rest of the bird:
> Its head which like your fist
> Is large, bald, beakless and blind.

These are two especially stark examples of the method that Simic sees operating in the poems of Vasko Popa that he says in the preface to his translations show an "elemental surrealism coupled undoubtedly with an animistic, myth-making approach to reality." Popa's poems, using the forms of riddles, proverbs, and jokes, present themselves as "magic formulas. If they enchant it is to make you see clearly. The language is that of definitions, of primitive books of genesis." We realize from such statements that Simic's style has its own origin not merely in a personal intensity of vision, but in a deep appreciation of what folklore has to teach.

By his own account, Simic spent several years in the New York Public Library reading all the folklore he could find. The effect of this study would be evident enough in his work without his acknowledgment of it. It has provided him with the dark atmosphere he exploits in a terse poem like "Butcher Shop," and equally with the fabulous material he exuberantly manipulates in the long catalogue poem "Concerning My Neighbors, the Hittites." To quote a typical passage:

> . . . Great are the Hittites.
> Their fathers are in cradles,
> their newborn make war.
> To them lead floats, a leaf sinks.
> Their god is the size
> Of a mustard seed so that
> He can be quickly eaten.
>
> They also piss against the wind,
> Pour water in a leaky bucket,
> Strike two tears to make fire,
> And have tongues with bones in them,
> Bones of a wolf gnawed by lambs.

Here and elsewhere the folk tradition has yielded Simic a store not only of images, but of poetic forms. Like Popa, he favors the riddle, the proverb, the question posed and answered askew, parallelism and antic repetition. In the use of such strategies the influence of Theodore Roethke may also be taken for granted.

In his earlier poems Simic's humor, even at its broadest as in recounting the habits of the Hittites, retains a peasant toughness, a menacing edge. *Dismantling the Silence* gains much of its power from dispensing with amenities; its landscapes are bleak and seem only incidentally touched by humanity. More than once Simic imagines the world as returned to its primeval state: "Whoever swings an axe," he writes, "Knows the body of man / Will again be covered with fur." "Hearing Steps," with its cast of migrating Mongols and wolf hunters, presents a similar premonition. One can see in such pieces traces of the political despair of the '60s, which made apocalyptic a fashionable mode. In a strong recent poem, "The Place," the political theme comes unequivocally to the surface:

> They were talking about the war
> The table still uncleared in front of them.
> Across the way, the first windows
> Of the evening were already lit.
> He sat, hunched over, quiet
> The old fear coming over him . . .
> It grew darker. She got up to take the plate—
> Now unpleasantly white—to the kitchen.
> Outside in the fields, in the woods
> A bird spoke in proverbs,
> A Pope went out to meet Attila,
> The ditch was ready for its squad.

Aside from any political implications, however, Simic's effort on such occasions follows a procedure he believes necessary for the artist, a backward leap of the imagination that will return it to the images that first nourished it. Another bit of Simic's prose, this time from the introduction to his Lalic translations, describes the poet as an explorer of "all that which came before thought and emotion but without which these two could not exist. In the deepest sense," he goes on, "the possibilities that allow us to create belong to our ancestors. We can do very little but great things can be done through us." There is nothing easy in this program. It requires considerable sophistication and restraint for a 20th-century poet to write from a primitive point of view, however willing he may be to surrender his consciousness to the power of the archetypes.

Simic's exploration of the springs of myth is convincing because it is conducted by means of an exciting exploration of language. While his mastery of English is beyond that of most native speakers, this poet's experience of writing in a language not his first must give him a special awareness of the innate mysteriousness of words. To be reminded of what peculiar things words are, if we are ever in danger of forgetting, we need only read closely a random page of the dictionary, from goat to god-daughter, or from kinkajou to kiss. The equanimity of definitions as they go about the business of pasting labels on reality in their studious, poker-faced way must seem weird and faintly scandalous as soon as we cease to take language for granted. Simic at no time takes language for granted. At his most serious he writes as if he were naming things for the first time: the words, one by one discovered and cunningly placed make and shape a world before our eyes. In a lighter tone he writes "Charles Simic is a sentence"—a sentence which the ensuing poem proceeded to parse.

In his latest book Simic's linguistic inventiveness illuminates a wider range of experience than before. *Return to a Place Lit by a Glass of Milk* (an almost over-characteristic title) is not as sternly unified as the collection which preceded it; but its variety of theme and tone largely make up for what it lacks of the earlier volume's force. Comic touches, at times quite broad, are more numerous and relaxed in their application; and there is a further, more important change as well. Human beings had rarely appeared as major subjects in *Dismantling the Silence.* Now Simic has come to admit them more often to his view of the world, including in the contents of *Return* . . . , a poem about his father and some remarkable love poems. This seems a healthy development. Although he had been doing amazing things with stones and cutlery, Simic was beginning to run the risk of repetition, even of self-parody. For example, the piled-up recipes in "Soup"—"A hiccup in aspic with paprika / Cold wind fried in onions / A roast of darkest thoughts"—compare unfavorably with earlier, less stylized catalogues. The addition of human characters has turned Simic in a new and venturous direction, preventing his verse from diminishing to a virtuoso's ritual gesturing.

The great bane of love poetry is stale diction, whether in the over-literary lyric, or the illiterate popular song. Love is blind; is it fated in poetry to be either pompous or inarticulate as well? In pieces like "Breasts" and "That Straightlaced Thing between Her Legs" Simic's active, individualized vocabulary is especially to be appreciated.

> . . . little black ember,
> skillet
> for my heart's
> hailstone,
> may my touch be
> the only dress
> you ever wear. . . .

By standing in vivid, ungainly contrast to the conventional language of love, Simic's words make us aware of how falsified and monochromatic a version of our emotions indifferent writers and the intrusive media have been pandering to us. Slapstick and subtle feelings, awkwardness and sophistication strike a balance in these poems, renewing in us a wonder at the complexity of our desires.

Another recent trend in Simic's poetry, formal rather than thematic, is its readiness to explore the possibilities of greater length. The earlier poems, in keeping with their impassive tone, were tight-lipped, rarely going much beyond a page. In the new book there is a more expansive architecture at work in several pieces, and the fantastic concluding narrative, "The Chicken without a Head," seems *over*-expanded; one feels for once that a little of the plumage might better have been plucked. The same criticism could not be leveled at *White,* the separately published poem, Simic's longest to date. One could argue whether it is in fact a single poem or an unusually cohesive sequence; but about its importance in Simic's canon there should not be much dispute. Anyone concerned with the fortunes of the extended poem in our time should read this one, ignoring the illustrations, which are unworthy of it, and the type-setting, which regrettably includes some errors. The poem has no difficulty in rising above its unflattering format. White, from which all the colors of the spectrum proceed, here represents the inscrutable source of all images which the poet, in his acts of making, must perilously explore. The sections of 10 lines each, with an elegant self-allusive circularity, chronicle a poet's repeated forays into this mysterious region.

> Out of poverty
> To begin again:
>
> With the color of the bride
> And that of blindness,
>
> Touch what I can
> Of the quick,
>
> Speak and then wait,
> As if this light
>
> Will continue to linger
> On the threshold.

So the book begins, and at its halfway point:

We haven't gone far.
Fear lives here too.

Five ears of my fingers
Against the white page.

What do we hear?
We hear holy nothing

Blindfolding itself.
It touched you once

And tore like a surgeon's stitch
Pulled quickly out of the wound.

"We hear holy nothing / Blindfolding itself." It requires sharp ears to do that. *White* shows at times an understanding of the creative moment, of the silence out of which the word is uttered, which is so acute that it deserves to be termed mystical. This is Simic's most austere and intellectual work thus far, and yet it succeeds as well as any of his others in stirring and retaining the reader's attention.

Much has been written lately about the crippling effect of self-consciousness upon artists. Simic seems to be able to keep his self-consciousness under control, employing it in making needful esthetic decisions, but effacing it when it threatens to become obtrusive or didactic. Other contemporary poets would do well to emulate this poise of his. Whatever effect his example may have upon our literature, however, Simic's career is bound to be a lonely one because of the singularity of his gift. Of this singularity he is thoroughly and unrepentantly aware:

Inside my empty bottle
I was constructing a lighthouse
While all the others
Were making ships.

TOMISLAV LONGINOVIC

Between Serbian and English: The Poetics of Translation in the Works of Charles Simic

> On the first page of my dream book
> It is always evening
> In an occupied country.
>
> —Charles Simic, "Empire of Dreams"

It is the Second World War. Yugoslavia is being dismembered by Germany for the first time. One little boy named Dusan Simic, born in Belgrade just three years before his hometown was to be bombed into oblivion by Hitler's forces, spends his evenings in an occupied country, busy with games whose childhood innocence stands in sharp contrast with the devastation of war. The apparent horror of such childhood experience is one of the moving forces behind the poetry of Charles Simic, one of the leading American poets today. The scene of devastation emerges in the half-light of evening, saturated with uncertainty, violence and hunger experienced by the poetic persona. The matter-of-fact tone precludes any sentimentalism from seeping into the poem, heightening the effect of veracity. It is clear that the war does not intimidate the little boy: he hides in shelters, goes for days without food and plays on the rubble-spattered streets with ammunition stolen from soldiers' corpses.

The gap between Dusan Simic and Charles Simic, the Serbian boy and the American poet, the native and the exile, is constantly being bridged by the interplay of language, dream and memory. The imaginative attempt of the American poet to reach the distant world of childhood is made possible by the process of translation which links the two identities. The poetic persona invokes a dreambook recovered from memory, an image that promises gathering of dreams, things and beings which are filtered through the layers of stories heard in Serbian and then inscribed in English. Both dreams and memory are recovered

From "Between Serbian and English: The Poetics of Translation in the Works of Charles Simic" by Tomislav Longinovic, *Modern Poetry in Translation*, n.s., no. 3 (1993).

through the language of a new country, retold or remembered to resist the destiny of exile and counter the power of forgetting. Exile is a tragic battle against forgetting, which gradually transforms the images and stories from the place of origin into dreamlike and often mythicized poetic constructions. Simic's poetry attempts to soften the work of forgetting by inscription, through a constant imaginary return to the perceived place of origin which is represented as a translation of "the first page of my dreambook."

> On the first page of my dreambook
> It is always evening
> In an occupied country.
> Hours before the curfew.
> A small provincial city
> The houses all dark.
> The store-fronts gutted.[1]

Childhood innocence is lost almost from the very start, and the poet ejected into a world at war. Time and space are condensed into the vision of catastrophe, first seen through the eyes of an exile and then through the eyes of a child. This double vision is resplendent with possibilities, since it is made possible by the interaction of the remembered image and language used to articulate it. The images of remembered youth are demanding a proper translation from the written sign, changing it and leaving a specific mark on the poetic English, not unlike the accent which the exile impresses on the language of the adopted country. This process of cultural translation is laden with uncertainties, since memory is often like a dream, susceptible to unconscious forces which turn any attempt at accuracy into illusion and contingency. In his latest collection, entitled *Hotel Insomnia,* Simic brings this experience of uncertainty to the foreground.

> The infinite number of lines
> That join to me things and beings,
> So that a diagram
> Of any moment in my life
> Looks like a child's scribble.[2]

The position of this poetic persona is central, yet uncertain, cast into fabrication of diagrams that can be adequately represented only as "a child's scribble." The centrality of the poetic "me" seems to be talking about the total memory device, a contraption that has the capacity of charting "a diagram of any moment of my life." The title of the segment is "Puppet," a simulacrum of a human always moved by the will and power of someone else. The destiny of a puppet is a parody of human destiny, where so much knowledge about the poetic persona remains concealed from the poetic "me." This "me" is joined to "things and beings" through "the infinite number of lines" which traverse the universe of language, reaching for the accurate translation of the world of memory.

Simic does not mourn the departure from the native country, since it is a getaway. Life in exile is experienced as salvation, and America is the place of happiness for the boy. But at the same time, humans are likened to puppets unable to know or control their own destiny. The horrific power of history often makes choices and decisions for them. This catastrophic vision of the world is forever branded into the memory of the poet: "It is always evening in an occupied country." Each return to the place of origin is a return to the place where a violent and unwanted separation took place between Dusan and Charles, the separation caused by the war and its contingencies. Many years later Charles Simic will write in his memoir:

> My previous life has taught me that making plans was a waste of time. My father used to ask me jokingly, "Where are we going to immigrate next?" Anything was possible in this century. The experiment was still in progress. People like him and me were its laboratory animals. Strangest of all, one of the rats was writing poetry.[3]

The poet wanders through the laboratories of history, trying to translate images and stories that existed before the Fall into horrors of war, time and language. History turns humans into experimental animals, who suffer but also laugh in the face of suffering. The rat who writes poetry has learned the art of uncertainty, meeting every new blow of history with an ironic sneer. But the rat soon notices that the art of roaming through the poetic sites of the mother tongue can be rendered in English. The process of translation, so important in Simic's poetic development, defines this relationship between Serbian and English. The origin of childhood memories is supplemented by the reading and translation makes one aware of language as a material force, capable of shaping the world of things and beings into a particular idiom, or as Simic puts it: "the way that people's experience of the self is reflected in words."[4]

The latest example is *The Horse Has Six Legs,* a personal selection of translations from Serbian done in the past few decades.[5] From Vasko Popa, a leading post-war poet of former Yugoslavia, whose spirited objects inhabit wondrous landscapes of Balkan folklore, to Novic Tadic, the latest discovery, whose native Montenegro is transformed into a grotesque horror worthy of Hieronymus Bosch, Simic has been attuned to the events on the poetic scene in the country of origin.[6] "The 1960s were a time of great translation activity in this country, and since I knew the language, I paid a visit one day to the New York Public Library on Forty-Second Street to read the Yugoslav poets," he writes in the introduction to the anthology:

> That's where I discovered their poetry and made my first translations of Popa, Lalic, and Nastasijevic. I wanted to share the poems with my American friends, but I was also fascinated by the process of translation. I had already begun to wonder what kind of poems I would have written had I started writing poetry in Serbian. Are the differences between two languages on the surface, or is it true what they say about language, that each one paints the world in a different way?[7]

The separation and exile appear as almost necessary conditions for this kind of insight, in which translation is not simply a process of transformation of one set of signs into another, but an almost alchemical transfiguration of one's linguistic and cultural origin into a medium for communicating with the world of actuality. The process of translation is fascinating because it bridges the gap between the two languages and articulates the poet's desire for wholeness. If one can reach into the poetic depths of the mother tongue and give them voice in English, then it might also be possible for the poet to imagine the place of his own origin, hidden in half-forgotten childhood in Belgrade. "I had already begun to wonder what kind of poems I would have written had I started writing poetry in Serbian."[8]

Doubt expressed in these lines reveals the presence of another within the poet, a poetic double who remains forever concealed in the silence of the mother tongue. The other's poetic activity is crucial for the process of translation of poems, cultures and identities.

> The aim of that discipline and technique [i.e., of translation] is to become an other, to speak in tongues. The dream of the translator is to experience a self that is on the verge of utterance, to catch it in the very instant before it has divided itself into *logos* and *melos*. I am thinking of that mouth where the great mother tongue is beginning to fork—infinitely.[9]

This "dream of the translator" reveals the desire of the poet for the prelinguistic space, where the self is not yet touched by the divisiveness of the world and its history. This imagined wholeness breaks down into *logos,* which belongs to the world of exile and stepmother tongue, and *melos,* tied to the tonality of the mother tongue. The infinite forking of the mother tongue is experienced as a loss of wholeness, detachment from the space of childhood, but at the same time as a necessary stage in poetic development. "To become an other" is an imperative for the poet who through the process of translation detaches himself from original identifications with native linguistic realities and begins to "speak in tongues." English is a realm of *licentia poetica* where the two selves merge into a poem which is both a translation and the original work of art. The poetic persona is no longer a petrified state of identity with the perceived origin, but a process of linguistic transmutation which enables the self to identify with endless chains of "things and beings." The early fascination with objects, present in the poetry of both Vasko Popa and Charles Simic, is the end result of this process of self-erasure which results in a sort of metaphysical humility when confronted with the inanimate world.

On the one hand, it is the process of cultural translation that brings into focus the illusory nature of our identifications with a self, family, nation, country, etc. On the other, the gradual loss of a mother tongue in exile forces the poet to constantly reinvent the present, since continuity with the past selves is not guaranteed. In an earlier poem, Simic invokes the mystery of separation from the mother tongue as the endless search to "recover the space" the poet has once known.

> It is true I'm forgetting the language I've known once,
> And that I bury myself in the bodies of women
> With a set of burglar's tools
> To recover the space I have known once.[10]

"Bodies of women" are faceless and multiple, since they serve as a screen for the projection of the poet's desire to recover that mythic space before the fall into identity and language, the maternal space which is experienced as non-conflictual and euphoric. The forgetting of the mother tongue prompts him to "bury" himself in the bodies of women, to experience the symbolic passing of the childhood self which now inhabits the space of memory. It is as if feminine bodies form a chain which connects the poet to the first link tied to the world of "things and begins"—the mother's body and the mother's tongue. The most curious element in these lines is "a set of burglar's tools," used to "recover the space" the poet has known once.

First of all, there is a metaphoric operation which puts these "tools" in the service of the poet's manhood, since it is with them that he "buries himself" in the bodies of women. This sense is strengthened by the fact that the tools are a burglar's, and therefore concealed, illicit and secretive, used in a game played between lovers. On the other hand, those tools are linguistic as well, since the only way of approaching the space of the gradually fading mother's tongue is by using the stepmother's tongue. Poems written in English are a tool for unlocking the doors to that secret and ever-receding space of childhood and memory. They are in effect a translation of that space, an attempt to come to grips with the uncertain quest for divided identity. "The problem of translation precedes literary works," writes Simic. "Or in the words of Heidegger, one stands in the midst of 'the essence of language which refuses to come to language.' "[11] In other words, Heidegger's "essence of language" is that which resists thing-for-word translation, but requires a different, poetic translation. The translator's dream is to grasp that scintillation of the poetic essence which refuses to be distilled into one or other of the linguistic codes which shape identity and the realities it forges to stay sane and alive. "Things" are hesitant to become named and therefore lose their "thingness." Both poetry and translation are seen as necessary approximations of the world of "things" that can turn against language to distort its conventions.

The poetics of translation can grapple with the untranslatability of our experience of "things and beings," since it is aware of its necessary failure from the very start. Since its aim is not to pursue a positive description of reality, but to give voice to the negative side of the human condition, Simic in 1978 embraces the "poetics of uncertainty": "Uncertainty is the description of that gap which consciousness proclaims: actuality versus contingency. A new and unofficial view of our human condition."[12] The gap between something that exists and the incidental force which causes it to exist is the source of uncertainty. It describes the human condition in the century of mass destruction, where the experiential becomes the experimental, and poet is called on to embody history's contradictions if he or she is to retain any relevance. But the very fact that the image of the gap is used to define this "new and unofficial view of our human condition," indicates that the process of translation constructs the poetic identity of Charles Simic. The contingency of his historical experience is pointing him in the direction of the actuality of "things and beings" that present themselves to the senses. The unresolvable problem of translation between the two realms, between memory that can be reached only through language and actuality that always eludes the linguistic sign, causes the poet to embrace uncertainty as the only absolute description of the human condition. The very nature of Simic's search is absolutist, determined by the existential desire to reach beyond the condition of exile and recover the space of elusive wholeness in childhood. But this search is doomed to uncertainty since childhood belongs to the other who has been traumatized and left many years ago in war-ravaged Belgrade. The space of childhood is visited again in "Tragic Architecture" from Simic's last collection:

> All of that in ruins now.
> Cracked, peeling walls
> With every window broken.
> Not even a naked light bulb left
> For the prisoner forgotten in solitary,
> And the school boy left behind
> Watching the bare winter trees
> Lashed by the driving wind.[13]

This is the story of that other self, "the school boy left behind" who continues to exist in the realm of perpetual catastrophe. "All of that in ruins now." Recent events in Yugoslavia give a prophetic echo to Simic's poetry, since they give the impression that the horror of history remained frozen for decades, only to become revived in the present. His childhood experience is repeated and multiplied today by more than a million children displaced by the civil war. "Cracked, peeling walls / With every window broken." This is again a description of the timeless present of suffering caused by abandonment, destruction and exile. The schoolboy is left behind like a "prisoner forgotten in solitary," a poetic other forever detached by exile, yet constantly revived by the current atrocities in the former Yugoslavia, committed by those whose certainty of their national identity and its "others" is often deadly. Those who, like Charles Simic, have understood the illusory nature of identification with the "blood and soil" of their native realm, as well as the suffering caused by wars and displacements, offer a vision of identity that is based on translation. This poetics of translation teaches one to embrace uncertainty and hesitation when confronted with "originals" whose ideology brings more violence and suffering in the name of the nation or the state. Simic's poetics of translation resists any form of linear or univocal concept of identity, since the presence of the "other" always undermines historical projects whose intention is to simplify, vulgarize and ultimately annihilate the complexities and differences between nations, cultures and selves that inhabit this world.

NOTES

1. Charles Simic, *Selected Poems, 1963–1983* (New York: Braziller, 1985), 121.

2. Charles Simic, *Hotel Insomnia* (New York: Harcourt Brace Jovanovich, 1992), 39.

3. Charles Simic, *Wonderful Words, Silent Truth* (Ann Arbor: University of Michigan Press, 1990), 53.

4. Charles Simic, *The Uncertain Certainty* (Ann Arbor: University of Michigan Press, 1985), 118.

5. Charles Simic, ed., *The Horse Has Six Legs: An Anthology of Serbian Poetry* (Port Townsend, Wash.: Graywolf, 1992).

6. Simic has also published a translation of the entire collection by Novica Tadic: *Night Mail: Selected Poems*, trans. Charles Simic, *Field* Translation Series 19 (Oberlin, Ohio: Oberlin College Press, 1992).

7. Simic, *Horse Has Six Legs*, 2.

8. Ibid.

9. Simic, *The Uncertain Certainty,* 119.

10. Charles Simic, *Biography and a Lament* (Hartford, Conn.: Bartholomew's Cobble, 1976), 14.

11. Simic, *The Uncertain Certainty*, 119.

12. Simic, *The Uncertain Certainty*, 91.

13. Simic, *Hotel Insomnia*, 13.

BRUCE BOND

Immanent Distance: Silence and the Poetry of Charles Simic

In Charles Simic's poetry, we glimpse human suffering from a strangely detached perspective, often lending hardship an aura of wonder. This detachment continues to irritate some readers who see in it remnants of a reclusive modernist excess, a failure to let the self become vulnerable, fit for responsible action. As further testimony to Simic's retreat into an invulnerable persona, critics point to his frequent ambiguities, his failure to commit himself to the human task of communicating. His austere language sounds less like a man speaking to men than a man speaking to himself. And a rhetoric which rarely accommodates itself to a reader not only mirrors but also creates a sense of isolation. What, we may ask, can be the value of such verse? But to refer to Simic's poetry merely as "detached" is simplistic. We cannot help but feel emotionally confronted by the scenes of suffering in his poems. While maintaining a quiet, understating rhetoric, Simic's poems simultaneously dramatize the most pressing needs. Thus, he creates a complex tone of detached involvement. That realm of experience which seems closest, most urgent, most charged by suffering, also feels strangely out of reach. No language can accommodate it. And rather than lapsing into a complacency with the imperfections of words, his poems express a desire for words to be more than arbitrary, to be disciplined by attentiveness. Such verse communicates in ways that poetry best communicates, by drawing attention to its failures but nevertheless attempting an effectively inclusive version of consciousness, "three-dimensional" rather than linear, full of our own sad and marvelous contraries. To attempt this with sensitivity is to recognize both the shortcomings and appeals of mimesis. It is to resist linguistic limits and human insularity, with the knowledge that such resistance is a painful, irresolvable, and constant source of wonder.

From "Immanent Distance: Silence and the Poetry of Charles Simic" by Bruce Bond, *Mid-American Review* 8, no. 1 (1988).

Simic refers to the immanent realm unyielding to language as "silence." Consciousness of the incommunicable nature of silence brings with it consciousness of solitude:

> Silence, solitude, what is more essential to the human condition? "Maternal silence" is what I like to call it. Life before the coming of language. That place where we begin to hear the voice of the inanimate. Poetry is an orphan of silence. The words never quite equal the experience behind them.[1]

We may puzzle over the implications of Simic's metaphor: if poetry is the "orphan of silence," then what can it tell us of its beginnings? Is the notion of prelinguistic experience little but a marvelous afterthought locked with us in our prisonhouse of language? Because consciousness cannot fully account for itself, such questions make their final appeal to awareness rather than consciousness, seeing rather than thinking. Since the advent of Derridean and other post-modern challenges to the notion of linguistic origin, it has become increasingly unpopular to allow undifferentiating awareness a role in informing the process of differentiation, of consciousness. Simic is aware that he holds a minority view:

> I'm one of those who believes that there is something that precedes language. The usual view is that there is some kind of equivalence between thought and language, that if you can't verbalize it you can't think it. I've always felt that there is a state that precedes verbalization, a complexity of experience that consists of things not yet brought to consciousness, not yet existing as language but as some sort of inner pressure.[2]

A sympathetic understanding of such pressure and its failure to find adequate expression enriches our context for reading Simic's verse. Silence, according to Simic's description, is generative, but it cannot generate its own likeness. This matters insofar as silence demands that it matters. In such a model of mind, language, though imperfect, is nevertheless responsibly bound to something outside itself. We are not in an intellectually dominated, self-referential world comprised of only signs. The body, for instance, demands a quality of attentiveness peripheral to the chatter of signification. Our hands become intimate with spoons and fork in a way that our language cannot. Or, stunned by significant loss, we may sense a gap between our tragic awareness and what can be said. Silence may offer an enlarged version of experience, the liberating sense of a spacious setting for our house of language, but it also burdens us with its impossible task. For Schöenberg's Moses in *Moses and Aaron,* this task is explicitly religious. Moses must try to communicate the Word of God to his people. For Simic, the sense of urgency comes not from the burden of divine authority but from that of human suffering, the most demanding physical and emotional needs.

Despite Simic's confrontation with human suffering, we may be tempted into a narcosis of wonder attracted to the otherworldliness of his poem-world. We may look on the bald realities of mutilation and poverty with a voyeuristic fascination. Simic's understating rhetoric and folk-tale settings often invite this. Voyeuristic fascination appears to be a central part of Simic's experience. But this fascination is coupled with a simultaneous sense of terrifying immanence. Simic remembers his childhood in Yugoslavia:

> There was a church which had a large yard, and there were dead German soldiers there, and so we'd go over there, and we'd take from the German soldiers the belts, the ammo-belts, helmets, war-junk such as kids can play with. . . . I don't have any nightmares about it. It was all part of this wonderful game we had . . . if you were writing a poem about it, one really has to capture that complicated game. That innocence. . . . There was something there, which I can't quite name, but I felt touched and disturbed. But it wasn't any of the obvious things: that here was a dead man, that this was War.[3]

Simic's poem "Pastoral," from the book *Dismantling the Silence,* creates a similarly complex feeling of detachment and disturbance. Whatever innocence we detect in Simic's unflinching rhetoric is tainted. In keeping with other pastorals, the poem explores through its setting a style of passion which is at once celebrative and sad, a mood which translates the idyllic into mortal terms. Nature's consolations become reminders of loss. Silence, like flesh, is grass:

PASTORAL

I came to a meadow
Where the grass was silence
And flowers
Words

I saw they were both
Of flesh and blood
And that they sense and fear
The wind like a knife

The poem uses a veneer of simplicity to convey its complex tone. Simic's syntax is bare; his diction, flat as the pavement. Little effort is made to persuade by dazzling. But to call the language "unrhetorical" is to discount the seductive weirdness of its surface. The speaker's quiet lack of astonishment is itself strange given the strangeness of his world. He is the deadpan observer of his own vastly unexplained condition. He does not actively seek out a meadow. He "comes" to it as though incidentally. But this incidental setting then turns into hypersensitized flesh and blood, neurotic imagery which asserts the pre-eminence of emotional life. Silence and language become embodied, humanized, vulnerable. Even the metaphor of the flesh is complicated by contrary feelings: little is more intimate than our own bodies, but little is more mysterious. The speaker then links together a causal chain of private events with apparent self-assurance:

So I sat between the word *truth*
And the word *gallows*
Took out my tin can
And spoon

Whistled for the word *love*
And she answered me
By and by in her sleep

There were also many other things
For which there was no word
Only a breath now and then[4]

Even the distance which the speaker experiences between himself and the anonymous woman is mitigated by an unaccountable intimacy. Her groggy, milk-toast responsiveness and the withholding of her identity contribute to our sense of her as remote. But the ambiguous pronoun "she" cuts two ways. While withholding her identity, it also suggests that the speaker is already familiar with her. She needs no introduction. It is as though we have been dropped into the middle of an ongoing relation which might make more complete sense if we could only trace it back to its beginnings. But the poem's resistance, its eclipsed origins, make it all the better model of consciousness.

The speaker asks the woman, not for love, but for the word "love." Given the poem's climate of fear, we might expect a request for the "real thing." But the word "love" turns out to be the choice most consistent with the poem's tone. The request for the word "love" is a request for a token rather than an emotional commitment. This particular word, "love," may signify human involvement, but we experience in the speaker's prevailing sense of isolation the gap between word and referent.

To complicate things further, love, though it may signify a form of human involvement, not only tolerates but thrives on isolation and ambiguity. Ambiguity becomes a source of love's wonder, a dark place for the amorous imagination to play. In his essay on the poetry of Benjamin Péret, Simic says:

> If Péret has a "metaphysics," it has to do with the interdependence of love and the marvelous. Each of his images is as earthbound as the act of love. No longing here for the Absolute, only an appetite for multiplicity. . . . Péret is the purest practitioner of Keats' negative capability. No one is more patient with the absurd, the inexplicable.[5]

Thus the act of love is an act of faith in the absurd: it draws its mystique and vitality from the very isolation and ambiguity its rituals set out to overcome. Words are the mythemes in such rituals. Rather than representing experience, they express a desire to represent it. Words do not overcome a sense of isolation. They express a desire to overcome it. Thus they are gestures of longing rather than vestiges of truth. And, as such, they become perennial sources of the marvelous.

In "Pastoral," words, like flesh, take on an odd material reality apart from the speaker himself. They, like the body, have a quality of immanent distance, being essential to the experience of self yet spatially apart. Separate from the stuff of his identity, the speaker is strangely anonymous, a self without a self. In his essay "Images and 'Images,' " Simic writes, "To be conscious is to experience a distancing. One is neither World, nor Language, nor Self. One *is* and one *is not*."[6] The self which is not the self is the self-neglecting observer, a point of view which cannot account for its own perspective. Such an observer, in some measure independent from what the self has to lose, resembles an invulnerable voyeur, a persona similar to the Yugoslavian child who sleeps untroubled by nightmares.

Such an invulnerable self is best identified by what it lacks. It is an absence, but paradoxically present in the sense that it is nevertheless experienced. We may recognize in Simic's notion of the self-which-is-not-the-self traces of Husserl's concept of the transcendental ego. Simic frequently nods to the German phenomenological tradition as influential. The transcendental ego (as opposed to the concept of the transcendental ego) does not deconstruct since it never "constructs" in the first place. It lies on the periphery of the play of differentiation. The deconstructionist view allows no room for an unconstructed self behind language. The term "ego" may be misleading since this ego is not an organizing center. It is more like a field, something closer to the silent meadow in Simic's poem. In an interview, Simic recalls Heidegger's metaphor of open spaces:

> I've always felt that inside each of us there is profound anonymity . . . whatever you meet, it is not yours though you enclose it. . . . [Heidegger] describes the division between the world as nothing, as what he calls the "open," and any act of conceptualizing. . . . Many of his texts are longings to experience that anonymity, the condition where we don't have an "I" yet. It is as if we were in a room from which paradoxically, we were absent.[7]

If we were to literalize what it is to be half-missing, we might wind up with a pathetic cripple. This is precisely whom we meet in Simic's poem "Great Infirmities" from *Classic Ballroom Dances*. We may recognize a characteristic economy and quietness to the rhetoric, the correlative to innocence playing its complicated game in a desperate situation:

> Everyone has only one leg.
> So difficult to get around,
> So difficult to climb the stairs
> Without a cane or crutch to our name.
>
> And only one arm. Impossible contortions
> Just to embrace the one you love,
> To cut the bread on the table,
> To put a coat on in a hurry.

I should mention that we are almost blind,
and a little deaf in both ears.
Perilous to be on the street
Among the congregations of the afflicted.[8]

The phrase "I should mention" on the surface implies urgency but functions conversationally as a prelude to an afterthought. The joke, of course, is that we might expect more than a postscript to talk about our near-blindness. Simic has a knack for grim humor, another strategy of emotional distancing which thrives on its simultaneous ability to disturb. In the above poem, Simic alternates between hyperbole—"Everyone has only one leg"—and litotes—"So difficult to get around." Such wildly modulating humor encourages us to take pleasure in ambiguity.

The poem also risks a small pun: "Without a cane or a crutch to our name." The phrase "a crutch to our name" suggests a crutch reaching to our name, a crutch for our name. As in "Pastoral," words arc made flesh, halve-able. The pun opens up a reading of the poem as a meditation on living in two worlds, the "sayable" and the "unsayable." Our missing halves complicate things horribly. Language offers no closure, no sense of, not only truth-telling, but sufficiency. To name is to embrace with one arm.

The poem's final stanza plays tricks on our depth perception to dramatize such frustrated desire. To draw close is to withdraw:

An immense stillness everywhere
With the trees always bare,
The raindrops coming down only halfway.
Coming so close and giving up.

The trees are bare for want of what never arrives. What is most desired fades as it approaches like a small object in a blur over the eyes. The result is absolute isolation. To name is to experience a distancing. No attentive effort can overcome this distance.

Finally, we may remain unconvinced that physical hardship is appropriately cast in Simic's terms. It may strike some as trivializing to concern ourselves with the limits of language when subsistence is at stake. By placing language in a state of crisis, Simic's poems suggest the fundamental nature of imaginative need. As Stevens tells us, it is the imagination which makes the world into something we can love. But imaginative need can never be equivalent to physical need. Though our world is shaped by a desire for imaginative flight, game playing, jokes, all the pleasures of abstraction and ambiguity, such marvels cannot overcome physical hardship. Simic's verse swings broadly between the miraculous and the hard. Both contribute to his spacious version of us as immanent and distant, as being in the flesh and being conscious of ourselves in the flesh. Rather than trivializing human need, Simic's verse gives us a model for the quality of inner attentiveness which breeds respect for human range, an expanse extending beyond the sacramental gesturings of language. A world in which words are given like bread involves us deeply because in it we recognize the unresolved dissonance in our own imaginations rude, venerating, straining our eyes.

NOTES

1. Charles Simic, *The Uncertain Certainty* (Ann Arbor: University of Michigan Press, 1985), 5.
2. *The Uncertain Certainty,* 61.
3. *The Uncertain Certainty,* 35–36.
4. Charles Simic, *Selected Poems, 1963–1983* (New York: George Braziller, 1985), 18.
5. *The Uncertain Certainty,* 99.
6. *The Uncertain Certainty,* 106.
7. *The Uncertain Certainty,* 62–63.
8. *Selected Poems,* 128.

MATTHEW FLAMM

Impersonal Best: Charles Simic Loses Himself

For Charles Simic this has been a very funny century—one joke after another, like that big one in the middle, the Second World War. Simic, raised in Belgrade, was seven when it ended. Asked to describe it, he begins with numbers: nearly two million killed in Yugoslavia, at that time a country of 16 million. He mentions Hitler, Stalin, civil war. But Simic's only warming up. It's not long before he sounds like his poems, where the irrational is a routine, and terror one of the punch lines.

"I was reading recently," he tells me, "about this guy who was sent back to Yugoslavia to be put on trial; he was part of the pro-Nazi Croation government. They started killing right away after the Germans came in—the first summer they killed something like 200,000 people. It really staggered me. I mean, what an enormous effort, of organization, of willpower, to kill that many people. It's no joke," he adds. "You've got to burn their villages, you've got to round them up, you've got to shoot them. Jesus, those guys were hardworking, busy, dedicated sons of bitches."

Simic's humor runs through all his poetry, from his celebrated first poems to those in his new collection, *Unending Blues*. It's a fatalistic, Eastern European humor, and part of why I find it hard to believe that he is really, through and through, an American poet. The question of nationality, as it concerns Simic, may seem moot. Although he speaks with a distinctly Serbian twist and looks Slavic enough, with a bit of the bulkiness I associate with characters in early Milos Forman movies, he has always written in English—11 books, some essays, and translations. It's an imaginative, precise, essentially native's English, one that's been recognized with an assortment of awards, including, since 1983, a MacArthur Fellowship. But nationality was not one of the

---

From "Impersonal Best: Charles Simic Loses Himself" by Matthew Flamm, *Village Voice Literary Supplement* (December 1986). Reprinted by permission of the author and *The Village Voice*.

things I wanted to discuss, partly because the poems themselves never mention it, but also because I once took a class with Simic. All semester I wondered what difference his background made on how he looked at poems. It was a little like the emperor's new clothes the way the subject never came up.

Some of Simic's "foreignness" has to do with trends in recent American poetry. In the late '60's and '70's, he was linked with the so-called neosurrealist school, whose poets, influenced by European and South American fabulists, were after a certain archetypal or mythic experience in their work. Simic's mysterious "utterances" about elemental things—a stone, a knife, "the invisible"—became some of the (over-used) models for this group. But he stood out, both for his inventiveness and for something distinctive and intimate about his voice. There's that irony, inseparable from an Eastern European's sense of history; the joke's on us whether it's the cosmos or a tyrant who's playing it. It's a curiously detached voice, removed from its author's self. Simic's "I" is always impersonal, collective—another difference from most other American poets.

I ask him about growing up (in Belgrade, then New York and Chicago) but Simic, who likes to talk, turns out to be only a little more open about his past in person than he is on the page. "It was your typical Eastern European war childhood" closes the subject. That he arrived here at 16 and was writing poems in English three years later he finds hardly worth noting. When I ask, finally, if he might be a Yugoslav poet in an American disguise, he answers simply, "I've been translated over there [in Yugoslavia]. They don't see me as one of them." These *are* old questions for Simic, but I am getting back more than just boredom. This is also his point of view, which regards the individual as anonymous, shaped by forces that couldn't care less about character. Which is the subject Simic keeps returning to: the ways we're affected all of the time by things we barely understand.

"One of the things in the poems," he says,"that for me personally has always been the issue, is that we live in a series of endless contradictions. Just take the view of the self, or of the dozens of theories of the universe. We have dozens of theories about everything. And the poor individual, if you're not inclined to believe in something easily, if you're a skeptic, if you have a sense of humor—then you have to make sense of it all, by yourself. It's a very heroic and incredible situation to be in. Very different from the Greeks, or from Mr. Hamlet, who had only a few options before him."

Simic likes the confusion; he's at home in it. So are his poems, which are best read as a self-portrait, in negative space: Simic tells us about his past all the time, by what he leaves out. It has to do with what he went through during his childhood, which included pilfering "war junk" from dead German soldiers, and going hungry after the war. But what's important is not that he suffered (he's described the war as "fun") but that ordinary expectations were shattered. Therefore his "I" has to find its own way—"make sense of it all," by itself—despite the tricks constantly played on it. The anonymity of the poems, their puzzled nature, their amnesia-like scattering of the few autobiographical details, all reflect the experience. He's writing about bewilderment, about being part of history's comedy act, in which he grew up half-abandoned in Belgrade and then became, with his Slavic accent, an American poet.

Simic's devotion to his themes has its drawbacks. He tends to write too many of the same kind of poems, to the point that his surreal asides and ironic send-ups seem merely glib. You have to pick and choose with Simic; fortunately, he has pretty much done the job for us in his *Selected Poems,* which fits 20 years of work into less than 200 pages, including poems (notably *White*) previously available only in small press editions. Just as important, though, *Selected Poems* shows how over the years Simic has become a sharper, more economical writer, while moving on to new ways of thinking about his past.

Early Simic seems to have nothing to do with the poet's personal life. The concerns throughout the first half of *Selected Poems* are "ancestral and archetypal": experience that predates history, or carries on regardless of it. Or, as Simic describes it in one of his essays, "to lower oneself one notch below language . . . to recover our mute existence." In *Dismantling the Silence,* Simic's first major collection, that means trying to observe the act of thinking, or knowing, just as it takes place, prior to any conceptions. The results are oracular, unexplained, and loaded with menace, as if to say there's always been history, it's in our blood. But there's anger in the work that has to do with Simic's staking out his territory; with his background, he couldn't have written any of the more conventional types of autobiographical poem. He has to respond to history—posed as the conditions of consciousness and its attempts to keep him confused, fogbound, Simic's way to truth was through chance. He followed only the random—and therefore pure—associations his mind made at that deeper level ("below language"), encountering ordinary things as if for the first time. A fork, for instance:

> It resembles a bird's foot
> Worn around the cannibal's neck.
>
> As you hold it in your hand,
> As you stab with it into a piece of meat,
> It is possible to imagine the rest of the bird:
> Its head which like your fist
> Is large, bald, beakless and blind.

"It was an attempt to go back to beginning," Simic says, "to go back to the things that one really loves—stones, household objects, objects of immense affection." Not surprisingly, in those days, he detested anything artificial (" '50's academic poetry, the school of Eliot and Lowell") or casual ("poems of the sophisticated, literate traveler—someone goes to Europe and writes about a painting"). Taking off from Roethke's *The Lost Son* (Simic credits Roethke and the Yugoslav Vasko Popa as his main influences), he went primitive—no people, no places, no literary trappings—and bragged about it. "Go inside a stone / That would be my way. / Let somebody else become a dove," begins "Stone," Simic's most famous poem of this period, and a kind of *ars poetica*. But he wouldn't stay this ornery for long. By the time of his second major collection, *Return to a Place Lit by a Glass of Milk,* he was writing poems and at least mentioning, if not describing, people. There's also a playfulness in *Return,* a sense of delight in letting the mind make discoveries, as in these lines from the lovely and ingenious "Watch Repair."

> Number 12 presides
> Like a beekeeper
> Over the swarming honeycomb
> Of the open watch. . . .
>
> Tiny golden mills
> Grinding invisible
> Coffee beans.

When the coffee's boiling
Cautiously,
So it doesn't burn us,
We raise it
To the lips
Of the nearest
Ear.

And that's real coffee, mind you, even if it's invisible. The poem's eerie power, entirely out of proportion to its size, derives from the sense it gives of being just the visible tip of another world, one that's the imaginative reverse of our own, metaphor its only fact.

Simic experiments with letting imagination guide him; the poems are exercises in exploration. But the desire to behold inspiration rather than its products, to visit metaphor at its source—as impossible as knowing what we think before we think it—reaches (mock) epic proportions in the mini-saga *White*. The poem, by Simic's standards, is immense. Some 250 lines long, it sits in the middle of the *Selected Poems*, the culmination of all his earlier phenomenological quests. Its theme is of a kind of marriage, "the White" being the muse, or bride, or Simic's poems. Her groom, though, can barely get a glimpse of her:

Touch what I can
Of the quick,

Speak and then wait,
As if this light

Will continue to linger
On the threshold

The series of short poems that follows tells the history of this romance while acting it out, the poor poet mixing riddles, ditties, incantations—anything to get a closer look. Not that his expectations are terribly high. Simic relishes a certain lowliness in himself, a peasant grunginess that's like a whoopie cushion to his metaphysics. He's just the opposite of White; little wonder she's always slipping away. A poem in which he repeats their wedding vows (meanwhile, she's nowhere to be found) matches her purity with his squalor. "Do you take this line / Stretching to infinity?" he is asked. He answers, "I take this chipped tooth / On which to cut it in half." In the end he gets to kiss the spot "Where her bridal train last rustled."

The bride does finally speak up, though, in "What the White Had to Say," which concludes the sequence. In contrast to the clipped stanzas of the previous sections, White, speaking metaphor, her native tongue, is leisurely (she's not chasing anybody) and direct (she's not confused). She explains to her poet that there's no use trying to contain her, she'll always have the jump on him: "I thought of you long before you thought of me." But the poem does more than wrap things up. It's an account of poetic inspiration, and not the sophisticated, literate kind. Inspiration is—metaphorically, which, with Simic, means literally—the source of life. It leads him out of darkness. That being the case, though, inspiration also owes darkness a debt. In Simic's world, neither desolation and joy nor violence and art are ever far apart. No surprise, then, that his muse was born a gun.

> Because I am the bullet
> That has baptized each one of your senses,
> Poems are made of our lusty wedding nights.
> The joy of words as they are written.
> The ear that got up at four in the morning.
> Still, the most beautiful riddle has no answer.
>
> I am the emptiness that tucks you in like a mockingbird's nest,
> The fingernail that scratched on your sleep's blackboard.

Beginning in the late '70's, the poems examine what actually happened. History enters the picture undisguised, along with people, places, and names, as in the title of Simic's 1977 collection *Charon's Cosmology*. He keeps his mythic tone, applying it to events from daily life. The book was a breakthrough for Simic, though one he describes with his usual understatement: "The earlier poems are phenomenologies of perception of consciousness," he says. "But at this point, I simply realized, yes, there was all this history I had lived. And I started writing poems which had that in mind. You get all the atrocities, all the craziness, all the killing—you know, all the things that happened in the 20th century." And nowhere more so than in "The Lesson": "It occurs to me now / that all these years / I have been / the idiot pupil / of a practical joker."

The poem chronicles the pupil's discovery of the dark bent of the universe, showing, as well, the temptation to believe in a benevolent order. He thinks, at first, he's part of a picaresque novel, the conclusion of which will be "given over / entirely / to lyrical evocations / of nature," but gradually, the things he finds to be real turn out to be the most mundane; in fact, he trusts these details either because they're too trivial to be part of the joker's pattern, or because they're painful and disturbing: "The haircut of a soldier who was urinating against our fence . . . the day / My mother and I had nothing to eat." The irony is pure Simic—the poet's traditional awakening turned inside out, the source of lyricism become the apparently meaningless. And it's a real lyricism, not a parody. The poem is touching, rather than cynical, the pupil almost found of his illusions, which have lingered on like a phantom limb. After all, the lesson never ends; he can still be surprised.

> for the first time
> in this long and terrifying
> apprenticeship,
> I burst out laughing.
> Forgive me, all of you!
> At the memory of my uncle
> charging a barricade
> with a homemade bomb,
> I burst out laughing.

Initially, the books that follow—*Classic Ballroom Dances, Austerities*—seem to be more of the same. But the changes in the work are subtler now. Simic has begun to reflect, not just on his past, but on his peculiar relationship to it. He's a poet who's forgotten his biography, but rather than simply reacting to that condition, as he did earlier, he recognizes it as just another joke. "Prodigy," in *Classic Ballroom Dances*, describes his predicament through a faintly comic reminiscence of learning chess in 1944. The poem gives a child's eye view of the war: the planes and tanks shaking the windowpanes are just part of landscape. But the child's clarity of vision—he remembers everything, down to the chipped paint on the black pieces—can be too much. Some things he has to forget. "I'm told but do not believe / that that summer I witnessed / men hung from telephone poles. / I remember my mother / blindfolding me a lot." That amnesia will be his handicap, as well as a source of inspiration, of even greater vision, as long as he can learn to live with it.

She had a way of tucking my head
suddenly under her overcoat.
In chess, too, the professor told me,
the masters play blindfolded,
the great one on several boards
at the same time.

Unending Blues, Simic's first book since the initial *Selected Poems*, shows him turning towards a more personally accessible poem, one with a bit less irony between himself and his feelings. The lines are longer, the language more discursive, the settings more specific. They're also rural instead of urban, the result, Simic says, of living in New England for the last 13 years (he teaches at the University of New Hampshire). The book includes landscapes ("Trees in the Open Country"), some relatively straightforward domestic love poems ("Dear Helen" and "To Helen") and a long meditation addressed to Emily Dickinson ("Birthday Star Atlas"), which shows the intellectual side of Simic's contact with New England. History appears more as topic, less as disturbing force within the work, though Simic can still conjure up haunting scenes. "Toward Nightfall" moves from country road, to grocery store, to rooming house, brooding over tragedy and how it affects us in an age when "in the proper Greek sense" it supposedly doesn't exist. Overall, though (and in spite of the title), *Unending Blues* is Simic at his most cheerful. Against this homespun landscape, Europe, with all its insanity, stands out sharper than ever before as comic relief. In "A Place in the Country," those old ideas are not only funny but positively soothing, having lost their power to mystify.

And the fire is roaring in the stove,

While up above in what are still called the heavens,
There's our own chimney smoke
Like an old time coachman's whip
For both the good and the bad angels.

JAY BARWELL

Charles Simic: Visions of Solitude

Charles Simic's visions of solitude are in a context unlike that of other contemporary writers. Writers such as Beckett, Sartre, Gabriel García Márquez, and John Gardner envision the ubiquitous solitude of suffering, hell, and condemnation that emerges out of the loss of personal identity in modern society. Charles Simic is committed "to celebrate and affirm life, no matter what horrors are seen," whether they be the irreversible loss of ideals, the "color of an idea / which will not complete itself in our lifetime" (*Dismantling the Silence* 78), or the loss of individualism within a society bound and cemented to the city where

> Two uniformed men
> stroll along the empty streets,
> solemn and slow
> they advance, stopping
> to look in shop-windows,
> into parked cars.
>
> One of them wears a brass whistle,
> the other hides a gun with a silencer.
>
> (*Silence* 77)

Simic sets the stage for an apocalyptic vision that affirms a return to humankind's origins as if in triumph, when "There's no one left on the earth."

Simic again prophesies our return to the primeval in "Hearing Steps." An historic allusion to the Mongols presents the possibility that humankind is only an extension of its origins in its primitive urge to migrate like the beasts. He suggests the apocalyptic sentiment by conjuring images of cyclic emergence:

> Perhaps, the time has come again
> To go back into the forests and snow fields, . . .

From "Charles Simic: Visions of Solitude" by Jay Barwell, *Manassas Review: Essays on Contemporary American Poetry, Charles Simic* 1, no. 2 (winter 1978).

Perhaps it is time to return to the solitude from which we came:

> Live alone killing wolves with our bare hands,
> Until the last word and the last sound
> Of this language I am speaking is forgotten.

Back to the silence. Totemic imagery in Simic's poetry reverts man to nothing more than animal. These images are a preamble to the isolated vision of returning to our "old resting place" (*Silence* 63):

> Whoever swings an ax
> Knows the body of man
> Will again be covered with fur.

We will hibernate "like the bears" and women's breasts "Will grow coarse. He who cannot / Grow teeth, will not survive." These are the "dark prophecies" the speaker gathers. The images are primitive, "historical probabilities," and very human. This return, a return without intellectual options, reaps solitude—a silent instinctual urge to remove ourselves from civility, to reckon with the images of "Sleep" (*Silence* 19) where we are judged by beasts: woodpeckers, hyenas, toads. Here, solitude is uttered as "I climb into deep wells" where only the "quiet end" is his song.

> . . . Nothing of us remains
> Almost nothing. I am whatever beast inhabits me.
>
> When the rain turns into snow
> Every beast shall see its tracks and wonder.

The closing image of tracks in the snow is an important one in Simic's work, recurring throughout both *Return* and *Silence*. The snow will return each year and beasts will continue to leave their tracks. In "Sleep" the suggestion of an inherent relationship between civilization and its animal origins is made through the beast's almost intellectual capacity for "wonder" or contemplation. A later poem generates the same symbolic linking of present with past, making use of the same image. The title poem, "Return to a Place Lit by a Glass of Milk" (*Return* 61), shows hands lying "open with tracks of animals / Journeying across the fresh snow. " The image carries us back to our origins and again suggests cyclic continuity over each "fresh snow." As the poem develops, the hand becomes a further symbol for our silent instincts which are perhaps as old as gravitational forces:

> As they come closer, as they touch,
> It is like two small streams
> Which upon entering a wide river
> Feel the pull of the distant sea.

We find ourselves being pulled, instinctually, into the sea, lost in "a room far back in time."

Any discussion of solitude, whether literal or metaphorical, cannot disregard man's fear, the instinct to shudder. Simic maintains that "Fear" (*Silence* 11) *is* an instinct by comparing each leaf on a tree to a man's fear of the unknown:

> Fear passes from man to man
> Unknowing,
> As one leaf passes its shudder
> To another.

Fear is a continuation, like heredity; it is a silent rustling that emerges out of the unknown until it becomes contagion without vehicle:

> All at once the whole tree is trembling
> And there is no sign of the wind.

Fear not only encompasses the unknown, but there are objects such as the knife and butcher's hook and ideologies such as religion in even the most primitive societies that make humankind a victim of solitude. The knife "beds down in the flesh" (*Silence* 37). There are knives whose honed blades reflect distorted images of man "like a funhouse mirror" (*Return* 67). Often the blades suggest the morose:

> There are knives that glitter like altars
> In a dark church
>
> Where they bring the cripple and the imbecile
> To be healed.
>
> (*Silence* 24)

The knife is an "invention," the blade "imagined by the hanged man / in that split of a second as he glimpses / with raised eyes the rope for the last time." The knife here reinforces a vision of solitude, the desperate hope of a man condemned to hang. An element of hopelessness prevails in this vision. The executioners witness the death, and in ironic contrast

> . . . go home at daybreak
> over the snow that makes no sound
> to cut the bread fresh from the oven.
>
> (*Silence* 76)

The knife may also be the "Father-confessor" (*Silence* 56) of an ideological comparison between Christianity and insanity as the priest becomes "A single shining eye / Of a madman. " We are to fear the knife as if it were a deified superior, or fanatic "madman." Our fear is then manifest as a revelation, "a candle" illuminating the secret halls of our origins:

> We go down
> An inner staircase.
> We walk under the earth.
> The knife lights the way.

It is a tool used to cut flesh, to pierce the barriers of time and space, and to guide us through these barriers like a star or a religion, or the meaning of a poem. Simic celebrates:

> If it's a poem
> You want,
> Take a knife;
> A star of solitude,
> It will rise and set in your hand.

Anointment, baptism, and crucifixion occur frequently enough in both collections to pay them particular attention here, especially as religion applies to Simic's mythopoetic vision of solitude. In "Soup" (*Return* 62), a sort of melting pot of the knowledge of our origins, he answers the question "On what shall we cook" this soup, how do we bring it to a boil? The cook suggests sarcastically that we try cooking it "On an oval locket with the picture of Jesus." Perhaps, he continues, we will eat it "With a finger which is the divining-rod." Simic's religious imagery supplements his own digging into the past. "Second Avenue Winter" (*Return* 9) contrasts the "great battles" of our past with the battle of the "old negro driver," a junkman whose "insanity . . . makes him keep / A horse in New York city." The speaker is led through "A million years of shivering and coughing." He endures, "With a slow shuffle / Of sweet sanctified thoughts, / Like a bearded pilgrim" and committedly assumes the role "Of a dumb and unknown animal sorrow":

> Its ritual and secret life
> Where I wish to be anointed.

As symbolized by the old negro junkman, man's instinct to preserve the past is accompanied with what Simic might have called *martyrdom,* a religious solitude—the irremediable torment of an individual who can see (in the lifelines of his hand) all that has gone before and all that is to come. As in "Solving the Riddle" the poet observes the palm:

> I take note of its crossroads and ditches.
> I travel crucified.
>
> (*Return* 28)

It is martyrdom, and it is not blind. There is a determination to continue, almost dutifully, to systematically unearth the riddle of our origins.

In an earlier poem called "Meat" (*Silence* 26) a transformation takes place leading the traditional vision of baptism into a visionary baptism of primitive solitude. This change begins with an image alluding to the crucifixion, how Christ, in his solitude, was hung up for man to observe.

> Hang the meat on the hook
> So that I may see what I am.
>
> In this pagan ceremony a pig is hanging
>
> Like the weight of a man
> Who has turned to go
> With grief in his heart.

The traditional vision is debased, turned into butchery. This vision emerges from within. It is the bloody vision of mankind, of the prophecies of religion which turn on us to blacken our vision of the future. Simic treats this vision as the solitude of religion:

> I am baptized in this sight,
> As when a child immersed in water
> Feels the hand of death
> At his throat.

Simic's vision of solitude is partially due to his excavation of images that serve his quest to answer the riddle of existence. He has dug for the substance humankind is made of, the universal quality in humanity that has endured through the ages. This search has led him only so far and, like the secret recipe for an ancient medicinal broth, he tries to comprehend the essence of man, recreating the "Soup" (*Return* 62) and laying out the directions:

> Take a little backache
> Melt some snow from the year of your birth
> Add the lump in your throat
> And the fear of the dark
>
> Instead of oil a pinch of chill

and then you "Swear loudly into it / . . . stir it with the night." As we add all the ingredients of our origins and attempt to blend them well, we find the quest for knowledge is almost futile—like finding the secret ingredient of the soup. We will inevitably philosophize "With two eyes that quarrel in the same head" until we finally "Grind each other into black pepper." The images of this poem are totemic. They present qualities of humanity: the backache of man's vain attempt to progress, the original sin suggested with the image of an Adam-like lump in the throat, and the instinctual fear of darkness. He commits humanity to the solitude of holding its breath as we

> . . . dive into the soup
> With a grain of salt between our teeth
> And won't come up
> Until we learn its song.

He accounts for the solitude an individual faces as an intrinsic seed of a society that, ironically, accepts everything with a "grain of salt." For Simic, solitude emerges from the limits of knowledge and the silence of being held under. The only knowledge of our origin we have gained is that it is an evolving continuation bridging the gap from past to present:

> . . . finally there's your grandmother
> Sweeping the dust of the nineteenth century
> Into the twentieth, and your grandfather plucking
> A straw out of the broom to pick his teeth.
>
> (*Return* 23)

The image of dust is a symbol of man's past, his antiquity, and the unavoidability of the future that sweeps from century to century. It forms "Into neat pyramids, / That have tombs in them, / Already sacked by robbers, / Once, long ago." The ancient image of a process that takes place and builds up slowly represents the solitude that man cannot remove himself from.

"Solving the Riddle" (*Return* 28) can only be contended with through the individual. There are no universal answers offered. The clues to the answer are "My clues / . . . my strings of omens." Yet they are not evidence enough in themselves, and react as if in a binary force making "one hand unearn / What the other earns." The futility of this force results in the speaker's efforts to affirm a solitude of alienation:

> Inside my empty bottle
> I was constructing a lighthouse
> While all the others
> Were making ships.

Solitude inhabits the deep subjective awareness of an identity that contrasts with the feelings and ideologies of others. It is the "Inner Man" (*Silence* 28) that senses this alienation:

> It isn't the body
> That's a stranger.
> It's someone else.

A sort of elusive spirit who, at night, sits alone and addresses his corporeal partner:

"Though you utter
Every one of my words,
You are a stranger.
It's time you spoke."

It is the detachment of the inner and outer selves that results in that solitude; yet, the individual within society must reveal his own elemental identity and assert that "I belong to no one" (*Silence* 5). Thus, knowledge of solitude reinforces the realization that the power of the individual depends upon the contrast of self with society. The self is only a fraction of the "Tapestry" (*Silence* 31) of civilization. Images of solitude, in this sense, portray a sense of loss: loss of the past, loss of belonging, loss of group identity. The tapestry is the presentation of civilization and its archetypes represented in a universal setting that "hangs from heaven to earth." The vision Simic gives is of an historic process toward humankind's anonymity:

There are trees in it, cities, rivers,
small pigs and moons. In one corner
snow is falling over a charging cavalry,
in another women are planting rice.

You can also see:
a chicken carried off by a fox,
a naked couple on their wedding night,
a column of smoke,
an evil-eyed woman spitting into a pail of milk.

He suggests that behind this surface of civilization is only "Space, plenty of empty space." The poem then goes on to ask "who is talking now?" and answers, "—A man asleep under a hat." Man is alienated, unaware of the action of the tapestry, but, the man's voice is the only voice audible. This seems a blind sense of knowledge.

And when he wakes up?
—He'll go into the barbershop.
They'll shave his beard, nose, ears and hair
To look like everyone else.

Equating civilization to a barbershop suggests that ultimately it is only in solitude that one can assert his or her unique voice. If civilization is a barbershop which makes the individual "look like everyone else," then the voice cannot help feeling isolated and even anxious towards the demand for conformity. If men and women are unique only in solitude, civilization places them in the midst of the silence presented by this tapestry. Only in his or her recovery of the past does one recover his or her sense of self.

By dwelling in the past, the mythic origins of its evolution, humankind becomes submerged in an unavoidable landscape of solitude. As Simic transforms the "concrete particulars" of his environment into a symbolic vision of continuity and alienation, the physical details about the landscape invariably assume primitive dimensions. The landscapes are bleak and seem only incidentally touched by humanity and we find few traces of the city community or civilized pastoral. Instead we encounter at one extreme a grotesquely luxuriant forest whose fossil "imprints of strange flowers" engender the same mystical echoes of "a star / Dead a million years" (*Silence* 3), and at the other extreme an extended Beckett landscape in which ". . . there's only his empty chair" (*Silence* 76). Examining the full implications of this imagery we realize that Simic's landscape, like Beckett's, is literally and figuratively a place to stand, an angle of vision that is characteristic of Simic. Its topography forms the landscape of solitude.

Traditionally the pastoral has been entwined in a realm of the idyllic and the magically romantic. As Simic seeks to discover life in an alien and perhaps threatening landscape, both time and space become esoteric. His treatment and development of solitude within the realm of the forest and fields contrasts with the traditional view. The images found in "Forest" (*Silence* 3) are visions of man's alienation and estrangement from his origins. The essence of this forest, its "termites, . . . roots and streams / Will stitch their chill into the heart of man."

> The human body will be revealed for what it is—
> A cluster of roots
> Pulling in every direction.

The speaker prophesies our return to the roots of trees and the fossils of their leaves, saying

> There'll be plenty of time
> When an acorn grows out of your ear
> To accustom yourself to my ways,
> To carve yourself a hermit's toothpick.

Thus he affirms his regard for humankind's origins by idealizing the solitude of the hermit.

The landscape of solitude develops into a psychology of heightened awareness. The "Invention of Nothing" (*Silence* 79) draws attention to the sublime realization of solitude, of being the only one left in a transient existence. As he writes, Simic is suddenly aware of his alienation from everything—"that nothing remains of the world / except my table and chair." At this moment he poses the question:

> Is this the tavern
> without a glass, wine or waiter
> where I'm the long awaited drunk?

The image is similar to the physical alienation from objectivity and psychological ambiance of Beckett's *Krapp's Last Tape* and the naked landscape and endless waiting found in *Waiting for Godot*. But Simic's character is eventually served wine, alleviating the pain of waiting. Simic goes beyond Beckett; he continues, "The color of nothing is blue," immediately negating total emptiness. There is a quality to nothingness and "I strike it with my left hand and the hand disappears." This contortion of surrealism allows the voice to lose its subjectivity, almost as if the end were nearing and the boundaries of time and space were to be transcended. He asks "Why am I . . . / . . . so happy?" and seems to realize that the solitude has blissfully intoxicated him as he proceeds to

> . . . climb on the table
> (the chair is already gone)
> I sing through the throat
> of an empty beer-bottle.

Perhaps the intoxication is only metaphorical, perhaps he actually got drunk and wrote the poem, either case leading to such revelations as solitude claims: hope, negation of pessimism, and the song of triumph.

Simic has entered a landscape of unknown psychological territory and his exploration reveals only nakedness and barren ground:

> The sky and the earth
> Are of the same impenetrable color.

There's no wind. If there are rivers,
They must be under the ground.
Of the marvels we sought, no trace.
Of the strange new stars, nothing.
There's not even dust. . . .

(*Silence* 66)

This geography is spaceless and imperceptible, yet uniquely primitive. Progress has not been made because there is no time, "There's not even dust." Yet the speaker has transcended the obstacles and he affirms this unknown territory:

I recognize you. You are all
That has eluded me.

May this be my country.

Throughout, Simic's voice is clear, quiet, and appealing. At his best his images are the apotheosis of solitude. Consciousness of the entropy of humanity demands, in his poetry, the detail that arouses and makes believable those distinguishable qualities of solitude that serve as hosts to the interiors of each of us. In amiable signature, Simic cheers solitude.

PART THREE *Metaphysician in the Dark*

Charles Simic is a sentence.

CHARLES SIMIC

From Notebooks, 1963–69

> Time, where are we, you and I, since I live in you and you do not exist.
>
> —Alphonso Cortes

★

O beau pays!
The monkey at the typewriter.

★

The art of making gods with ear wax. Venus, for example, in full splendor of her naked beauty.

Went to see Mrs. Murphy and ask her if she could make a teeny black dress for my goddess? Her ears turned cherry red. When she calmed down, she let me measure her waist with a piece of red thread bit off at the end.

★

In my childhood women mended stockings in the evening. To have a "run" in one's stocking was catastrophic. Stockings were expensive, and so was electricity. We would all sit around the table with a lamp in its middle, the father reading the papers, the children pretending to do their homework, while secretly watching the mother spreading her red-painted fingernails inside the transparent stocking.

★

I went to see Ionesco's *Bald Soprano* with B. It was being shown at the small theatre on the Lower East Side. There were only six people in the audience, and that included the two of us. They gave the performance, anyway. When it came to the love scene with the woman who has three noses, the actors got carried away on the couch. Their voices went down to a whisper. All of a sudden, they began taking their clothes off. I could feel B.

trembling. I was afraid to touch her . . . I don't remember where we went afterwards, what we said, or what came after that scene in the play. Nothing, except that the streets were covered with newly fallen snow.

★

A scene from the 50s French movie which still delights me:

A fly gets shut in a room with three armed thugs and a woman gagged and bound who watches them with eyes popping. In front of each man on the table there's a sugar cube and a pile of large bills. No one stirs. A naked bulb hangs from the ceiling by a long wire so they can see the fly count its legs. It counts them on the table, it counts them on the wall, then it just sits at the end of someone's nose.

Of course, that wasn't exactly the way it was in the movie. I worked on it over the years, making delicious little adjustments, as one does with a poem being written in rigorous meter and rhyme.

★

"This thing came from a maximum security penitentiary," she told me. I could not say what kind of metal it was made of. I could see it had been bent and straightened badly. It had been a part of something, but I had no idea what that could be. I put my tongue against it, and was surprised by how cold it felt.

"One writes the dates of one's imprisonment with such an object," I said.

"One must keep it concealed at all times," she added.

The man who left it with her was her lover for a week. That was many years ago.

"He used to scratch my back with it," she told me.

She wore a flowered silk robe and red Turkish slippers on her bare feet. They kept falling off when she crossed her legs. I wanted the thing. I kept wondering if she would give it to me, if I asked her for it, if I pretended to plead.

Her robe was slightly open. The thing lay on the table between us. Outside it was beginning to rain. She got up to close the windows and I put the thing in my pocket. It was raining so hard, the room had darkened. Now we could not see the look in our eyes.

★

I leave the dentist after what seems an eternity in his chair. It's an evening in June. I'm walking on a tree-lined street full of dark, whispering trees. The streets are badly lit, but there are people everywhere strolling close to each other as if they were all lovers. The thought crosses my mind that I'm immensely happy.

★

"I have the impression," she said to me one day, "that in my life there have been more nights than days. It was like night came, and then, just as the new day was about to break, another night would follow immediately in its wake.

"I forgot the face of my great and only love because it was always so dark. I would sit looking at his face which the shadows had already obscured. Only his naked shoulders kept their ghostly whiteness. I wanted to touch them, but I no longer had the right.

"It was much too dark now. My memory is a store specializing in the fashions of the eclipse. My love and I are trying on all the suits and dresses, but the mirrors work only dimly. They hold only vague outlines of some clothing of another era."

★

"My history is at the mercy of my poetry." (Marx revised.)

★

I thought "nosology" had to do with noses. Something like a science of noses. Many noses coming to be examined. The pretty nosologist is measuring them and making entries on a sheet of paper.

Nature? The perfect nose, for example, crossing the street in our neighborhood. Or the perfect nose in a lobby of a grand hotel lighting a gold-tipped cigarette behind some potted palm tree?

Nosology, unfortunately, has nothing to do with noses.

★

A tower of cliches fell upon the two lovers. You could only see a solitary arm or a leg sticking out of the rubble. The foot that was in her mouth was not mine. The ace was not up my sleeve, but over my eyes, etc.

★

"He seeks the secret and meaning of Time," we are told upon entering. If we weren't told, we'd say he's just staring out of the window at the rain. His mother wants us to walk on tiptoes. "Make yourselves at home," she tells us using improvised deaf-mute signs.

"Povera e nuda vai, Filosophia," wrote the Italian poet Petrarca. Steady rain, then the sound of distant thunder over Manhattan.

★

There was a maid in our house who let me put her hand under her skirt. I was five or six years old. I can still remember the dampness of her crotch and my surprise that there was all that hair there. I couldn't get enough of it. She would crawl under the table where I had my military fort and kept all my weapons. I don't remember what we said, if anything. Just her hand, firmly guiding mine.

★

In a park, dangerous to the public after dark, the soapbox speaker shouting: "Everything I say has been misunderstood!" Something to do with justice in the world, with forces of evil. . .

O century of bad dreams! They all want us to bite their morgue attendants' nails for them, and we refuse to!

★

When my grandfather was dying from diabetes, when he had already one leg cut off at the knee and they were threatening to do the same to the other, his old buddy, Savo Lazanic, used to visit him every morning to keep him company. They would play chess and talk.

One morning my grandmother had to leave him alone in the house as she had to attend a funeral of a distant relative. That's what gave him the idea. He hopped out of bed and into the kitchen where he found candles and matches. He got back into his bed, placed one candle above his head and the other one at his feet. Then he lit them. Finally, he pulled the sheet over his face and began to wait.

When his friend knocked, there was no answer. The door being unlocked, he went in, calling from time to time. The kitchen was empty. A gray cat slept by the cold woodstove in the livingroom. When he entered the bedroom and saw the bed, the lit candles, the sheet—he let out a wail, and then broke into sobs as he groped for a chair to sit down.

"Shut up, Savo," said my grandfather from under the sheet. "Can't you see I'm only practicing?"

★

The exiled general's only grandson was playing war under the table, cheeks puffed to imitate bombs exploding. The grim daughter wrote the old man's memoirs. There was a smell of bad cooking, the view of a busy highway through the window.

The general was in a wheelchair. He wore a bib and smoked a cigar. The daughter was smiling in a welcome way that made her small teeth show.

I liked the general better. He remembered a distinguished East European prime minister pretending to wipe his ass with a peace treaty, the captured enemy officers drinking heavily and toasting some cabaret singer from their youth.

★

In Chicago, in 1950s, there was still an old woman with a street organ and a monkey. She turned the crank with both hands while the monkey went around with a tin cup. Some tune that made our grandmothers in their youth sigh.

If the woman was a hundred years old, she must have known the cow that started the Great Fire. Later she married the Sicilian with the street organ. He kissed her every night with the monkey still on his shoulder.

The animal I saw looked young and full of mischief. He wore a coat with brass buttons which must have come down to him from his great grandfather, or thereabouts. That day, they had for an audience a small boy who looked fearful, but also curious.

His beautiful mother kept pulling his arm. The old woman had her eyes raised heavenward in a manner favored by saints at the time of their martyrdom.

★

The night of my farewell dinner in Chicago, I got very drunk. At some point, I went to the bathroom and could not find my way back. The restaurant was large and full of mirrors. I would see my friends in the distance, seated at the table, but when I went toward them, I would come face to face with myself in the mirror. With my new beard I did not recognize myself immediately. I would even apologize before realizing who it was. I finally sat down at an old man's table. He said nothing, and I lit a cigarette. Time passed. The place was emptying. The old man, who could have been an undertaker, pushed his wine glass toward me. I would have remained with him indefinitely if one of the women from our table did not find me and lead me outside.

★

They sit on the table, the tailors do. At least, they used to. A street of dim shops in Belgrade where we went to have my father's coat narrowed and shortened so it would fit me. The tailor got off the table and stuck pins into my shoulder. "Don't squirm," my mother said. Outside it was getting dark. Large snowflakes fell.

Years later in New York, on the same kind of winter afternoon, a dry-cleaning store window with an ugly, thick-legged woman standing on the chair. She's having the hems of her skirt pinned by the gray-headed Jewish tailor who kneels before her like a beseeching tutor.

★

> "Truth brushes me with its wing!"
> "It's not a wing but a dog comb," we tell him.

★

Young black woman in pink haircurlers, arms crossed on her chest, as she leans out of the first floor window to speak to a boy on a bicycle. A beer bottle raised to his lips, he's taking a long swig before offering her what's left. He has to reach up, and she has to stretch down a little, just opening, one big naked breast slipping out for all to see—before she gets hold of the beer.

★

I got the idea of sleeping on the roof on hot nights from my mother and father. That's what they did during the War, except it wasn't a roof but a big terrace on a top floor of a building in downtown Belgrade. There was a blackout, of course. I remember immense starry skies, and how silent the city was. I would begin to say something, but someone—I could not tell for a moment who it was—would put a hand over my mouth.

Like a dark ocean liner adrift on the dark sea—that's how it felt when clouds were racing over our heads. We were sailing full speed ahead. "Nearer to the infinite," I remember my father whispering.

★

Ideas to make your hair stand up, just as if you were to stick your finger in a socket.

"The external world," she assures me, "is the work of our sense organs."

"Sweet Jesus! Does that mean our sweaty, naked bodies, being a part of the external world, are merely the work of our sense organs?"

"Not so loud, you fool," she says as she pulls the covers up to her chin. "Our sense organs themselves are the products of our sense organs."

"In that case," I say pulling off her covers, "if I understand you correctly, we might not even be here!" But, she just glares at me and calls me stupid.

★

In that huge city there's a woman he has met the night before. She has left his bed in the morning, telling him only that she works as a secretary in an office just off the Grand Central Station. That afternoon, he gets the bright idea to go and find her as she leaves the office at five. Against infinite odds, knowing neither the building nor the street she works on, he decides to look for her.

And that's what he does. He stands on the corner of 42nd Street and 5th for more than two hours searching the faces in the crowd for a fleeting glimpse of her. At times, he thinks he sees her. His heart jumps! He rushes, pushing people aside, only to overtake a complete stranger, someone equally beautiful, equally ethereal.

When the streets begin to empty, he walks around the neighborhood still full of hope. "I'm practicing magic" he thinks. The night has now fallen and the more he walks the fewer people there are on the street. He's certain, however, that when he rounds the next corner, she'll be there.

He's astonished that she is not. And yet, with each disappointment, he feels closer to her. She's working late, it occurs to him. There are still a few lights on the upper floors of these dark buildings. Her accounts won't balance to the last penny. Any minute now she will step out of a dark doorway. He can already hear the rustle of her dress, the sound of her heels as she rushes off in the opposite direction, never to be overtaken.

★

Chance is . . . "the humorous master." (Ernst)

★

"You look like Franz Schubert," a crazy looking woman told me as we were introduced.

At that same party, I spoke to a lawyer who insisted we had met in London two years ago. I explained my accent to a doctor by telling him that I was born in Gary, Indiana, and grew up among people who didn't speak English.

There was a girl there, too, who was blind. She kept smiling sweetly. Her mother told me that I reminded her of her brother who was hung by the Germans in Norway. She had witnessed the atrocity and was going to give me the details, but I excused myself telling everyone that I had this sudden and terrible toothache that required immediate attention.

I became more and more lucid the later it got. Everybody was already asleep. I tried to wake J., but she drew me down on her breasts sleepily. We made love, and then I talked to her about philosophy, to my heart's content, while she slept.

CHARLES SIMIC

From Notebooks, 1980–84

My father remembers a fly that wouldn't let him sleep one summer fifty years ago.

★

Another story about time. This one about how long it took them to quit their cells after realizing the jailers were gone. Even then, they thought it best to remove their shoes and tiptoe out of that Gestapo prison in Milan.

He was still tiptoeing that night, crossing a large empty square. The moon was full above the abandoned palazzos. His heart was in his mouth.

"Just like when I was a kid," he says. Returning home late and sneaking past his father's and stepmother's bedroom, afraid he'll wake them out of their passionate embrace.

★

Ars Poetica: trying to make the jailers laugh.

★

Celestial bodies aligning themselves so a ray of light may find my old shoes. It's all finally about astronomy, it occurred to me. Even shoes!

★

He suffered and she suffered. Everybody they knew suffered, but they were not supposed to show it. Even the children, even the dogs kept quiet. On the Street of Ten Thousand Sufferings not a peep. Ten thousand kitchens and in them ten thousand women with clenched teeth. Not like today—when everybody whines, etc.

★

The huge crowd cheering the Dictator; the smiling faces of little children bringing flowers. How many times I've seen that? The one with blonde braids curtseys surrounded by high boots of the dignitaries and tightly leashed police dogs. The sky is cloudless. The holiday flags are flying high. I look in vain for someone with a troubled face.

★

The country doctor provided the waiting room: twelve dragon-clawed chairs and a coat-tree bare except for a single gray mitten in its branches. Also, an aquarium rigged up to resemble a tropical forest. Blue bubbles ascending languidly among the hair-lipped, pin-eyed flowers of some nightmarish species. Schools of razor-thin minnows shimmering among them.

I couldn't take my eyes off them, but then I noticed a young woman biting her nails in the corner. She smiled to herself, and shrugged, without looking at me.

★

Approaching Manhattan at night, I always think of the old Polish and Ukrainian scrubwomen wielding their mops in the brightly lit towers of high finance. That's how I remember them, anyway. The one in a flowered dress who dusted off the portraits of the grim founder and his clever offspring. The old black man who ran the elevator at night, and who'd bow to her like a headwaiter in a fancy restaurant, to make her laugh, and show her missing tooth in front.

★

The cold made me remember this, too. A shabby gray overcoat twice my size which they made me wear. It was wintertime, and my mother couldn't afford another one. People on the street would stop to watch me. The overcoat trailed the ground and made walking difficult. That day I had reached the corner, and was waiting to cross, when a young woman mistook me for a beggar. She gave me a small coin and hurried away troubled, obviously a stranger in the city.

★

Enigmas make Cynthia beautiful. "I was Bigfoot's Love Slave," say the headlines she's reading.

★

Northwood with night falling. Professor of Philosophy barking up the wrong tree. His bête noire curled up, he thinks, in its highest branches.

★

We were on our third bottle of wine when he said he was going to show me pictures of his girlfriend. Earlier he had been telling me about what a wonderful person she was. To my surprise, the photographs spread out on the table were of a naked woman shamelessly displaying herself. Leaning over my shoulder, he praised her small, shapely breasts and the rich hair in her crotch, until I felt aroused. It was an odd situation. My host was an older man, a cardiologist of great renown, whose pregnant young wife was asleep in the next room. "Do you want to meet her," he asked me, pointing to one of the pictures, and I told him that I did, realizing that that's what he wanted me to say.

A few weeks later, the three of us had dined together. The woman was, indeed, beautiful in a severe kind of way. Like a bearer of bad news in a hospital waiting room—I thought for some reason. We talked about arts and politics, superficially and without enthusiasm. He was ordering another bottle of champagne, when I abruptly excused myself as if I had to go to the washroom, and instead when home.

★

It was a window with a view of a large office with many identical desks at which men and women sat working. A woman got up and walked the length of the floor with papers in hand and stopped where a man rose to meet her at the other end. He waved his arms as he talked, while she stood before him a while to realize that man was yelling at that woman.

★

Two young birch trees wrestling in the wind. The crow in the snow as a referee.

★

The face of my daughter lit by a table lamp while she sucks a finger pricked by a compass, a drop of blood already fallen on the black numerals of the difficult homework, as she worried whether to hand it, just as it is, to the stern old nun who'll make her stand and wait for the verdict before the whole class. . .

The spring-day bright with sunlight; the nun's small, tight fist clouding the answer.

★

They look like scholarly comic book dealers. Their names should be Morpheus and Phantasos. They stand in their long winter overcoats outside the horse-players hangout. A crow-headed Emperor rules their universe. His subjects are white mice, and an occasional human.

Across the street, two fat sisters keep a candy store, stale and close with many dusty jars of hard candy and spy on the neighborhood.

There's also a kid on his way to school who looks like a monkey because he tells delicious lies.

★

In a line at the porno-flick with Saracens, Chinese, Vikings, ex-Nubian slaves. Winter dusk; snow mixed with rain. Inside the huge open crotch of one Cassandra Jones. The smell of wet feet below, and up on the screen her fake black eyelashes blinded by love.

★

Where they nail old women to crosses. Where little children lick lollipops in shape of a death's head. Where they wouldn't trust God, the father, himself . . .

★

Beneath the shadow of moving airplanes we were eating watermelon. While we ate the bombs fell on Belgrade. We watched the smoke rise in the distance. We were hot in the garden and asked to take our shirts off. The watermelon made a ripe, cracking noise as my mother cut it with a huge knife. We also heard what we thought was thunder, but when we looked up, the sky was vast and cloudless.

★

Once I adored a philosopher, a pretty one. We walked the country paths bowed as if going to the funeral of a lofty idea. "It's like sneaking up on a question mark with a butterfly net," I remember her saying. And then also: "Logic is a fairy tale in which the Prince and the Princess live in reasonable happiness."

★

The poor continue to reproduce themselves obstinately. The details are not seemly, drunk as they are, and the small children watching from their beds, the ones God doesn't love except in Sunday School stories.

There are heated dinner debates as to the degree of their discomfort, and whether their misfortune is predestined or self-imposed. Everyone agrees there's something beautiful in saying their name. However, the unremitting monotony of their daily diet is not a fit subject right now. A relief to have the door shut after such a guest. "They must like it that way!" someone yells after the departed, while the others laugh and shake their heads. "The poor have a way of spoiling everything," thinks the hostess in a pretty new white dress on which a couple of greasy stains have inexplicably appeared. Like fingerprints! A strange thumb and forefinger.

★

It's your birthday! The child you were arrives tomorrow. You'll meet on the street as the day breaks. He wants to take you by the hand, but you won't let him.

"You've forgotten something," he whispers. And you . . . quiet as a mutt around an undertaker . . . since, of course, he doesn't exist.

Nothing is his new name. He has nothing to do with words.

★

Strafford Orpheus assuaging the fierceness of wild beasts with his new kazoo.

★

Emerson was the cow from which their milk was drawn. Who said that?

★

On the street corner the card trickster was shuffling his three cards using a large cardboard box as a table. The cards fluttered. It looked like a cock fight. Five of us watching with heads buzzing with intricate calculations and visions of riches. The day so cold everyone's hat pulled down over the ears . . . Time to place bets.

★

I told the well-read young girl on the train that I was a Russian Prince in exile. We were somewhere between Cleveland and Buffalo in a darkened coach full of sleeping people. I whispered and she whispered. I described our house in St. Petersburg, the terrors of the Revolution, the death of my father by the firing squad which the whole family had to witness. Later, we were even necking a little. The year was 1958. I was twenty years old, and she no more than sixteen.

★

The "repose of philosophy" as far as the eye can see. The few who died laughing turned into little white flowers.

★

Back-slapping Republican party regulars at a money-raising shindig. Big Bill, Big John, Big Daddy—I forget the name—mouth full of false teeth. Glad to see you! Pushing through a crowd of well-wishers. Yes Sir, the old lard-face and the silver-haired missus on his fat arm. The Veterans' band striking up a hot number! Regretfully, one of the instruments out of tune. Most likely the pinhead with a slide trombone. He must weigh less than a hundred pounds, and has that hangdog look when his cheeks go puff.

★

I caught a peek at the mortician's wife nursing the mortician's new daughter, and her breast was huge.

★

The Golden Mountain doesn't exist. The Golden Mountain is three thousand feet high.

★

The suitcase on the railroad tracks they were afraid to come near. Far from any station, on a stretch of track bordered by orchards where they were stealing plums that afternoon. The suitcase with its many colorful labels of what must have been world famous hotels, did not seem real to them. During the war one heard of bombs, special ones, in shape of toys, pens, soccer balls, exotic birds—so why not suitcases?

"I always wondered what was in it?" she told me.

We were talking about the summer of 1943 of which we both only had a few clear recollections.

★

One of those postwar scenes: A baby carriage pushed by a hump-backed old woman; her son sitting in it, both legs amputated. She was haggling with the grocer when it got away from her! The street so steep—off it went at increasing speed! The cripple waving his crutch, the mother screaming for help, and everybody else grinning—they might've been at the movies. Some moon-faced comedian of the silent screen about to go over a cliff. One knew it would end well. One was surprised when it didn't.

★

Two old friends talking about how some people look like animals. The bird-like wife of so and so, for example. The many breeds of dogs and their lookalikes. The one who is a cow. The one who is a tigress, etc. "And what about me?" says one to the other. "You look like a rat, Marshall," says my father to his friend, after which they just sit drinking without saying another word.

★

Driving around Pennsylvania, I came upon, what seemed, miles and miles of railroad yards. Old freight cars overgrown with weeds and no town nearby. Huge black clouds over them like those the coal engines used to leave in their wake.

★

The old bridegroom pisses in the bloody toilet bowl. The child bride studies the spots where he bit her tiny breasts. He likes the way the hairs curl on his thick, cigar-shaped pecker. With a blanket over her head, she pretends to be asleep. Luckily, on the street the fire-engines come shrieking. Somewhere the sky reddens in the pitchy, brain-chilling night. Overcoats thrown over their pajamas, the lovers of the tragedies crowd the streets to where a naked babe is being thrown out of a highrise window.

★

My mother heard a man plead for his life once. She remembered the stars, the dark shapes of trees along the road on which they were fleeing the Austrians in a slow-moving ox-cart. "That man was terribly frightened," she says. The cart went on. No one said anything. Soon they could hear the river. In the silence of the night they could hear the river they were supposed to cross.

★

You make summations to phantom juries, o bird, grand and solitary among the evening trees. The cloudy heavens with their pale palaces and columns for the children at the breast, rapt at the way the silence deepens despite your voice.

★

Guess-your-weight expert in a long-tailed red coat and a lion-tamer's hat. His prop a bathroom scale on the sidewalk. A giggly, long-legged girl is about to step on it to please her beau who wants to bet. The crowd of idlers nosing in for the outcome. The one in charge maintaining his grave deportment. Just like a dimestore sphinx!

★

I remember reading about a Baptist Minister somewhere in the Midwest using a homemade electric stool to shock little kids into listening to God's word. The stool was wired to a 12-volt battery and a wire screen was placed over the seat. The Reverend said he got the idea from a magazine. One kid complained it hurt till he came and took a bath. He said it was still fun with everybody laughing so much. His mother and father explained that there ain't much for the young ones to do around there on summer evenings.

★

N. ruminates. R. gorges himself. P. takes cat-naps. The plot thickens. Nadine barges in wearing only a bikini. She wants to know what they think of her. They think she ought to turn around, except for N. He continues to rack his brains, and raise his eyes piously to the ceiling from time to time.

★

I propose a supreme work of conceptual art. Shoot dictionaries into outer space. Then shoot some armchairs. One of each falls on one of the moon's deserts. We can see them through the telescope. The shadows lengthen as the lunar evening approaches. Now everybody close their eyes and think of the words and their definitions tucked in between the crimson covers for the long night.

★

The master and his idiot disciples are sharing a pitcher of beer. He smokes, and they take turns coughing. When the big-assed waitress approaches, he asks for some pretzels in such a way so that all can see his tongue is made of gold.

★

In a field next to the town dump, they ate picnic lunch, and then the heat made them take their clothes off.

There was an old tub thrown in the tall weeds where she went to sit and pretend to wash herself. He danced around her playing the beer bottle as if it were a goatherd's flute.

When some buzzard flew over them, she threw her head back so that her bare breasts rose in full sight above the rusty rim.

He was on the ground, looking for a thorn in his hairy foot, his cock standing stiff between his legs.

★

They read Emerson's essay "Nature" in the literature class of the local junior college, Jose and Felicia who thought of themselves as being madly in love. Their excuse was they were helping each other study the difficult text the night before the final exam, so they hid in an abandoned apartment. It was winter and it was cold there with all the windows broken. They used a flashlight to underline in red everything they thought important. On the stairs, someone very drunk was singing when he was not arguing with himself. Then, it got very late and very quiet. There were even a few stars visible from where they sat on the floor. "The universe is unimaginably big," said the instructor with a bad cough. The battery was dying. It was not easy to understand the stuff about nature being the symbol of the spirit. There were rats in the dark, but for now they were only listening, only stargazing like themselves.

CHARLES SIMIC

Charles the Obscure

Late one night, as the half-moon rode high above the church of St. Mark, I grabbed my balls passing a priest. This happened in Belgrade when I was twelve years old. I was skipping along without a care in the world when he came around the corner. He assumed I was about to greet him—he was even inclining his head benevolently—when I did what my friends advised me to do when meeting a priest. He stood there steaming in his cassock for a moment. Then, it was my turn to be surprised. Plump as he was, he went after me with extraordinary quickness, waving his arms about and shouting: "You little creep! You little son of a bitch!" His cussing terrified me even more than the chase he gave me. I ran without looking back.

At home the photographs of my great-great grandfathers and uncles awaited me on the living room walls. On my mother's side, I had several priests and one bishop in my ancestry. I've never seen in a wanted poster a more murderous collection of mugs. They had huge black-and-white beards that grew even sideways. Their eyes were bulging. The photographer must have warned them not to move and they obeyed. Flies crawled inside their ears during the long exposure. Their noses itched terribly. That evening their eyes followed me with unusual grimness. They all knew what I had done.

The meanest looking of the lot was my grandfather's father. It was public knowledge that his children hated him. My grandfather did not permit any mention of priests or religion in our house when he was around. When my grandmother died later that year, he informed the family that there will be no priest officiating in the cemetery chapel or at the gravesite. A scandal, people whispered. Everybody crossed themselves just thinking about it. A couple of aunts decided to disobey his wishes. The priest would appear at the gravesite while the coffin was being lowered, and my grandfather, so the theory went, would be too

---

From "Charles the Obscure" by Charles Simic, *New Letters* 60, no. 4 (summer 1994).

overwhelmed with grief and sorrow to object to a short prayer being said.

That's not what happened. Just as the gravediggers were fussing with the ropes, and the family and friends were standing with bowed heads, the priest materialized in his vestments, a prayer book in hand, already blessing us and mumbling a prayer. To everyone's astonishment, the old curmudgeon lunged at him. Before we had time to realize what was happening, grandpa had the priest by the scruff of the neck and was marching him away from the grave. As if that wasn't enough, one of my weeping aunts ran after them, grabbed the tails of grandfather's coat and started pulling him back. She had the strength of ten and so did he. A tug of war ensued and lots of yelling. The old man was trying to kick her without turning and letting the priest go. Unfortunately, my mother rushed me and my brother away before we could see and hear more.

★

If you were to ask anybody in my family if God exists, they would have given you a puzzled look. Of course he does, they'd reply. This meant, in practice, attending the church only to baptize, wed and bury someone. Bonafide atheists probably mention religion and God more frequently than my mother ever did. My father, however, was a different story. He didn't mind entering churches. Russian churches, Black churches, old Italian churches, austere New England churches, Byzantine churches, all that was admirable. The same is true of me. He liked the pomp and music, but even more he liked an empty church. I saw him a few times get down on his knees to pray, but he had no use for organized religion, or every other idea that has sought to take its place. As far as he was concerned, Communism and Fascism were visions of the nastiest aspects of Christianity. "All that orthodoxy, fanaticism, virtue by decree," he'd complain. They were all enemies of the individual, forever peddling intolerance and conformity. He had serious philosophical interest in Islam, Buddhism, Hinduism and Christianity, but no desire to join any congregation of the faithful. Belief in God was something private, like sex. If you did not believe in anything, as I often told him was the case with me, that was all right, too.

★

"Come on," she yanked my arm, "let's go. They're just a couple of hicks," she assured me, but I had to take a better look at the street preachers.

The young woman with thick glasses pressed a Bible to her heart; the horse-faced fellow by her side strummed a tuneless guitar at the edge of a large Saturday night crowd. They preached and sang hymns as if dogs were biting their asses.

My friend had enough. Without me noticing, she had split. I was left in custody of their Jesus who, by the sound of it, had too many lost sheep already to worry about. His great love always spurned—"Sweet Jesus," they hollered, trying to drown out an ambulance crying its heart out somewhere in the dark city beyond the brightly lit movie houses and penny arcades all around us.

Hell! I was deeply moved.

★

"Give me two wings to fly away!"

America is God crazy, as everyone knows. It's impossible to be an American writer without taking that into account.

Driving just after daybreak early one spring morning through West Virginia, I'm listening to the radio. Someone is playing scratchy old Black gospel records. The station is fading and coming clear in turn; the car is speeding down the empty road, and I'm wondering who is choosing the records so impeccably, so mysteriously, given the odd hour. Beyond the enjoyment, the emotion is gripping me, I have a sudden realization: They mean every word they say. Every word. They sing so beautifully, and so wildly, because they believe the Lord is in their midst right then and there.

It has always seemed obvious to me that we are alone in the universe. I love metaphysics and its speculations, but the suspicion at the core of my being is that we are whistling in the dark. Still, I have tears in my eyes every time I hear good church music. Never has the human heart been so pure, I think. Perhaps divinity can only be experienced by those who sing together? The God who comes or does not come to the solitaries is a different one.

"Without this mystery, the most incomprehensible of all, we are incomprehensible to ourselves," said Pascal, in a different context.

Sing and shout, Reverend! is my advice. Do that little dance step while the choir behind you sways and slaps its tambourines, and the old lady on the piano and the scrawny kid on the electric guitar nod to each other with approval. There's no doubt about it: "Except for music, everything is a lie," as Cioran says.

★

One day I finally admitted to myself that I'm hopelessly superstitious. You do not believe in God, I said to myself, so how come you believe in bad luck? I have no reply to that. Do we make our Fate, or is our Fate an independent agency? Calvin at least knew who arranged our destiny; I do not.

This head full of contradictions walking on two legs, is this the modern version of holy foolishness? Let's hope so.

In the meantime, the worries of a crumb overlooked on death's dinner plate. . . .

★

I was always attracted to mystical and esoteric doctrines that propose the unknowingness of the Supreme Being, the ineffability of the experience of His presence and the ambiguity of our human condition. Ambiguity, that great carnivore. If I believe in anything, it is in the dark night of the soul. Awe is my religion, and mystery is its church. I include here equally the mysteries of consciousness and the torments of conscience.

If not for conscience would we ever consider the possibility of the independent existence of evil? Nothing explains the world and the people in it. This is the knowledge that makes us fall down on our knees and listen to the silence of the night. Not even a dog or an owl is brave enough to interrupt it tonight. Being and nothingness, those two abstractions, how real, how close they feel. In such moments I want to reach for my chessboard. Let them play each other, and I'll sit and watch until the first streak of light slips under the door and crawls to my feet without waking the dust.

★

Many years ago, Vasko Popa took me to visit the women's monastery Mesic, near his hometown, Vrsac, on the Yugoslav-Rumanian border. We had a long lunch at a young poet's house and did not leave till five in the afternoon. I don't remember much about the drive, since we were talking a lot, interrupting each other with stories and jokes; but all of a sudden there was a high wall at the end of a dirt road and a closed iron gate. We left the car outside the gate and pushed it open just enough to squeeze through. What we found inside was a veritable jungle, as if the grass had not been cut all summer, and the trees had grown wild over the years without being trimmed and thinned out. We followed what was once a road, and now a narrow path in the twilight calm broken occasionally by the sound of a bird or a cricket. We did not speak. After a mile or so, we saw through the trees several large houses and a small Byzantine church. We walked to the largest of them, knocked, opened the door, peeked inside, even announced ourselves, but only silence came out to welcome us. It was so quiet, our steps became cautious. We walked on tiptoe on the way to the next house. Through the open door, we could see six nuns sitting in a circle with heads bowed. Vasko knew the name of the prioress and called out to her. She jumped, and the nuns followed after her in joy and delight to see him. The prioress who was old, Vasko had told me, used to be in her youth a lady in waiting at the royal court, and was exceptionally well educated. Vasko sent her French books. She was just reading Camus and immediately wanted to talk about him with us.

We were then given a tour by the prioress and a tall, skinny young nun. We visited the church, which was under repair, to see some surprisingly fine frescoes, and then slowly, because of the prioress' age, we climbed to the small graveyard above the church. The sun had just set. "I'll be soon resting here," the prioress told us, laughing. We smiled in reply. One could almost envy the prospect.

Then we were led back to the large house we had first come to. This we heard was one of the local bishop's many summer residences. He had not stayed in it for the last thirty years, but everything was kept in readiness for his arrival. We sat in a large living room with the prioress and the skinny nun drinking homemade brandy, while being sternly examined by former bishops in sooty old paintings. Only one table lamp had been lit. Vasko talked and so did the old woman, but the rustling of so many leaves muffled their voices, and then all of a sudden, there was complete silence. Here was peace of a world outside time, the kind one encounters at times in fairy-tale illustrations, in which a solitary child is seen entering a dark forest of gigantic trees.

After a while I listened only to the silence deepen, the night continue to hold its breath.

★

"Every poem, knowingly or unknowingly, is addressed to God," the poet Frank Samperi told me long ago. I remember being surprised, objecting, mentioning some awful contemporary poems . . . . We were filing subscription cards in the stock room of a photography magazine and having long philosophical conversations on the subject of poetry. Frank had been reading a lot of Dante, so I figured, that's it. He is stuck in fourteenth-century Italy.

No more. Today I think as he did then. It makes absolutely no difference whether gods and devils exist or not. The secret ambition of every true poem is to ask about them even as it acknowledges their absence.

BRUCE WEIGL

The Metaphysician in the Dark: An Interview

Bruce Weigl: How has the fact that you're an immigrant affected the way you see the world, especially as a writer? How has that immigrant point of view, that particular angle of vision, served you as a writer?

Charles Simic: Enormously, I'm sure. "Displaced Persons," they used to call us. Left their homelands because of war or tyranny. For Western Marxists we were traitors. They were building paradise on earth in Eastern Europe and we wanted nothing to do with it. So, right away, outcasts, people who depend on charity, who look different, speak the language with a heavy accent, etc. You learn not to take things for granted. "Where are we going to immigrate to next?" My father used to ask me. He was only half joking. Life is unpredictable. Anything can happen. . . . That's the historical and autobiographical context of my poetry.

BW: What does it mean to you who watched the German bombs fall in Belgrade when you were three years old, who learned English in Paris at the free night school classes, and who arrived in New York with not much more than your immigrant's bundle, what does it mean to you to be an American poet?

CS: It's fairly obvious I think. I have no choice. The Yugoslavs know I ain't one of them. The language I think and dream in is English. My favorite writers are Americans. I spent the last thirty-five years watching baseball on TV. I mean, this is the only place on earth where I feel at home. I have memories of the other life, but no nostalgias.

BW: What kind of relationship do you have with our language? How, since those early days of writing in Chicago, has that relationship changed?

From "The Metaphysician in the Dark: An Interview with Charles Simic" by Bruce Weigl, *American Poetry Review* 20 (September–October 1991).

CS: English is the language I know well and yet I speak it with an accent. I can't write or talk very well in Serbian. English, I have the impression, I still have to learn. I'm sure that native speakers don't have that much self-consciousness. Actually, it's hard for me to know. I write better and I'm more inside the language than I was twenty years ago, but perhaps that is to be expected of anyone who is a poet?

One thing I'm certain, though. When I was young and just starting to write in English, Serbian words would often come to mind and create difficulties. Now that never happens. All my verbal options are in English.

BW: Did your journey from Yugoslavia, a journey that eventually led you to New York, make you a poet? Did the experience of immigration somehow compel you to ask the kind of questions only poetry can answer?

CS: Probably. Who can tell? I knew guys with identical backgrounds who became engineers. On the other hand, the experience of immigration did compel me to ask and continue to ask certain questions about the twentieth-century history.

BW: Why, how did you begin to write poems? Can you recall making a conscious decision that writing poems was what you wanted to do, the way other people decide to be butchers or firemen or shirt salesmen?

CS: I started writing poetry because I caught a couple of my friends doing it. I wanted to show them that I can do it better. There were girls involved. I wanted to make an impression. It started me reading poetry in a big way. I found I liked it a lot. Everything I wrote, however, stunk. I couldn't figure out why. So I kept writing and reading and throwing things away, but I never said to myself, "I want to be a poet." I had no confidence in my abilities. I still don't.

BW: Back when you "caught a couple" of your friends writing poems and tried it yourself, what did you hear in your head that led you forward gradually into poetry?

CS: I am afraid I don't remember what poetry meant to me then precisely. I liked reading it. I had some vague notion that I could pour my heart into a poem and make myself and others cry. I also, I suppose, wanted to be amusing and clever. That's how I understood rhyme, anyway.

BW: How do you discover, or invent, whatever the case may be, the forms for your experience? the forms to contain the mythic imaginative regard you clearly have for the world, and for the self in collision with history?

CS: "Form is the extension of content," said Creeley, and Levertov changed it to "form is the revelation of content." I agree with them. So it's not *an invention*—something out of nothing—but a discovery of what is already there. In my experience (content) myth lurks, and so does history. Poetry is the archeology of the self. The bits and pieces one keeps digging up belong to the world—everybody's world. It's a paradox that has always amused me. Just when you think you're most subjective, you meet everybody else.

BW: How do you reconcile the larger forms of history and the litany of terrors (including those you witnessed as a child during the war in Yugoslavia) with the more exclusive forms that are art? In other words, why write poems in the late twentieth century?

CS: Already Hölderin asked the question: "And what are poets good for in a destitute time?" And Heidegger replies: "In the age of the world's night, the abyss of the world must be experienced and endured. But for this it is necessary that there be those who reach into the abyss." I continue to believe that poetry says more about the psychic life of an age than any other art. Poetry is a place where all the fundamental questions are asked about the human condition. As for our age, the world has never been a more complex place. God is dead, we say, but our TV preachers talk to him all the time. Such contradictions are everywhere. Our situation is impossible and therefore ideal for philosophers and poets.

BW: When you say that "poetry says more about the psychic life of an age than any other art," and that "poetry is a place where all the fundamental questions are asked about the human condition," it seems to me that here you're arguing for the utilitarian nature of poetry; is that true? If so, could you elaborate. For instance, if poetry can provide us with this wealth of significant information about a particular age, why doesn't poetry have more readers? Or are there enough readers?

CS: I see your point, but "utilitarian" has awful connotations. It's like those people who say that poetry is good therapy and recommend its practice for the mentally disturbed. I had something else in mind, actually. It seems pretty obvious to me: In great poetry one asks the fundamental questions about the human condition. It's hard to get far in reading or writing poetry without asking who am I and what does it all mean? Poetry is a way of knowledge. The words it uses are a mirror of the age in which it is being written. Each word a little mirror—a fun house mirror probably!

Now to the second part of your question as to why more people don't read poetry. I suppose for the same reasons more people don't read philosophy. Philosophy is important, was always important, but very few people in any age have read it. No point kidding ourselves! The human animal is lazy. Thinking is work and so is poetry—and by thinking I don't mean fiddling with a computer or scheming how to screw your neighbor. . . . You notice how all those imported Eastern philosophies, when they come to the West, reduce their theologies to the simplest possible terms? A two-word mantra and off you go! That's all you need, kid! Imagine if someone actually tried to make them study the great Hindu and Buddhist philosophers and poets?

I think poetry has enough readers.

BW: You also said that "our situation is impossible and therefore ideal for philosophers and poets," and once, many years ago when I was your student, I remember you saying (this stayed with me) that when I realized the impossibility of writing poems, then I would begin to write. Could you elaborate on both of these points? Why does this impossibility, in both cases, nurture poetry? How? Can you give me some examples of what you mean here from your own work or from the work of others?

CS: Well, to think otherwise would be sheer vanity. The actual situation is this: one "superfluous human being," as they used to say in the nineteenth-century Russian literature, in the midst of all and everything—the humankind, history, literature, the infinite universe—is attempting to talk back in a dozen or so lines of poetry. No wonder people say the poets are nuts! The world so big and the poem so teeny. And yet—it's been done! The history of literature is full of examples: The impossible is possible.

Remember Dickinson's:

> and I alone —
> A Speck upon a Ball
> Went out upon Circumference —
> Beyond the Dip of Bell.

And she didn't even know—although she suspected—the unimaginable hugeness of the known universe. . . . That's the part I love: it's "known" but it cannot be imagined. . . . Anyway, once I remember myself, once I savor the full implication of my predicament, words come out of the astonishment—the comic astonishment! The long sequence *White* is written in that spirit. Many other poems too, I'm sure.

BW: You once said that the difference between Milosz and most American poets is that when Milosz sees a tree, he knows it can also be used to hang people. Are you suggesting that because of Milosz's experience with confronting the brute facts of history directly—his experience in Poland of course—he has insights into things that distinguish him from our recent American poets? Do you think that your particular experience, your memory of the Nazis in Belgrade, or the American bombers overhead, and what that experience did in terms of shaping your imagination, your personality, also distinguishes you from your contemporaries? Clearly you stand apart from all other contemporary American poets for more than just stylistic reasons; I'm trying here to get at the reasons for that.

CS: I've been asked repeatedly about that, and if I give a slightly different answer each time, it's because I'm still thinking about it and finding new angles. Sure my childhood in Yugoslavia during the war was decisive, but that's not the whole story. There has been plenty of history since then to make me what I am. The Vietnam War, for example, had a tremendous impact on me. I was in active Army reserve during the early days—was almost called in. My brother ended up there. I walked the streets of New York scared shitless, and I thought about my childhood. That war reminded me of that other war—actually the Civil War in Yugoslavia in the years 1941–1945. Even today when I read about Lebanon, I have a pretty good idea what that's like. So, the subject is constantly on my mind, and that gets into the poetry in various ways.

Let's put it this way. I'm a culinary mixture. My soul-stew was made of various ingredients. It's murky down there in the pot. I can't see all that's there, but I lick my plate clean every day.

BW: With regard to a question Rod Santos asked you in an interview about the comic element in your work you said, "More likely my situation is comic. It's 'the amazement of the thinking spirit at itself' and its predicament—or so said Schlegel. One just has to laugh at the extent of our stupidity." I'm also interested in the comic element throughout your work, especially in the earlier books. Is it fair to describe that element as "grotesque"—as in Baudelaire's "grotesque laughter?" or ironic? What is it specifically about the way you regard the world that allows this element to find its way so often into the poems?

CS: Horace Walpole said: "The world is a comedy for those that think, a tragedy to those that feel." Since we are capable of both, I can't conceive of literature which excludes one or the other. If I have an ambition in poetry, and a dream, it is to write a great comic poem.

The suffering of the innocent is, of course, tragic, but as for the rest—it's pretty funny. Look at most of our leaders in political and intellectual life with their vanity, gullibility, greed, malice—they could be stock characters out of classical comedy. The genius of comedy—it seems to me—is in the profound insight that dopiness is at the heart of much human activity. For instance, so many of the participants in the so-called Irangate matter strike me as complete fools. They are the same guys who are eternally buying the Brooklyn Bridge or those wonderful tenderloin steak mines in Colorado that W. C. Fields purchased in that movie.

As for the grotesque—the word doesn't mean a hell of a lot to me. In fact, I don't care for it. One thinks of the fantastic, the gratuitously exaggerated. My poems seem "grotesque" because I like to juxtapose high and low, the sacred and the profane, as they call it, but not because I'm trying to create an effect. I just think the world is like that.

BW: I want to shift gears here a bit and move from questions of style and theme to questions of form. There has been much talk lately, and I would refer specifically to an article in *The Hudson*

Review by Dana Gioia, about the so-called "new formalism." In most of this talk, critics point to several younger poets who write in traditional forms and argue that the return to these forms might be a response to the so-called "formlessness" of free verse. What are your feelings about this "new formalism?"

CS: Well, their ideas of prosody sound like they're coming from Victorian school books—or perhaps cookbooks? Bring back the old cookie cutters, etc. What is it that Sidney says in *Apology?* "One may be a poet without versing, and a versifier without poetry."

It's plain to me that the prosody of Pound and Williams, and of their followers is more subtle and beautiful than that of someone like Yvor Winters. Winters knew the history of English prosody, but his dream was to sound like an Elizabethan.

My point is that a lot of thinking has been done on the subject of prosody by some of our best twentieth century poets, but there's not much evidence that the "new formalists" have read any of it.

BW: I know that you're a poet who has always been concerned with the nature of the line in poetry, traditionally formal or otherwise, so I wondered if you'd talk a bit about the elements of form in your own work?

What are you concerned about with regard to the formal elements of the line? the stanza? the poem as a whole? And what is the relationship between your formal tendencies and what you're trying to say in the poem?

CS: Valéry says something like: "We understand each other only as a result of the speed with which we pass over words." Pound speaks of verse consisting of a variation and constant. Frost says that there are basically two meters in English, iambic and loose iambic. All these make sense to me. Line is the place where we make music and direct attention.

I also believe in Creeley's "form is the extension of content," and Stevens emphasizing that "the essential thing in form is to be free in whatever form is used. . . ."

There are a lot of such (seeming) contradictions in poetry. I always felt poetry is made half-way between speech and song. It's a question of nuances, of course, and it depends on how you hear the poem. Do you want it spoken, declaimed, intoned, or sung?

Duration, symmetry, their interruptions; the ear and the eye working together; the exactness of utterance; the poet measuring by the means of words—is what I think prosody is about.

BW: What do you believe the relationship is between what goes on, generally speaking, in the free verse tradition, and what came before in a more traditionally formal (accentual/syllabic) tradition?

CS: No good verse, as it has been said is free. "If number, measure and weighing be taken away from any art, that which remains will not be much." I think Plato said that. The prosody of the best of the moderns is an extension, a series of innovations and discoveries about recurrence and duration. It doesn't replace anything. At its best, it incorporates the whole poetic practice since the Greeks and Romans.

BW: Charles O. Hartman, in his book *Free Verse: An Essay on Prosody,* writes that "to perform its basic function prosody does not require meter." In this relatively simple statement there is contained, I believe, an important distinction that those who detract from free verse or open forms fail to recognize: that prosody and meter are two distinctly different things. What, in your mind, does prosody consist of?

CS: Prosody is a range of options. It is both tradition and deviation from. It has to do with language attempting to recover experience. The history of prosody writes the poem. Your mother tongue writes the poem. Still, meter is not always necessary. Think of prose poems! There's no question there's such a thing. I think the distinction I made before applies. Prose poems are spoken in a certain way, not sung.

BW: It seems to me that the free verse tradition can roughly be divided into two distinct categories: narrative and lyrical. Conversely, Norman Dubie once wrote that there is also a poetry of our time that can be called "lyrical/narrative." If we think of lyricism as the kind of poetry that is brief, subjective, marked by a highly imaginative regard for the world, concerned with melody and emotion, and creating for the reader a single, unified impression, I'd say it's fair to describe your work generally as lyrical. However, now that we have your autobiographical statement in *Antaeus,* we can go back to those elusive poems and see that you were actually referring, and often, to your own experiences, only in more oblique ways than most of the rest of the poets of your generation. The question then is this: how would you describe your poetry? and how do you manage to combine the elements of the narrative with the elements of the lyrical in your work?

CS: The best way I know, I guess. I like the conciseness of the lyric and I like to tell stories—an impossible situation! Brevity has always impressed me! A few striking images, and goodbye! I've learned a great deal from symbolist poets as well as from blues singers. How to say everything with the minimum of words is my ideal. I know it's possible—and every time it happens I think it's a miracle, but I couldn't draw you a road map as to how I got there.

BW: Hartman also writes that "free verse required, and implies, a new awareness of prosody as part of the communication a poem offers to its readers. . . ." I hate that word "communication," but I think I know what he means here. A formally metrical/numerical poem means in a very specific way, setting up certain expectations in the readers' mind. How is that different in a free verse poem? and how does a free verse poem accomplish what more traditional forms accomplish in the effect of their metrical patterns?

CS: I heard something the first time I read Williams' *Asphodel,* but it took me years to fully understand what was happening.

People often say that free verse is unmusical, but I think the problem we are talking about, really, has to do with music. As you know, there are trained musicians who play classical music with distinction but who cannot hear anything in modern music—or God forbid, jazz! It's very puzzling, and I don't know why that is.

BW: I know you're a serious fan of blues and jazz, that you've listened to this music for many, many years, that you have an extensive collection of this music and that you see in it a regard for the world that you seem to aspire to as a poet.

Could you talk about first, what it is in this music that interests you not only as a fan of the blues, but as a poet?

And secondly, could you talk about why, if this music means so much to you does it have such an abstract effect upon the poems? Or does it? There are others to whom jazz and black American music was important poetically—Leroi Jones for one, Michael Harper more recently, but they allude to the music in much more overt ways. They recall the names and the faces of jazz. You seem to be after something different; what is it?

CS: Well, I'm also serious about classical music. I drove a couple of my early girlfriends away with my love of Mozart. There's no point intellectualizing this. I listen to music because I love music. I grew up with all kinds of music including jazz. Would I give up my poetry if I could play tenor sax like Ben Webster? It's a tough choice. There's a largeness of soul in the best of jazz. It's full of life, recklessness, intuition, humor, sense of form, drama—all things I admire.

Blues is the finest example of native lyricism we have. How are you going to write a lyric poem if you don't know the blues or some fine old country song? That's why so much recent poetry is so prosy. No sense of the song.

Of course, describing the experience of listening to jazz is not easy. What usually happens in poems is that one names the musicians and the reader is supposed to dig it. Like I say "Bird," and you say "oh yeah!" The point is how to appropriate some of the manner of jazz and blues, etc. But even there one can only go so far. There's a difference. Poetry is not music.

BW: You have also been a painter in your lifetime so far, and spent time hanging out in New York with some early abstract expressionists, and the drawings that accompany the long poem *White* are of course yours, so I wanted to hear what you had to say about the relationship between painting and poetry. What do they have in common? what can painting teach you about being a poet? etc.?

CS: You learn how to look. Ordinarily we see very little. Paying attention is very difficult. Drawing is a tremendous discipline. People tell me my poetry is very visual, full of images. It's through painting that I got introduced to modern art. First in Oak Park Public Library, and then in the Chicago Public Library. I read all those books on Impressionism, Cubism, Expressionism, etc. That's how I discovered Surrealism, Dada. You couldn't find that kind of information if you read *Kenyon Review*. The world literary quarterlies struck me as terribly boring in comparison. Poets should know everything, and painting is one of the most beautiful things in the world.

BW: So, you're a serious student of music of all kinds but especially the only truly American music, blues and jazz, you were a painter at a particularly interesting and exciting time in American painting in the last fifty years, you are widely read in philosophy and know more about Heidegger than most guys teaching graduate seminars on the stuff, and you also have a gift for reading in other languages, especially French, and you end up, of all things, writing poems. What is it about poetry that allows you, or forces you to choose it above a life of music, or painting, for example?

CS: There was never any choice. I can't really draw. I can't think, and I certainly can't play a musical instrument. Some critics would also say that I can't write poetry. If someone told me when I was twenty that I was going to write and publish many poems, I would have thought they were nuts. I wrote poetry already, but I also played basketball. I mean, it would've been like someone telling me you'll be in the NBA someday! It's a complete mystery to me how it all happened. So, there's no poetry "allowing" anything. I do it because I have to, and because I can never get it right.

BW: Earlier you alluded to Dickinson, and I know you admire in her poems their compactness and their simultaneous ability to suggest the whole universe, and you said that that sense of awe displayed in Dickinson where "words come out of astonishment" was something you tried for in the long poem *White*. Could you elaborate? What is it exactly about Dickinson that you hear? And could you talk more about *White*? What were your trying to do there formally and conceptually that Dickinson could help you with?

CS: Dickinson intuited that a poet is a "metaphysician in the dark," to use Steven's phrase. Her metaphors point to cosmologies. Her universe is ultimately empty. To think that way is both exhilarating and frightening. *White* is an attempt to think the limits of the imagination through metaphors. Dickinson does that. She wasn't the only one I had in mind, though. Frost, Melville, Hawthorne, Stevens are there too. I'm always talking to them.

BW: I'd like to talk a little more about music. In his enigmatic "Ars Poetica," Milosz writes that "The purpose of poetry is to show ourselves how difficult it is to remain one person," or something like that. And though I can't articulate it, I have a strong sense of what he means by that. What is the purpose of the blues? how is that purpose similar to the purpose of poetry?

CS: I don't like the word "purpose." It implies intention, desired result, etc. And I'm not sure what Milosz means. My old hero Breton used to put it much better: "Poetry is made in bed like love, " he said.

As for the blues, it exists because people sing. Everywhere in the world people sing. If they're oppressed, they sing even better. In the upper classes, as you know, it's not polite to whistle or hum. The houses of the rich are very quiet. The poor, on the other hand, are either hollering at each other, or blasting the radio and singing. If people didn't sing in showers, there'd be no poetry either.

BW: You don't like the word "purpose" for the way it implies "intention, desired result, etc." However, your poetry, especially as we move into the work of the last six years or so, seems absolutely intent on changing the way the reader sees the world. You have a fix on the reader, a design on the reader. Isn't that Wordsworth's "worthy purpose," and Shelley's utilitarian poetry?

CS: Design is a better word. It brings out the contriving aspect of it, "the splendid insincerity" that Nabokov claimed guided the makers of chess problems. You have a chessboard on which only a few figures are left and are told "the white mates in two moves." Impossible, you say! When you solve the problem six months later, you are astonished by the ingenuity, the sneakiness, the elegance, the beauty of it! All this is very far from "worthy purpose."

BW: You said that the "point is how to appropriate some of the manner of jazz and blues, etc. . . . But even there one can only go so far." And of course you're talking about appropriating the manner of jazz and blues into poetry. I may be thick skinned, but I don't understand what you mean by that. What is it that can be taken, or borrowed, or learned from jazz and blues that can help you as a poet?

CS: It's hard to talk about one art in terms of another, so my answer will be a little approximate. First, I like the sensibility of the blues singer, the way he or she experiences this country. I'm interested in what they see, and how they put it together. I admire their brevity, their purity of heart. So much world, and so few words and notes. . . . A tough look at life. No slobbering, no self-pity.

Jazz is much more varied and much more complex musically. There are so many different kinds of jazz—it's hard to generalize and do justice to such a vast range. Let's just say you take someone like Lester Young, his immaculate sense of phrasing and time. The way he falls behind the beat, the way he constructs a solo, etc. It's all a matter of exquisite sense of form. Plenty to learn there.

BW: It's occurred to me, in trying to think about free verse and the forms of free verse, and in trying to teach this stuff, that free verse is to poetry, to the traditions of poetry that have come before us, what jazz is to music, especially with regard to the expansive and inclusive forms of each. Does that make any sense? Is that an analogy that can lead us anywhere interesting?

CS: I suppose so, but I wouldn't extend the analogy. As I said earlier, it's dangerous to make comparisons between the arts. You think you're saying something insightful about identities while you're really ignoring vast differences.

BW: It seems to me that very often narrative is not a significant aspect of the blues, that often in old blues songs, what is at work is something different than narrative (as in popular music say), something that has more in common with lyric poetry than with other forms of music in terms of a lyrical juxtaposition of the tragic with the comic; does that make sense to you? is that perhaps what draws you to the Blues? that view of our lives?

CS: Yes, yes! The tragic and comic under the same roof. They'll accompany the most tongue-in-cheek verses with a mournful tune, or vice verse: The words are tragic but the tune is a dance. I love that! A lot of folk music does that, though not in every culture. I know people get upset when there's too much mixing up of the two. They want either one or the other. Mixing tragedy and comedy is a great transgression in their view. Serious art is very serious. Well, I don't think it needs to be.

BW: I want to jump back here for a moment to something else you said about Dickinson. You said that "Dickinson intuited that a poet is a 'metaphysician in the dark,' to use Stevens's phrase. Her metaphors point to cosmologies. Her universe is ultimately empty." I'm particularly struck by that last statement, that her universe is ultimately empty because I have that same sense reading much of your poetry, especially reading your selected poems chronologically; the sense that you begin with an empty universe then gradually and with great care begin to people that universe with the archetypal characters of your imagination, and you begin to furnish that universe with an oddly mythical cityscape. Could you respond here, or am I out in left field?

CS: Like God—says the unbeliever—I always wanted to start from scratch. First the stones, roaches, and maggots, and then the bare-assed Adam and Eve. Actually, I had no idea the poems would turn out that way. Like so many twentieth century sceptics I wanted to reconstitute everything, to reexamine my and everybody else's view of things. The rest just followed.

BW: In a recent essay, "Reading Philosophy at Night," you wrote the following: "Whoever reads philosophy reads himself as much as he reads the philosopher. I am in a dialogue with certain decisive events in my life as much as I am with the ideas on the page. Meaning is a matter of my existence. My effort to understand is a perpetual circling around a few obsessive images. . . ." I want to try to link what you say here with a discussion of biographical references in your poetry.

This is not an interesting question when it comes to most contemporary poetry because the free verse tradition seems to nurture self-referential poetry, seems to too easily invite autobiographical references; of course sometimes that's interesting, and sometimes it's not. But in reading over a hundred reviews and essays about your work, it's become clear that most critics have been unable or unwilling to discuss these elements. The obvious reason for that reluctance or inability, seems to me, to have something to do with the indirect, mysterious way you bring these elements into your poems. This is not as complicated a question as I'm making it. What are those "few obsessive images," that you perpetually circle around?

CS: It's not just me. It's the rule. Every poet, every writer is obsessed and returns again and again to a few, decisive images.

For example, I talk about people hanging from telephone poles because I once saw people hanging from telephone poles. I'm still amazed that I actually saw them, that it was a nice day, that one of the executed had a shoe missing. I can spend the rest of my life thinking about that, and of a few other things that made an equally powerful impression on me. However, I've tried to write poems which would not depend on the reader knowing about my past. I want to make a poem, not talk about my life.

BW: In another essay, your long autobiographical piece that *Antaeus* published last year, you speak in very candid, very direct and personal ways about your life. I don't remember you ever doing that before in print. And your most recent collection, *Unending Blues,* is the most obviously personally referential book you've written. Have poems become more directly autobiographical, or have we simply finally learned how to read them?

CS: Yes and no. They *sound* more autobiographical. They're certainly based on things I did, but I'm far more interested in the fiction. The "I" is many fictions. The object is always "truth," but not the literal one.

Emerson says: "There's properly no history, only biography." I see what he's getting at, but I think it's not that clear-cut. There's History too, independent of my life and your life. I'm more interested in history than in autobiography.

BW: What surprises me, confuses me at times, baffles even me about your writing on philosophy is the way in which you always manage to infuse a concrete, physical ontōlogy side by side with the conceptual one. In one sentence you're quoting Wittgenstein on the nature of how things are in the world, and how mystical it is that the world exists, and in the next sentence you're talking about some pebbles that you'd looked at as a child lying in a ditch, the German bombers flying overhead. How does philosophy become graspable to you? How do you get inside of it?

CS: It's very simple, really. You're reading Plato and your back itches. You're reading Wittgenstein and the smell of the bean soup your wife is making in the kitchen comes to distract you . . . In the midst of a very difficult passage that requires all of your concentration, you catch yourself thinking: "Did she put smoked sausage in it, or is it something else I'm smelling?"

I was always aware of the comic aspect of it. The way one is many things at the same time. As I tried to say in that essay, philosophy begins to make sense to me when it includes its opposite. In other words, no Plato without scratching. That's the human condition.

BW: You also say that in philosophy (and in poetry and history as well) you see, "in the sense of being able to picture and feel the human weight of another's solitude. . . ." What is it specifically about philosophy that allows you this special seeing?

CS: Because the one who thinks is alone. The greater the thinker the greater his solitude. What poetry brings to philosophy is, of course, imagination. Poetry imagines the place and the circumstances in which the thinker thinks. In that sense poetry is a kind of seeing too. It sees how it feels to be thinking the supreme thoughts about the nature of things.

BW: How *does* it feel to think those supreme thoughts?

CS: It feels good. This is all I ever wanted to do.

BW: Now I want to get back to some further discussion of the so-called New Formalists. Since we last talked about this, several months ago actually, a great deal more rhetoric about new formalism has filled the air. A magazine called *Crosscurrents* devoted an entire issue to the poetry and critical thought of this group of poets; there also have been several more defenses, or explanations of the new formalism published in magazines, and here I'm thinking especially about Paul Lake's essay in the *AWP Newsletter* called "Toward a Liberal Poetics: Thoughts on the New Formalism." What do you think is the real basis for this movement, if we can call it that, in American poetry?

CS: Lack of talent. The poems in that issue of *Crosscurrents* are embarrassing. If these people could write as well as Merrill and Wilbur, I would take them more seriously. But when you have third-rate poetry accompanied by pronouncements on form and free verse that are totally ignorant—what is one to say? It's a fool's paradise.

You note these people never talk about imagination. They are perfectly happy—as their poems show—to recycle the same old tropes providing they rhyme. Rhymed platitudes—that's their ideal. Timothy Steele is the only one who is an exception in that group.

BW: Do you think that the free verse tradition has contributed to a kind of artistic collapse in our poetry? That the loosening or opening up of form has led us into a solipsistic abyss?

CS: Of course. All the bad things in the twentieth century are to be attributed to free verse. It's all the fault of W. C. Williams, as Bruce Bawer pointed out in a recent *New Criterion.* If only Williams and Pound had imitated Tennyson, sons would still call their fathers "Sir." We would still have THE GREAT WESTERN VALUES and the Modern Poetry would never have happened.

Look! Most free verse being written today is lousy. That's the way it is. There's very little good poetry written in any age. At the same time, most people who complain about free verse don't have a clue as to what it really is. The older I get the more I realize that most things written about literature and the other arts are complete nonsense.

BW: There are those on both sides of this issue who would argue that the matter at hand is a political one; Wayne Dodd recently called formal poets the "Reaganites of poetry," for example. Do you attach any political significance to an argument for a return to traditional formalism?

CS: I don't, but they do. People like this guy Bawer are always making connections with an armed squad at his side and at his command going with a red pencil through one of our poems.

BW: It seems to me, inherent in the manifestos that have been coming out of the new formalists' camp, or, the "expansionists" as they now call themselves, is a not so subtle suggestion that we should also return to the "New Criticism." They obviously haven't embraced the French critics, and conversely, they argue that they want to move away from what they see as a too impressionistic criticism associated with free verse. Any thoughts on this?

CS: I don't think New Criticism is a problem. I like much of it for the seriousness with which they approached poetry. Ransom and Warren have major limitations, but they also have wise things to say. The poems in *Crosscurrents* wouldn't fare very well in a close reading.

Again, there's so much intellectual laziness. We've talked about the excellence of Charles O. Hartman's book on free verse before. It's been out for a number of years. Does anybody pay attention to it? Of course not. Even if there were a dozen works explicating the tradition of free verse, they would still be ignored, because that simple-minded notion of form and tradition has a deep appeal for someone who truly, when all is said and done, doesn't really understand what poetry is.

BRIAN C. AVERY

A Simic Bibliography

My thanks to Charles Simic, Bruce Weigl, and Charles Seluzicki for their help in compiling this list.

Works by Charles Simic

What the Grass Says. San Francisco: Kayak, 1967.

Somewhere among Us a Stone Is Taking Notes. Kayak, 1969.

Dismantling the Silence. New York: Braziller, 1971. "With a note by Richard Howard."

White. New York: New Rivers Press, 1972.

"Where the Levels Meet: An Interview with Charles Simic." *Ohio Review* 14, no. 2 (winter 1973): 49–58.

Return to a Place Lit by a Glass of Milk. New York: Braziller, 1974.

"A Conversation." Interview by George Starbuck. *Ploughshares* 2, no. 3 (1975): 78–91.

Biography and a Lament, Poems 1961–1967. Hartford, Conn.: Bartholomew's Cobble, 1976.

Charon's Cosmology. New York: Braziller, 1977.

" 'Moments Worth Preserving and Playing Again': An Interview with Charles Simic." Interview by Rod Steier. *Manassas Review: Essays on Contemporary American Poetry, Charles Simic* 1, no. 2 (winter 1978): 11–15.

Classic Ballroom Dances. New York: Braziller, 1980.

White. Durango, Colo.: Logbridge-Rhodes Press, 1980.

Austerities. New York: Braziller, 1982.

Weather Forecast for Utopia and Vicinity, Poems 1967–1982. Barrytown, N.Y.: Station Hill Press, 1983.

"An Interview with Charles Simic." Interview by Sherod Santos. *Missouri Review* 7, no. 3 (1984): 61–74.

Selected Poems, 1963–1983. New York: Braziller, 1985.

The Uncertain Certainty: Interviews, Essays, and Notes on Poetry. Ann Arbor: University of Michigan Press, 1985.

Unending Blues. San Diego: Harcourt Brace, 1986.

"Between the Languages: An Interview with Charles Simic." Interview by Nina Zivancevic. *Poetry Flash*, October 1987, 1.

The World Doesn't End. San Diego: Harcourt Brace, 1989.

The Book of Gods and Devils. San Diego: Harcourt Brace, 1990.

Selected Poems, 1963–1983: Revised and Expanded. New York: Braziller, 1990.

Wonderful Words, Silent Truth: Essays on Poetry and a Memoir. Ann Arbor: University of Michigan Press, 1990.
"*The Metaphysician in the Dark*: An Interview with Bruce Weigl." *American Poetry Review* 20, no. 5 (September–October 1991): 5–13.
Dime-Store Alchemy: The Art of Joseph Cornell. Hopewell, N.J.: Ecco, 1992.
Hotel Insomnia. San Diego: Harcourt Brace, 1992.
"A Conversation." *Another Chicago Magazine* 26 (1993): 187–95.
"Charles the Obscure." *New Letters* 60, no. 4 (summer 1994): 21–27.
The Unemployed Fortune-Teller: Essays and Memoirs. Ann Arbor: University of Michigan Press, 1994.
A Wedding in Hell. New York: Harcourt Brace, 1994.

Works about Charles Simic

Ackerson, Duane. Review of *What the Grass Says. Dragonfly* 2 (summer 1969): 30–32.
Allen, Frank. Review of *The World Doesn't End. Library Journal* 114 (March 15, 1989), 74.
Allen, Frank. Review of *Unending Blues. Library Journal* 111 (December 1986): 116.
Altieri, Charles. "From Experience to Discourse: American Poetry and Poeticism in the Seventies." *Contemporary Literature* 21 (spring 1980): 191–222.
Atlas, James. "Autobiography of the Present." Review of *Return to a Place Lit by a Glass of Milk. Poetry* 125 (February 1975): 295–302.
Atwan, Robert. *"Unending Blues." Los Angeles Times Book Review,* 7 December 1986, 8.
Balakian, Anna. *Surrealism: The Road to the Absolute.* Rev. ed. New York: Dutton, 1970. Pp. 25–26.
Balakian, Peter. "The Trauma of Memory." Review of *Classic Ballroom Dances. American Book Review* 4 (July 1982): 2.
Bedient, Calvin. "Burning Alone." Review of *Selected Poems. Sewanee Review* 94 (fall 1986): 657–68.
Behm, Richard H. "A Study of the Function of Myth in the Work of Four Contemporary Poets: Charles Simic, Galway Kinnell, Gary Snyder, and Robert Duncan." Ph.D. diss., Bowling Green University, 1976.
Benedikt, Michael. "Critic of the Month." Review of *What the Grass Says. Poetry* 113 (December 1968): 188–215.
Bennett, Bruce. "Poems Magical, Poems Mordant." Review of *Austerities. Nation,* 12 March 1983, 314–15.
Berman, Paul. "Brief Encounters." Review of *Weather Forecast for Utopia and Vicinity. Village Voice,* 28 February 1984, 46.
Bizzaro, Patrick, ed. *Manassas Review: Essays on Contemporary American Poetry, Charles Simic* 1, no. 2 (winter 1978). Includes:
    Allen, Dick. "The Poet's Descent and Crossing: *Charon's Cosmology.*" Pp. 55–61.
    Barwell, Jay. "Charles Simic: Visions of Solitude." Pp. 33–44.
    Biographical note. P. 5.

Bizzaro, Patrick. " 'I Am Whatever Beast Inhabits Me': Introduction for Charles Simic." P. 7.
"Charles Simic: Bibliography." Pp. 63–67.
Gallo, Louis. "The Cosmos according to Charon: Simic's New Book." Pp. 49–53.
Johnson, Joyce. "The Flight from the Familiar: *Biography and a Lament* and *Dismantling the Silence*." Pp. 17–23.
Robson, Deborah. "Some Experiments in Alchemy." Pp. 25–31.
Smith, Arthur. "Definitions." Pp. 45–47.
[Steier, Rod]. " 'Moments Worth Preserving and Playing Again': An Interview with Charles Simic." Pp. 11–15.

Blazek, Doug. "Anti Matter! Small Presses." Review of *What the Grass Says*. *Nola Express*, 6–19 February 1970, 3.

———" 'I Was Out after That Speck Which Imbeds Itself in Each Moment We Live.' " Review of *Somewhere Among Us a Stone Is Taking Notes*. *Book Review* 13 (August 1970): 7.

Bond, Bruce. "Immanent Distance: Silence and the Poetry of Charles Simic." *Mid-American Review* 8, no. 1 (1988): 89–96.

Breslin, Paul. "How to Read the New Contemporary Poem." *American Scholar* 47 (summer 1978): 357–70.

Bromwich, David. "Book Reviews." Review of *Return to a Place Lit by a Glass of Milk*. *Georgia Review* 30 (winter 1976): 1021.

Carruth, Hayden. "Here Today: A Poetry Chronicle." Review of *Dismantling the Silence*. *Hudson Review* 24 (summer 1971): 320–35.

Charles, John W. Review of *Dismantling the Silence*. *Library Journal* 95 (1 April 1971): 1273.

"Charles Simic: Poems and Comment." *Ironwood 7/8* 4, nos. 1–2 (1976). Includes:
Carpenter, James K. "Charles Simic: *White*." Pp. 72–84.
Walker, David: "O What Solitude." Pp. 61–67.

Christensen, Paul. "Charles Simic." In *Contemporary Poets*, ed. James Vinson and D. L. Kirkpatrick, 782–83. New York: St. Martin's, 1985.

Cole, William. "Trade Winds." Review of *Return to a Place Lit by a Glass of Milk*. *S/R World* 23 (March 1974): 43.

Contoski, Victor. "At the Stone's Heart." Review of *Dismantling the Silence*. *Modern Poetry Studies* 2 (1971): 236–40.

———. "Charles Simic: Language at the Stone's Heart." *Chicago Review* 28, no. 4 (spring 1977): 145–57.

———. Review of *What the Grass Says*. *New American and Canadian Poetry* 5 (December 1967): 41–43.

———. Review of *White*. *Quixote* 8, no. 3 (March 1974): 22–23.

———. *"Somewhere Among Us a Stone Is Taking Notes." New American and Canadian Poetry* 15 (December 1971): 23–36.

Cooley, Peter. "Self-Reflections." Review of *Return to a Place Lit by a Glass of Milk*. *North American Review* 259, no. 3 (fall 1974): 70–71.

[Cramer, Hilton.] "Notes and Comments: A Pulitzer for—What?" *New Criterion* 8, no. 10 (June 1990): 1–2.

Crenshaw, Brad. "Charles Simic." *Critical Survey of Poetry, English Language Series*. Ed. Frank N. Magill. 6 vols. Inglewood Cliffs, N.J.: Salem Press, 1982: 2590–98.

Czubakowski, Janusz. "*Dismantling the Silence*." *Women's Wear Daily*, 26 January 1971, 12.

D[acey], Philip. Review of *Dismantling the Silence* and *White*. *Crazy Horse* 11 (summer 1972): 27.
Davison, Peter. "Poets of Exile and Isolation." Review of *Selected Poems*. *Book World (Washington Post)*, 13 April 1986, 6–7.
Dobyns, Steven. "Some Happy Moments, Some Very Tall Language." Review of *Unending Blues*. *New York Times Book Review*, 18 October 1987, 46.
Economou, George. Review of *Weather Forecast for Utopia and Vicinity*. *World Literature Today* 58 (autumn 1984): 609–10.
Elledge, Jim. Review of *The World Doesn't End*. *Booklist* 85 (1 March 1989): 1087.
F.W. Review of *Classic Ballroom Dances*. *Mid-American Review* 1, no. 1 (1981): 186–88.
Fenza, D. W. "News and Views: Totally Miffed about the Pulitzer." *Associated Writing Programs Chronicle* 23, no. 1 (September 1990): 21–22.
Flamm, Matthew. "Impersonal Best: Charles Simic Loses Himself." *Village Voice Literary Supplement*, December 1986, 18–19.
Foucherau, Serge. "La nouvelle subjectivité." *Lettres Nouvelles (Mercure de France)*, December 1970–January 1971, 159–62.
Funsten, Kenneth. Review of *Selected Poems*. *Los Angeles Times Book Review*, 16 March 1986, 9.
Goldensohn, Lorrie. "Love's Progress: Women, Sex, and Poetry in the Seventies." *Agni Review* 10–11 (1979): 222–42.
Guimond, James. "Moving Heaven and Earth." Review of *White*. *Parnassus: Poetry in Review* 1 (fall–winter 1972): 114–15.
Hart, Henry. "Story-tellers, Myth-makers, Truth-sayers." Review of *The Book of Gods and Devils*. *New England Review* (Middlebury, Vt.) 15, no. 4 (fall 1993): 192–206.
Hart, Kevin. "Writing Things: Literary Property in Heidegger and Simic." *New Literary History* 21 (autumn 1989): 199–214.
Ha[zo], S[amuel]. "Literature: American Poetry." *Britannica Book of the Year, 1972*. Encyclopedia Britannica, 1972: 427–28.
Heilker, Paul. "Rehabilitating the Essay: An Alternative Form for Composition Instruction." Ph.D. diss., Texas Christian University, 1992.
Hildebrand, Tim. *"Somewhere Among Us a Stone Is Taking Notes." Mandala* 6 (1971): 55–56.
Hitchcock, George. "A Gathering of Poets." Review of *Return to a Place Lit by a Glass of Milk*. *Western Humanities Review* 28 (autumn 1974): 403–9.
Hoffman, Daniel. "To Give a Book of Poetry Is to Pay a Compliment." Review of *Dismantling the Silence*. *Sunday Bulletin*, 5 December 1971, sec. 2:8.
Holden, Jonathan. "Poetry and Commitment." In *Style and Authenticity in Postmodern Poetry*. Columbia: University of Missouri Press, 1986.
Hudzik, Robert. Review of *Classic Ballroom Dances*. *Library Journal* 105 (1 November 1980): 2331.
Hufstader, Jonathan. "Coming to Consciousness: Lyric Poetry as Social Discourse in the Work of Charles Simic, Seamus Heaney, Tom Paulin, Tony Harrison, and Rita Dove." Ph.D. diss., Harvard University, 1993.
Ignatow, David. "Three Poets." Review of *Charon's Cosmology*. *New York Times Book Review*, 5 March 1978, 14.
Jackson, Richard. "Charles Simic and Mark Strand: The Presence of Absence." *Contemporary Literature* 21 (winter 1980): 136–45.
Janas, Marci. "The Secret World of Charles Simic" Review of *The Book of Gods and Devils*. *Field* 44 (spring 1991): 67–76.

Johnson, Halvard. "Living on the Home Planet." Review of *Dismantling the Silence. Minnesota Review* 1 (fall 1971): 123–28.

Johnson, Kent Linwood. "Strategies of Saying: Essays and Paraessays on Formal Semantics in Twentieth Century Poetry." Ph.D. diss., Bowling Green State University, 1991.

Kalstone, David. "Poetry Has Made Friends with Everyone." Review of *The Contemporary American Poets, American Poetry since 1940* (ed. Mark Strand, New American Library, 1969). *New York Times Book Review,* 13 February 1972, 3.

Katz, Bill. "Little Presses." *Library Journal* 97 (15 December 1972): 3993–94.

Lee, Al. "Poetry: Two Anthologies." Review of *The Young American Poets* (ed. Paul Carroll, Follett, 1968). *Village Voice,* 5 June 1969, 17.

Libby, Anthony. "Gloomy Runes and Loony Spoons." Review of *Selected Poems. New York Times Book Review,* 12 January 1986, 17.

Lipari, Joseph A. Review of *Selected Poems. Library Journal* 110 (15 September 1985): 84.

Longinovic, Tomislav. "Between Serbian and English: The Poetics of Translation in the Works of Charles Simic." *Modern Poetry in Translation,* n.s. 3 (1993): 167–74.

Loonie, Janice Hays. Review of *What the Grass Says. Opinion,* August 1968, 10.

Maio, Samuel Joseph. "Creating Another Self: An Analysis of Voice in American Contemporary Poetry." Ph.D. diss., University of Southern California, 1986.

Matthews, William. Review of *What the Grass Says. Lillabulero* 2, no. 1 (winter 1968): 41–43.

May, Boyer James. "Towards Print: Selected Poetries: Immediate Ancestries." Review of *What the Grass Says. Trace* 66 (1967–68): 313–14.

McClatchy, J. D. "Figures in the Landscape." Review of *Classic Ballroom Dances. Poetry* 138 (July 1981): 231–41.

McDuff, David. "Poetry Chronicle I." Review of *Unending Blues. Stand* 29, no. 4 (autumn 1988): 61–69.

Miller, Philip. "Simic's 'Cabbage.' " *Explicator* 51, no. 4 (summer 1993): 257–58.

Mitgutsch, Waltraud. "Metaphorical Gaps and Negation in the Poetry of W. S. Merwin, Mark Strand, and Charles Simic." In *On Poets and Poetry: Second Series.* Salzburg Institut für Anglistik und Amerikanistik, Universität Salzburg, 1980. Pp. 3–30.

Molesworth, Charles. "Fondled Memories." Review of *Classic Ballroom Dances. New York Times Book Review,* 12 October 1980, 14.

Moramarco, Fred. "A Gathering of Poets." Review of *Dismantling the Silence. Western Humanities Review* 25 (summer 1971): 278–83.

Morton, Kathryn. "A Spate of Poets New and Old." Review of *Dismantling the Silence. Virginian Pilot,* 28 March 1971, 71.

Muratori, Fred. Review of *White: New Version. Northwest Review* 22, no. 3 (1984): 121–25.

Murray, Michele. "Two Cheers for the Little Ones." Review of *What the Grass Says. National Catholic Reporter,* 5 June 1968, 9.

Naiden, James. "*Dismantling the Silence:* Poet Employs Harsh Imagery." *Minneapolis Star,* 30 July 1971.

Oberg, Arthur. "Strategies for Existence." Review of *Dismantling the Silence. Shenandoah* 22, no. 4 (summer 1971): 100–107.

Offen, Ron. "Poetry Scene." Review of *Return to a Place Lit by a Glass of Milk. Panorama—Chicago Daily News*, 20–21 April 1974.
Older, Julia. "High Latitudes: Recent Books from Four New England Poets." Review of *Unending Blues. Literary Review* 31 (1988): 358–62.
Orlich, Ileana A. "The Poet on a Roll: Charles Simic's 'The Tomb of Stéphane Mallarmé.'" *Centennial Review* 26, no. 2 (spring 1992): 413–28.
Palencia, Elaine F. Review of *Charon's Cosmology. Library Journal* 102 (15 May 1977): 1192.
Pinsky, Robert. *The Situation of Poetry*. Princeton University Press, 1976. N. 178.
Plumly, Stanley. "Of Lyricism, Verbal Energy, the Sonnet, and Gallows Humor." Review of *Classic Ballroom Dances. Book World (Washington Post)*, 2 November 1980, 11.
Prine, Jeanne Suzanne. "Inside and Outside: The Romantic Tradition from Wordsworth to Wright." Ph.D. Diss., University of Georgia, 1990.
Pritchard, William H. "Aboard the Poetry Omnibus." Review of *Weather Forecast for Utopia and Vicinity. Hudson Review* 37 (summer 1984): 327–42.
Pybus, Rodney. "Poetry Chronicle II." Review of *Selected Poems. Stand* 29, no. 3 (summer 1988): 72–80.
Raab, Lawrence. "On the Edge of Silence." Review of *Dismantling the Silence. American Scholar* 40 (summer 1971): 538–42.
Review of *Dismantling the Silence. Kirkus Review* 38 (15 November 1970): 1283.
Ransmeier, J. C. Review of *Somewhere Among Us a Stone Is Taking Notes. Human Voice* 7, no. 2 (1971): 110–11.
Rector, Liam. "Poetry Chronicle." Review of *Selected Poems. Hudson Review* 39 (autumn 1986): 501–15.
Revell, Donald. " 'The Deep En-leaving Has Now Come': Ammons, Matthews, Simic, and Cole." Review of *Unending Blues. Ohio Review* 41 (1988): 116–32.
Review of *Austerities. Virginia Quarterly Review* 59 (winter 1983): 20.
Review of *Charon's Cosmology. Booklist* 73 (1 June 1977): 1553.
Review of *Charon's Cosmology. Choice* 14 (October 1977): 1055.
Review of *Charon's Cosmology. Kirkus Review* 45 (1 May 1977): 533.
Review of *Charon's Cosmology. Nation*, 11 November 1978, 517–19.
Review of *Classic Ballroom Dances. Publisher's Weekly*, 22 August 1980, 38.
Review of *Classic Ballroom Dances. Virginia Quarterly Review* 57 (winter 1981): 25–26.
Review of *Dismantling the Silence. Booklist* 67 (1 May 1971): 724.
Review of *Dismantling the Silence. Kirkus Review* 39 (1 January 1971): 13.
Review of *Dismantling the Silence. Publisher's Weekly*, 14 December 1970, 34.
Review of *Return to a Place Lit by a Glass of Milk. Choice* 12, no. 1 (March 1975): 78.
Review of *Return to a Place Lit by a Glass of Milk. Kirkus Review* 42 (1 January 1974): 46.
Review of *Return to a Place Lit by a Glass of Milk. Virginia Quarterly Review* 51 (spring 1975): 56.
Review of *Selected Poems. Publisher's Weekly*, 26 July 1985, 160–61.
Review of *Weather Forecast for Utopia and Vicinity. Publisher's Weekly*, 28 October 1983, 67–68.
Review of *The World Doesn't End. Publisher's Weekly*, 3 February 1989, 101.
Robinson, Edgar. "Nine Kayak Books." Review of *What the Grass Says. Chicago Review* 20, no. 1 (1968): 116–26.
Rogers, David. Review of *Austerities. World Literature Today* 57 (summer 1983): 461.

Rogers, Dell Marie. "Difficult Brilliant Poetry." Review of *Dismantlirg the Silence. News and Observer (Raleigh, N.C.),* 5 September 1971, 8.

Rosenberg, L. M. Review of *Austerities. Chicago Tribune Book World,* 12 June 1983, sect. 13:36. Syndicated as "From 5 poets: Delights and Disappointments." *Philadelphia Inquirer, Sunday,* 27 April 1983, 7.

Sack, Lisa. "Charles the Great." Review of *A Wedding in Hell. Village Voice Literary Supplement,* November 1994, 35.

Schiff, Jeff. "Sleep, Simple One, Sleep." Review of *Classic Ballroom Dances. Southwest Review* 66 (summer 1981): 330–33.

Schmidt, Peter. "*White*: Charles Simic's Thumbnail Epic." *Contemporary Literature* 23 (fall 1982): 528–49.

Seluzicki, Charles. "Charles Simic: A Bibliographic Checklist," *American Book Collector,* n.s. 3, no. 4 (July–August 1982): 34–39.

Shaw, Robert B. "Charles Simic: An Appreciation." *New Republic,* 24 January 1976, 25–27.

———. "Life among the Cockroaches." Review of *Classic Ballroom Dances* and *White (A New Version). New Boston Review* (March/April 1981): 27–29.

———. "The Long and Short of It." Review of *Dismantling the Silence. Poetry* 119 (March 1972): 342–55.

———. "Short Reviews." Review of *Unending Blues. Poetry* 150 (July 1987): 226–41.

Söderberg, Lasse. "Charles Simic." *Lyrikvännen* 35, no. 1 (1988): 41.

Standford, Derek. Review of *Dismantling the Silence. Books and Bookmen* 17 (December 1971): 70–71.

Starkey, David. Review of *The World Doesn't End. Southern Humanities Review* 25 (winter 1991): 101–2.

Stepanchev, Stephen. "Voices of the New Generation." Review of *The Young American Poets* (ed. Paul Carroll, Follett, 1968). *New Leader* 51, no. 20 (21 October 1968): 21–22.

Stitt, Peter. "Imagination in the Ascendant." Review of *Austerities. Poetry* 143 (October 1983): 39–52.

———. "Staying at Home and Going Away." Review of *Selected Poems. Georgia Review* 40 (summer 1986): 557–71.

———. "The Whirlpool of Image and Narrative Flow." Review of *Unending Blues. Georgia Review* 41, no. 1 (spring 1987): 192–208.

Stuart, Dabney. Review of *Return to a Place Lit by a Glass of Milk. Library Journal* 99 (15 March 1974): 761–62.

Taylor, William E. "Simic, Snodgrass, etc." Review of *What the Grass Says. South* 1, no. 1 (1969): 46–50.

Thomas, Harry. Review of *Selected Poems. Boston Review* 11 (April 1986): 28.

Thurley, Geoffrey. *The American Moment, American Poetry in the Mid-Century.* New York: St. Martin's, 1977: 225–28.

Vendler, Helen. "Silence of the Spider." Review of *Dismantling the Silence. Christian Science Monitor,* 15 April 1971, 63.

———. "Recent Poetry: Ten Poets." Review of *Charon's Cosmology. Yale Review* 67 (autumn 1977): 72–90. Reprinted as "Ten Poets" in *Part of Nature, Part of Us, Modern American Poets.* Cambridge: Harvard University Press, 1980, 335–72.

———. "Totemic Shifting." Review of *The Book of Gods and Devils, Hotel Insomnia,* and *Dime-Store Alchemy. Parnassus: Poetry in Review* 18, no. 2–19, no. 1 (1993): 86–99.

Wakoski, Diane. "Songs and Notes." Review of *Somewhere Among Us a Stone Is Taking Notes. Poetry* 118 (September 1971): 355–58.

Walker, David. "Stone Soup: Contemporary Poetry and the Obsessive Image." *Field* 13 (fall 1975): 39–47.

Weeks, Ramona. "A Gathering of Poets." Review of *Somewhere Among Us a Stone Is Taking Notes. Western Humanities Review* 24 (summer 1970): 295–301.

Williamson, Alan. " 'Fool,' Said My Muse to Me . . . ' " Review of *Charon's Cosmology. Poetry* 133 (November 1978): 100–107.

———. "Pasts That Stay Present." Review of *Austerities. New York Times Book Review,* 1 May 1983, 15.

———. "Silence, Surrealism, and Allegory." *Kayak* 40 (November 1975): 57–67.

Winslow, Pete. "Reader's Checklist." Review of *The Young American Poets* (ed. Paul Carroll, Follett, 1968). *Independent,* 15 December 1968, 43.

Woesner, Warren. "Inner Passages." Review of *Dismantling the Silence. Abraxas* (summer 1971).

Wood, Susan. "Bards of America." Review of *Classic Ballroom Dances. Book World (Washington Post),* 11 December 1977, E6.

Young, Vernon. "Poetry Chronicle: The Light Is Dark Enough." Review of *Classic Ballroom Dances. Hudson Review* 34 (spring 1981): 141–54.

Young, David. Review of *Classic Ballroom Dances. Field* 24 (spring 1981): 83–96.

Zweig, Paul. "The New Surrealism." *Salmagundi* 22–23 (spring–summer 1973): 269–84.

———. Review of *Return to a Place Lit by a Glass of Milk. Village Voice,* 4 April 1974, 33–34.

POETS ON POETRY

Annie Finch and Marilyn Hacker, General Editors
Donald Hall, Founding Editor

New titles

Elizabeth Alexander, *Power and Possibility*
Ed Dorn, *Ed Dorn Live*
Laura (Riding) Jackson, *The Failure of Poetry, The Promise of Language*
Reginald Shepherd, *Orpheus in the Bronx*

Recently published

John Ashbery, *Selected Prose*
Annie Finch, *The Body of Poetry*
Alice Notley, *Coming After*
Charles Simic, *Memory Piano*
John Yau, *The Passionate Spectator*

Also available, collections by

A. R. Ammons, Robert Bly, Philip Booth, Marianne Boruch, Hayden Carruth, Amy Clampitt, Douglas Crase, Robert Creeley, Donald Davie, Thomas M. Disch, Tess Gallagher, Dana Gioia, Linda Gregerson, Allen Grossman, Thom Gunn, Rachel Hadas, John Haines, Donald Hall, Joy Harjo, Robert Hayden, Edward Hirsch, Daniel Hoffman, Jonathan Holden, John Hollander, Paul Hoover, Andrew Hudgins, Josephine Jacobsen, Mark Jarman, Galway Kinnell, Kenneth Koch, John Koethe, Yusef Komunyakaa, Maxine Kumin, Martin Lammon (editor), Philip Larkin, David Lehman, Philip Levine, Larry Levis, John Logan, William Logan, William Matthews, William Meredith, Jane Miller, David Mura, Carol Muske, Geoffrey O'Brien, Gregory Orr, Alicia Suskin Ostriker, Ron Padgett, Marge Piercy, Anne Sexton, Karl Shapiro, Charles Simic, William Stafford, Anne Stevenson, May Swenson, James Tate, Richard Tillinghast, C. K. Williams, Alan Williamson, Charles Wright, James Wright, and Stephen Yenser